Eminent
Hungarians

Translated from the Hungarian by
Bernard Adams

Krisztián Nyáry

Eminent Hungarians

Corvina

Thanks to Zsuzsi for the idea and everything else.
K.Ny.

The chapters of this book first appeared in Hungarian in
Igazi hősök – 33 magyar (Corvina, 2014)
Merész magyarok – 30 emberi történet (Corvina, 2015)

Design by Fruzsina Kun

Published in Hungary in 2017
by Corvina Books, Ltd.

1086 Budapest, Dankó utca 4-8.
www.corvinakiado.hu

ISBN 978 963 13 6410 1

Printed in Hungary

Contents

Introduction

Seven out of every ten people are prepared to deliver a lethal electric shock to a person in a laboratory if they are given a sufficiently firm order. Seven out of ten are prepared to humiliate their fellow man dressed as a prisoner – or to stand by and say nothing while someone else does – merely because they are dressed as warders. As a result of the celebrated socio-psychological experiments conducted by Stanley Milgram and Philip Zimbardo we can state the proportion of mankind that is prepared blindly to obey an evil order: seventy per cent. A series of sociologists have interpreted these experiments and attempted to understand why unquestioning obedience makes monsters of good people. Is it a desire to conform, peer pressure, fear or lack of self-confidence? It is certainly worthwhile devoting much thought to this question, but to me this is not what really matters. What interests me is the remainder, the thirty per cent. Those who venture to oppose the majority, who do the right thing even though they are in the minority. Who do not yield to that magnetic force that Zimbardo calls the Lucifer-effect: it seems devilish, but is very, very human.

My heroes have played important parts in the history of Hungary over the last two centuries. They have, however, not been military leaders, rulers or statesmen, but private individuals who have shaped the world around them. All the same, through what happened to them the reader can glimpse the most important trends in the recent past and find examples of how one can remain human under dictatorships and during wars, or simply when the indifference of society cripples something intrinsically good. To simplify the matter greatly, the tales that I tell have three sorts of people in them: aggressors, that is, those that enact and enforce harsh laws; victims, those that suffer the aggression; and heroes, who do not know what to do but do it all the same. These roles – especially in the tempestuous history of Hungary – are frequently exchanged: aggressors can, under a different régime, easily become victims, while victims become heroes and vice versa. The sum total of these visible actors in the tales, however, is a small minority compared to those that comprise a fourth group. These are the invisible majority: those that avert their gaze out of indifference or in fear, keen to save their skins, too lazy to act. These are those who could easily alter the course of events even in the most acute conflicts, but do not. We know them. At most moments in our lives we are reckoned among them ourselves.

Being heroic and brave is simple, says Philip Zimbardo; he came from the poor quarter of New York, and there learnt that what is really hard is to overcome one's own indifference, prejudices and fears. We do not like to be the first to act for fear of the possibility of failure. We think that someone else is better suited than ourselves, and that in any case it is too late: if there ever was the right moment to take action, it has passed. We would like to be among the heroes, but we will not risk finding ourselves among the victims instead. This book tells of Hungarians who had the nerve to take the first step, who chose the harder way and stood for justice even when outnumbered. Hungarians who acted when need arose, or simply dared to go all the way and thus set examples for others.

Olivér Halassy merely demonstrated – the first in the world to do so – that a physically disadvantaged person can reach the top of the Olympic pedestal. Vilma Hugonnai struggled for twenty years for women to be allowed to graduate in Hungary: she fought for her cause even when the majority ridiculed her. The courageous army officer Imre Reviczky was the first to deal kindly with the Jewish, Romanian and Ruthenian forced labourers under him. He addressed them as 'gentlemen' and 'comrades in misfortune' when sneering and humiliation were the rule. That was the first step, and from that followed the rest, the saving of thousands of lives.

They were all heroes, not because of their blind disregard for opposition but because they had the courage to consider the possibility of a course of action other than that expected of them by the majority, and if there was another – more courageous, more humane or more in keeping with their inner scale of values – they took it and remained faithful to it. And they were all Hungarians, because they took their decisions as Hungarians at crucial moments in Hungarian history, just as those that tried to stop them were Hungarians too. Some of them could trace their ancestry back to Hungarian aristocracy in the Middle Ages, and there were some that were proud to choose Hungary to be their country. Irrespective of that, their Hungarianness was the circumstance that defined their views of themselves and shaped their destinies, even if many of them had to live part of their lives abroad, and though there were always some that did not even consider them to be Hungarians. But elsewhere, in other cultures, among different people, their rewards would have been different.

They acted in accordance with very firm, definite inner scales of values, and in comparison their political outlook was of secondary importance. Both the left-wing Sára Karig and the conservative Géza Soos alike took it as obvious that they should stand up for the persecuted in 1944. The faith of Áron Márton, the exiled Roman Catholic bishop, and of the *nemzetőr* rabbi Lipót Löw alike was important for the understanding of their personalities, but it was their humanity that caused them to go beyond the narrow confines of the official stance of their respective churches.

Some of my heroes are known only to few: László Kozma, for example, who worked on the development of the first Hungarian computer both in the death-camp of Auschwitz and in the prison of the Hungarian communist police. There are those whose names are familiar only from street-names, such as Manó Gozsdu, after whom the well-known Budapest entertainment district is named: he dedicated his life to reconciling the Hungarian and Romanian peoples. There are those too whose most significant deeds are known to many, such as Ignác Semmelweis, the doctor who defeated puerperal fever; it is seldom mentioned, however, that the man who saved the lives of so many mothers was literally murdered.

There appear in the book an aristocrat who renounced wealth and title, a Gypsy artist born in poverty, and Hungarian patriots of German, Greek, Jewish and even Syrian origin. I write of persons in the churches who were persecuted under regimes that described themselves as Christian, and of convinced, starry-eyed communists whom the communists murdered. Among my heroes there are life-savers who risked their lives for others during the Holocaust when they could have lived in peace and safety. Of course, one cannot apply the same criteria – it would make no sense – to the heroic Lutheran pastor Gábor Sztehlo, who risked his life to save persecuted children, and the fencer Ilona Elek, the first to prove that in Hungary women too could become Olympic champions. There are sure to be readers who will question whether Uncle Róbert, the man of dubious honesty who set up free soup-kitchens for the poor during the great financial crisis, may feature in the same list as István Angyal, who assessed every situation in life on a moral basis and was executed by the communists. My answer is simple: these thirty people are my personal heroes, my selection of them has been completely subjective. One might give accounts of many hundreds of lives or more, all equally exemplary, but here and now these have been the most significant to me.

In none of their cases did courage mean lack of fear. They had their fears, like most people, of defeat, failure or disgrace. But they were more afraid that their humanity would be found lacking if they did not confront inhumanity. "I was not afraid of death but of becoming completely warped physically and spiritually", said Sára Karig, who was sent to the *gulag* for her honesty. "I did no more than any God-fearing, decent man would have done", was how László Ocskay put it, having been forced to leave Hungary after saving several thousands of his Jewish compatriots.

Personally, I can think of no "Eminent Hungarians" more deserving of the title than these.

Krisztián Nyáry

Blanka Teleki in about 1860.
Although her will provided otherwise she is buried in Paris.

Blanka Teleki

The forty-seven-year-old countess was expecting to be executed. The window of her cell was almost completely bricked up so that she should not be able to see the sky, but all the same she could hear perfectly well if someone was executed in the prison yard. She was not allowed visitors, and other than the guards only the interrogator might open the door. He gave her an account of every execution, and intended that she and her accomplice should not evade their destiny. On 22 June 1853 officers dressed in funereal splendour knocked at the door of the cell where Blanka Teleki had been incarcerated for eighteen months and led the prisoner in silence to a large room. The walls had been draped in black for the pronouncement of the verdict and a crucifix placed above the long table. When she and her companion, the thirty-two-year-old Klára Leövey, stood before the military judge drummers began to beat slowly on drums shrouded in black. Both of the accused were certain that the sentence was to be death. But they were expected only to break down: the sentence of the imperial and royal military tribunal of Pest was not summary execution. Blanka Teleki was condemned to ten years imprisonment in chains for creating a girls' school that disseminated revolutionary spirit, translating and circulating prohibited books, sheltering political refugees and other crimes. She did not believe that she would be able to survive the term. If she confessed her guilt and begged for mercy there was every likelihood of the punishment being significantly reduced. She, however, was not so disposed and endured the sufferings with head held high. *A woman of rare intellectual ability and education, and, it must not be omitted, firm intent and inexhaustible endurance* wrote the military judge of her. She was committed to Kufstein, the harshest prison in the Habsburg Empire. It was only after her release that she died of the diseases that she contracted there. She had stood for daring, new-fangled ideas in the matter of education, politics and the emancipation of women. Perhaps also in love.

HUNGARY IN THE HABSBURG EMPIRE. After the expulsion of the Turks from Hungary and Transylvania in 1699 the Kingdom of Hungary enjoyed a limited independence in the Habsburg Empire. The National Assembly of the noble Estates functioned in the capital Pozsony (today Bratislava, Slovakia), but the Emperor of Austria bore the title of King of Hungary. By the start of the nineteenth century clashes between the Hungarian nobility and the Viennese court had become on-going, and whether the king summoned or dissolved the National Assembly depended on the international political and economic situation of the moment. From the 1830s on the so-called Reform Parliament passed laws that sought to bring about civil transformation. The leading proponent of reform was the conservative-liberal aristocrat Count István Széchenyi. Beginning from the 1840s opposition politicians centred around Lajos Kossuth were no longer satisfied with economic reforms, and had their sights on a struggle for the greatest possible political independence.

Countess Maria Bianca Clara Emerica Anna Carolina Teleki of Szék was born in 1806 at Kővárhosszúfalva, in northern Transylvania. On her mother's side she came from the newly ennobled but very wealthy and highly enlightened Brunszvik family. Her mother, Karolina, and her sisters Jozefina and Teréz while still young girls had the entrée to the cultivated aristocratic salons of Vienna. Beethoven had been a guest in their mansion at

Martonvásár, and was rather attracted to Jozefina Brunszvik. The youngest girl was Karolina, and her hand in marriage was sought by Imre Teleki, of the most important aristocratic family of Transylvania – now struggling with material cares but having a line going back to the Middle Ages – and both families thought the marriage would be a mistake. In Martonvásár it was hard to accept that her young husband would take Karolina, accustomed to society life, off to a lonely, remote mansion in a poor village. Imre detested worldly show; he was an eccentric, a scholar, who had in his desk drawer both historical works in Latin and old-fashioned works of literature.

TRANSYLVANIA AND HUNGARY. In the Middle Ages Transylvania, with its mixed Romanian, Magyar and German population, was part of the Kingdom of Hungary. During the Turkish wars it became an independent principality, paying tribute to the Turks while being governed by ethnically Magyar princes and – to a degree unparalleled elsewhere in Europe – guaranteeing freedom of religious observance. From the late seventeenth century Transylvania was an independent territory in the Habsburg Empire. By that time the most numerous nationality were the Romanians (mostly of servile status) while the aristocracy were mostly Magyar and the citizens of the free towns were both Magyar and German. The re-unification of Transylvania with Hungary was an important aim of Hungarian politicians, but was only achieved in the revolution of 1848–49. As the Hungarian revolutionary government was reluctant to grant political rights to the Romanian population, the latter sided with the Austrians in the Freedom War.

Although the parents differed in all manner of things, in one thing they agreed: their children had to have the broadest possible education. Governesses and tutors came one after another in their house, and the children Blanka, Emma and Miksa were free to choose books from the vast library. Blanka showed talent for painting and music, and so while she was still a child a music teacher and a drawing master were engaged for her, and when she was in her teens she was sent to stay with a great-aunt on her father's side in the biggest town in Transylvania, Kolozsvár (Cluj-Napoca, Romania), to study painting at a higher level. A tall girl with a beautiful, melancholy face, there she managed to fall in love with Count Ottó Degenfeld, five years her senior. The young people were planning to marry, but for some unknown reason the count's mother prevented it. Blanka was deeply hurt by this and said that she would never marry. Her parents thought it better to send her to Buda[1] to forget her disappointment and stay with an aunt on her mother's side. There she was able to meet almost daily the person who exercised the greatest influence on her later life: Teréz Brunszvik. Her aunt regarded her as her spiritual child, and not only drew her into the setting-up of the first institution in Central Europe for the care of young children but also took her with her on journeys to Pozsony[2] and Vienna, thus introducing her to numerous key figures in aristocratic circles that were urging political reform.

We do not know precisely what happened in the third year of her stay in Buda, but in any case the young countess sank into profound melancholia and therefore her aunt sent her home to Transylvania. There she often crossed swords with her conservative father: *What life means to us – living for others, being useful to others – to him means nothing. He thinks that living for others is stupidity and a waste of time. So we are in a state of permanent quarrel* – she wrote to her aunt. She began to be rather interested in affairs of public life, especially the improving of the position of women, though even then she saw as her main goal becoming a painter.

At first she continued her painting studies in cities in Germany, Switzerland and Italy, and then in 1838 went to Paris with her brother. There she met an influential young aristocrat, Count Auguste de Gerando, and not long afterwards married him. A French relative helped her to be accepted as a pupil by the well known painter Léon Cogniet, and a promising career as a painter might have lain ahead if her mother had not suddenly fallen ill. She left

Paris and went home to her mother who, despite her careful nursing, died early in 1843. Blanka never went back to France but settled in Pest, close to her aunt, and although she never gave up painting henceforth she regarded the cause of "national advancement" as more important. She believed that the rise of Hungary was inconceivable without cultured women active in public life, and for this she considered the creation of an educational system modern in spirit to be necessary. All that was reckoned venturesome thinking in those days, when even the doors of secondary schools were closed to girls.

Blanka decided to set up an institution for the education of girls on the lines of foreign boarding-schools that she had known. She shared her plan with the governess Teréz Karacs, who held similarly modern educational views, and with her planned the workings of an ideal girls' school. In December 1845 an article on her programme, entitled *Manifesto on the education of upper-class Hungarian women* appeared in *Pesti Hirlap* (Pest News-sheet), the paper owned by Lajos Kossuth, leader of the liberal political opposition. The author was Blanka, and she proclaimed her programme like a man, signing it "an upper-class man". The call for the education of women in Hungarian did not arouse much response, but lack of interest did not cause her to waver. Six months later, this time in her own name, she announced her plan to establish the institute and its curriculum. At this more attention was forthcoming. For example her father, Imre Teleki, on learning that his daughter, countess that she was, meant to set up a school for girls, tried to have her declared mentally ill. Rejection was almost total in aristocratic circles, as the education of girls contradicted all tradition. As the school was about to open no one even enrolled. Nevertheless Blanka asked the representative of the Viennese court for permission for it to function: *Education somehow makes one human, brings us calm, earthly happiness, prepares a way for a better life*, she wrote.

For lack of pupils the prospects for the institute seemed so poor that Teréz Karacs signed a contract to work in the provinces and recommended in her stead Klára Leövey. At the end of summer, however, Blanka rented the second floor of an apartment house and had been paying the cost to no purpose for months by the time that the first pupil arrived. Although from the end of 1846 a stream of new pupils arrived the teaching staff was the more numerous and so the project was always losing money. The school was reckoned novel not only because it taught girls but also because it made no use of physical punishment or even humiliation. Blanka herself took a share of the teaching, was always among the pupils, took meals with them and indeed sat in at classes too. She was present at the lessons given by the twenty-one-year-old Pál Vasvári, who was popular not only among the pupils but also in the circles of the radical youth of Pest. He was a member of what was later known as the March Youth – a political group of university students, writers and intellectuals, which was considered the driving force of the revolutionary movement.

Vasvári embodied the masculine ideal of the age: he was tall, blue-eyed with thick dark curly hair, and always spoke excitingly in a resounding voice. According to a contemporary: *He could do as he pleased with the hearts of his hearers*, and so it is not surprising that his teen-age pupils too wrote him enthusiastic homework. There is every indication that the founder of the school was unable to oppose his charm and patriotic writings, and gradually fell in love with the teacher twenty years her junior. We do not know whether Blanka's affection was returned, but it is certain that we regularly find Vasvári at her side in the fateful moments in the years that followed.

On the day when the revolution broke out in Pest, 15 March 1848, Klára picked up a copy of *The National Song* off the pavement in the street and took it with her into the school. The first woman to declaim the poem in public – in front of her pupils – was Blanka Teleki. A few days later the pupils drafted their own demands on the lines of the twelve points, including the right of women to go to university and have the vote.

REVOLUTION AND FREEDOM WAR. On 15 March 1848 revolution broke out in Hungary, one of the wave of risings in Europe. In the streets of the larger towns and of Pest and Buda – then still separate entities – citizens and youthful intelligentsia directed the course of events, a National Guard was formed, and the twelve points containing radical political demands were printed as was the *National Song* by the young poet, Sándor Petőfi. Alarmed by the revolution, the Austrian court appointed an aristocrat of the Opposition, Lajos Batthyány, Prime Minister. A year later the Hungarian Parliament enacted the dethronement of the House of Habsburg and the secession of Hungary from the empire. Lajos Kossuth became head of state as regent. The Austrians succeeded only with the help of the Russian tsarist army in winning the armed Freedom War that had begun. The end of hostilities was followed by bloody retribution, in the course of which Batthyány and the military leaders in the Freedom War were executed. Lajos Kossuth and several associates went into exile, and István Széchenyi committed suicide in a mental hospital near Vienna. Hungary remained under strict military rule until the 1860s.

Blanka Teleki did not only encourage the spread of radical ideas from the sidelines: her article: *First reform, then the emancipation of women* was not only the first Hungarian document to demand equal rights for the sexes, but in the eyes of the aristocracy it represented the most republican voice in the revolution – it is no surprise that it too met with very little response. When the Austrian army was approaching Pest Blanka sent the girls that were still living in the school home at their parents' request, and on New Year's Eve 1848 finally closed its doors. By this time she was unquestionably the great lady of the revolution: she followed the government as it fled from the imperial forces, travelled to Debrecen in eastern Hungary and was present at the Declaration of Independence from the Austrian Empire. At the end of April Pál Vasvári raised a force to drive back the Romanian insurgents, who were allied to the Austrians, and called on Blanka to assist in the dedication of a banner.[3] The countess ceremonially handed the silver-embroidered red banner to Vasvári in front of six hundred volunteers, and he took his leave of her, most warmly desiring that they meet again after the fighting. They never saw one another again.

Blanka followed the government to its new seat at Szeged too. There she read in the paper that Vasvári had fallen in battle against the Romanians. Klára Leövey was present and sighed: *What the country has lost in him!* Blanka's only reply was: *And what have I lost!* Next day the two of them set out to try and recover his remains for burial. They were not successful. Klára withdrew to her native town, and in December 1849 Blanka moved into a smallish mansion, a family property in Pálfalva, Transylvania. The house was dark and damp, the garden muddy and neglected: not a welcoming home, but the exile soon considered it her paradise, and as she lived there in retreat she offered refuge there to many. She supported materially the publication of several revolutionary publications, at the same time distributing banned books. She was preparing to write the history of the Hungarian revolution in collaboration with the French historian Jules Michelet, and therefore sent information on the suppression of the Freedom War to her sister in Paris. In her replies Emma shared with her sister news of the emigration. And more besides. On 31 March 1850 Emma posted the little manuscript book in which she had compiled the history of the Freedom War for her children. It was not Blanka that read the carelessly posted package, however, but according to the manuscript annotations the Austrian Minister for the Interior, and indeed the imperial Prime Minister himself too.

Investigation into Blanka began that very day. Detectives read every letter sent to or from Pálfalva, at the result of which she was placed under surveillance as she was suspected of setting up a 'political laboratory'. All her writings were confiscated in a house-search, which she endured with dignity. They came for her in the night on 13 May 1851 and she was arrested together with her pupil and sometime servant, the seventeen-year-old Erzsi Erdélyi. She had to harness up her own carriage to be taken to prison. When the imperial official tried to sit beside her she informed him that she did not travel in such company, and so he sat on the box all the way to the prison. The interrogations took place with the approval of the highest Austrian government circles, and they intended to make a terrible example of the high-born Hungarian woman.

Two months later Klára Leövey too was arrested and taken to the military prison in Pest, the *Újépület* (New Building). In October the countess followed her, as did Erzsi Erdélyi, who was strictly and separately guarded as state's evidence. The prisoners were held in the notorious fifth block of the Újépület, the windows of which overlooked the place of execution. Blanka was kept in solitary confinement for eighteen months, and not interrogated. A year after their arrest Erzsi Erdélyi broke down and did what was asked of her: she made a confession accusing Blanka, after which she was released immediately. The military judge, Col. Ignatz Bilko, did his all to prove Blanka guilty of a capital offence and for the proceedings to end with a death sentence. But it was in vain: of a hundred witnesses only the said servant girl, a minor, testified that Blanka had intended to foment revolution.

Relatives with good connections at court sent word to the countess that if she asked for clemency she could regain her freedom. "Clemency? I don't know the word", she sent back. Only after that was she interrogated, in February 1853, and in May a charge was preferred. According to this, five years previously the whole revolution had started from her educational establishment, and she had plotted with Klára Leövey and her sister in Paris for a fresh outbreak of revolt and the secession of Hungary from Austria. A real show trial got under way: in the questioning Blanka refuted every untruth but admitted all that was true. Klára was sentenced to five years imprisonment in chains, Blanka to ten. After hearing the verdict the accused only said: "This has been lies and fabrication from start to finish". In the end, at the request of her relatives the Austrians reduced the sentence so that she did not wear chains at all times. On 20 June 1853 the convicts set out for Kufstein. When they were handed over to the guards at the gate of the tower the military escort too burst into tears. Everyone was sure that the two women would not live to see the end of their sentences in the harshest prison in the empire. Blanka Teleki thought so too: "What a shame I have no art materials", she said at the prison gate. "How nice it would be for the dying to paint their coffin!"

Three hundred steps led up from the gate to the cell in the tower from the heavily barred window of which hardly anything could be seen of the sky. In the alpine cold the cell could not be heated to above six degrees. Despite the circumstances the commandant of the castle, a Hungarian, tried to treat the prisoners decently. He allowed them to have food brought in at their own expense, to do handiwork, and to walk in the castle yard for two hours a day. After a few months the Hungarian guard was relieved and the new Austrian commandant cancelled all privileges and even forbade them to write or receive letters. The women were subjected to two humiliating searches a day, and the guard regularly opened the door with "Still alive?" Their health deteriorated seriously because of the lack of food, air and exercise.

Despite all her suffering her fellow prisoners only heard Blanka weep aloud once, when Klára ended her sentence and she was left alone. As the guards did not consider that she would survive another winter in Kufstein she was transferred to the prison of Laibach (today Ljubljana, Slovenia). She was given a big, well-lit cell, but her eyes had grown accustomed to darkness and could not bear the light, and her sight was completely ruined. In 1857, on the occasion of the birth of an heir to the throne, the Emperor Rudolf declared an amnesty for political prisoners. Blanka was freed after six years, half blind and with serious lung disease.

After returning home she was placed under police surveillance and constantly surrounded by informers. She nursed Klára Leövey with typhus for some months, then fell sick herself. While she was ill she decided that she would stay no longer in enslaved Hungary and meant to move to France, but in the end, only months later, received a passport to travel to Munich. She lived on, a sick woman, for another five years. In the autumn of 1862 the doctors recommended "sea air" for her delicate lungs, and with Klára she set off for the French coast. In Paris they stayed with Emma Teleki, but could go no further. On the morning of 23 October Blanka could no longer rise from her bed. She was delirious with fever for a long time, then saw figures standing round her bed, and all she said was "Hungary". Minutes later she was no more. The creator of Hungarian women's education, the most significant woman in the Freedom War, had died at the age of fifty-six. She was buried in the Montparnasse cemetery, and despite her last wish is there still.

The principle of liberty, fraternity and equality has been proclaimed. In consequence the emancipation of women is brought under consideration, sometimes seriously, sometimes scornfully. We are delighted at both. (…) We are children, minors, not only in the eyes of the law but also of the spirit. We cannot yet escape from petty self-interest, we seek liberty in externals. (…) Spiritual liberty will produce its own fruit in time in societal relationships too. (…) The revolution demands people. Bring up your daughters to be people, not ephemera to be married off at the earliest opportunity, as if a woman, like a butterfly, has attained the ultimate goal of her destiny when the párta[4] is taken from her head. (…) Awake, my female fellow citizens! The age is changing life at breakneck speed, let us be firmer, and may the three sacred words equality, fraternity and liberty become reality!

Blanka Teleki,
First reform, then women's emancipation
Életképek, May 1848

"If the Hungarian is lost, the Romanian will be lost tomorrow."
An 1844 portait of Gozsdu.

Manó Gozsdu

In 1826, not long after opening his office, the young Pest law-yer decided on a bold step. For the first time in the history of Hungary he submitted a plaint written in Hungarian instead of the prescribed Latin. This was reckoned an unusually patriotic ac-tion, anticipating by ten years the establishment of Hungarian as an official language. The German-speaking members of the city council were not at all pleased, but the twenty-four year-old law-yer's Hungarian writer friends certainly were. The lawyer that stood up for the Hungarian language, Manó Gozsdu, had been born a Romanian, and considered himself both a good Hungari-an and a good Romanian. He was therefore regarded by Romani-an nationalists as a traitor in the service of the Hungarians, and by Hungarian nationalists as a Romanian separatist. His belief was that the two peoples were destined to work together, because "in opposing one another, both must be lost". He became the most important cultural sponsor of Romanians in Transylvania and Hungary, and even 140 years after his death Hungary and Roma-nia still disputed his inheritance.

He was born in Nagyvárad (today Oradea, Romania) to a Roma-nian merchant family of Macedonian origin. In the home Roma-nian was spoken, together with Greek for Balkan business part-ners, but Serbian and Hungarian too were not unknown. Atanasie

Gozsdu was able to apply serious amounts of money to the education of his children. His son Emanuel was born in 1802, and after finishing the Romanian school in Várad was enrolled at the Hungarian-language Catholic grammar school. By the time that he entered law school in Pozsony he logically wrote his name in Hungarian form, Gozsdu Manó. From there he went to the law faculty in Pest, taking his degree in 1824. He became an articled clerk in the office of Mihály Vitkovics, which was also a centre of Pest literary life, and that let its mark on his entire career. Vitkovics was considered a reviver of both Hungarian and Serbian literature, and his dual cultural affinity caused him no problems. Numerous members of the intelligentsia, Hungarian and Serbian alike, were frequent visitors to the house in Szerb utca. The lively intellectual milieu so swept young Gozsdu away that he too began to write verse in Hungarian. We know nothing of his attempts at writing in Romanian, but following Vitkovics's example he felt it important to cultivate his native language as well as Hungarian. He went regularly to Atanáz Grabovszky's Romanian literary salon, where he made friends with Romanian intellectuals from Transylvania and Hungary.

In 1825 Gozsdu opened an independent lawyer's office in Pest, but did not give up writing verse. In the following year a few of his poems actually appeared in the journal *Szép-Literatúrai Ajándék* (Fine-Literary Offering). The most successful of these was a lament on the death of a certain Miss Zs. Ny., presumably in memory of a youthful love who had met a tragic end. After that perhaps he himself recognised that he had greater talent for legal language as he brought out no further verse, whereas his successful speeches in defence were often published. He acquired a name, and a steadily growing fortune, in criminal proceedings in particular. Public affairs, primarily the assertion of laws concerning the use of language, interested him from the beginning. That was why he resolved to petition the councils of Pest and Buda in Hungarian. The courageous but unlawful act was much talked about, and according to one Hungarian appreciation the lawyer of Romanian origin had advanced the cause of Magyarisation in what was at the time a largely German-speaking city.

NATIONALITY IN HISTORICAL HUNGARY. The Kingdom of Hungary was a multiracial state from the early Middle Ages on, but until the nineteenth century the question of mother tongue was of secondary importance to religious differences or the division between noble and ignoble. Until 1836 the official language of the country was Latin! After the expulsion of the Turks the Habsburg rulers proclaimed a large-scale programme for the resettlement of the areas that were left depopulated, and spontaneous immigration helped this. In the course of the eighteenth century the population almost trebled, and large German, Slovak, South Slav and Romanian minorities entered Hungary. There had been a significant Romanian population in Transylvania at the end of the Middle Ages, and by the early nineteenth century this had risen to fifty per cent. As the Magyar movement for independence from Austria gathered momentum, so did political movements among the non-Magyar 'nationalities', which found a natural supporter in the Viennese court. Friction came to a head in the Freedom War of 1848–49. After the Austro-Hungarian 'Compromise' of 1867 the Hungarian State forged its own agreement with that part of the Kingdom that now constitutes Croatia, but it was a long time before the rights of the other ethnic minorities concerning use of language and education in the mother tongue were recognised.

By the 1830s Gozsdu was considered the most successful lawyer in Pest. He married Anastasia Pometa, widow of a Buda merchant, a man of Macedonian-Romanian extraction like himself. With his money he bought a number of properties, among them an empty plot on the main street in rapidly developing Pest, Königsgasse (now Király utca), which we can now recognise from the name Gozsdu-udvar, the group of buildings that now stands there. Step by step he became the spiritual leader of the Romanian community in Pest-Buda. When in 1836 the Orthodox Church community in Pest almost split in two – the Greek speakers wanted to keep the church registers exclusively in Greek and the Romanians in Romanian – Gozsdu brought about peace between them by proposing that the documents be written in Hungarian. He donated ever larger sums from his constantly increasing wealth to Hungarian and Romanian cultural aims. On one occasion he bought an ancient Hungarian charter, regarded as a rarity, and presented it to the Hungarian Scientific Society, and on another he financed the Romanian-language publications of Buda University Press. It was with his support that the first Romanian periodical in Buda appeared, *Biblioteca românesca*, as did the equally important annual *Calendarul Românesc,* to both of which he contributed items.

Although he held no elective position his views and words became decisive in Romanian circles in Hungary. It went therefore without saying that on 1 May 1848 the Romanians of Pest, on whose proposal a vote of confidence in the Batthyány government was passed, gathered in his house. For this reason there were many in the ranks of the Transylvanian Romanians that regarded Gozsdu as a traitor. It was thanks to the passions that were aroused that when he stood in the Parliamentary elections of 1848 almost the entire Romanian population of Oravica (Oravița in south-west Romania) was massacred. Gozsdu took as a personal failure the bloody conflict between the Transylvanian Hungarians, who supported the revolution, and the Romanian insurgents, who were loyal to the emperor, and decided to withdraw from public life. After the revolution had been suppressed the Austrians wanted to make use of him for their own ends by appointing him imperial agent in Bihar county, but he declined the offer. It was said of him that in the days of political retribution he protested against absolutism by listening to solemn Hungarian music.

In those years he concentrated on his legal and commercial activity. He obtained permission to divide up the land in Königsgasse, built warehouses, and let them out profitably. His outspoken speeches in court were talked of in the streets of Pest for days. When repression had eased he too returned to political life. In 1861 he was appointed Lord Lieutenant of Krassó county in Transylvania, and later chief secretary of the Upper House of Parliament. It was at this time that he made his famous speech on the interdependence of the two peoples: *The God of the peoples of the world has ordained for the Hungarian and Romanian peoples that they must live together in an eternal union; together they have a glorious future, but in opposing one another both must be lost.* Not everyone was pleased to hear words proclaiming pacification; the Romanian politician Vincenţiu Babeş, for example, openly called Gozsdu a bad Romanian who had gained his position by Hungarian largesse. In a furious response Gozsdu stated what he understood by patriotism: *There is not on the whole globe of Earth a better Romanian and a better Hungarian patriot than myself.* In Krassó county, where there was a Romanian majority, liberal rules on use of language were accepted on his proposal: *Both Hungarian-speaking and Romanian-speaking patriots alike are recognised as true brothers.* When the king dissolved Parliament Gozsdu was offered to remain in post as Lord Lieutenant, and in fact his name was mentioned at court as a future Chancellor of Transylvania. All that he said to those around him was: *If a constitutional Lord Lieutenant puts into effect the absolutist measures of an unconstitutional government he may not be regarded as a constitutional Lord Lieutenant, and rather than be seen in that light I prefer to resign.*

He withdrew from public life for a second time. As an experienced lawyer, his services were sought by a series of rapidly developing Hungarian enterprises, and thus he became chairman of the Pest Insurance Company and of the Concordia Steam-mill Company, and a member of the boards of a number of others. His private life too changed. His wife died in 1863, but at the age of sixty he remarried that same year. His second wife was Melania Dumcia, daughter of a director of a Romanian bank in Buda. As no child was born to either marriage he applied all his time and money to supporting Romanian culture. He collected and published a volume of Romanian folk-songs thirty years before the collecting journeys of Zoltán Kodály and Béla Bartók, and had them translated into Hungarian under the title *A Garland of Romanian Folk-poetry*. He went back into politics before the Compromise at the request of Ferenc Deák. He assisted in drafting the law on nationality, and supported Deák's proposed text that referred to the Hungarian nation as one and undivided. He explained this to his Romanian critics thus: *There is a nation, not nations. (...) By independent free nation is meant the whole population, irrespective of language.* When he stood in the parliamentary election in Bihar county the local Romanian peasantry cheered him when he went canvassing. In his response he said to the crowd: *My brothers! You say 'Long live Gozsdu', but I say 'May he live only as long as he works in your interests and to your benefit, and the minute that he ceases to represent your interests may Gozsdu live no more!'* On that occasion the lawyer from Pest won a brilliant victory and became a member of the Parliament that voted for the Compromise. At the coronation he received the Knight's Cross, as did Ferenc Liszt, which shows that his person was reckoned emblematic of the court and the political élite.

THE COMPROMISE. The repression and political absolutism that followed the defeat of the 1848–49 revolution began to ease when the Austrian Empire suffered defeats in the Franco-Austrian War of 1859 and the Seven Weeks War of 1866. The young Emperor Franz Joseph wanted to establish internal peace in his realm. The leader of the Hungarian opposition, Ferenc Deák and his associates regarded the implementation of the laws accepted in the 1848 revolution as the basis of discussions, and endeavoured to maximise Hungary's political independence. Under the political agreement of 1867, known as the Compromise, a new federal state came into being named the Austro-Hungarian Monarchy, with Franz Joseph, Emperor of Austria and King of Hungary, at the head. In the federation only foreign affairs, military affairs and finance were directed jointly, and in other spheres decisions were taken by the sovereign national governments and parliaments. An amnesty was granted to those that had fled abroad after the revolution and they were allowed to return. It is characteristic of the period that portraits of the ever more popular 'Ferencjóska' and of Lajos Kossuth, who was living in voluntary exile in Turin, hung side by side in many homes. The period of dualism lasted until 1918 and brought unparalleled economic and cultural prosperity, but the adherents of full independence – among them Kossuth – saw the Compromise as a betrayal.

In the years that followed, the Romanian political and cultural élite of Hungary once again met regularly in Gozsdu's house in Pest. The more radical Romanian leaders, however, continued to consider their Deák-collaborator host a renegade Magyar-lover and a representative of a bygone age. In his old age, however, Gozsdu gave a tremendous impetus to Romanian culture, and there was hardly a literary or historical work that was published otherwise than at his expense. In addition to numerous books and periodicals he bore the cost of reproducing the portraits of the three Hunyadis, whom he regarded as heroes of Hungarian and Romanian history alike. He died at home in Pest in 1870 at the age of sixty-seven, a few days after being elected a member of the Supreme Court. His admirers erected a memorial to him in the Kerepesi cemetery, and the main weekly in Budapest devoted a whole page to his obituary. It was not known, however, that even after his death several charitable acts would be linked to his name.

Only after his will was published did it emerge that he had donated all his enormous wealth to charitable purposes. He had created a foundation *having in mind the assistance and flourishing of the joint Hungarian fatherland, the Eastern Orthodox Church and the Romanian people*, and his last wish was that its funds must be applied to educational goals. Young Romanians living in Hungary, having a knowledge of Hungarian and practising the Orthodox faith might profit by its scholarships. *Fundatiunea lui Gozsdu* was one of the biggest private foundations in the whole Monarchy, and in ad-

Today the Gozsdu-court is the most fashionable multicultural place of entertainment in Budapest.

dition to a portfolio of various investments its most valuable possession was the real estate in Király utca. The administrators of the foundation demolished the warehouses that Gozsdu had built there and in their place erected a row of completely individual apartment buildings. The intention was to let the upstairs apartments to well-to-do middle class tenants and the business premises on the ground floor to silversmiths and jewellers – with the revenue going to the educational purposes that Gozsdu had outlined. It comes as no surprise that after the First World War a dispute over the foundation's Budapest property broke out time and again between the Romanian and Hungarian states, and has only recently been resolved.

Many of the Romanian political élite of the twentieth century have had Gozsdu's foundation to thank for their free education, including some who did not stand up for the rights of the Hungarian minority in Transylvania, such as, for example, Octavian Goga and Petru Groza, later to become Prime Ministers of Romania. The Pest lawyer who was the first to submit a plaint in Hungarian, and who, according to his admirers, at all times held two flags in his hands, would probably not have been pleased at that. But perhaps he would have smiled at knowing that the complex of buildings erected on his land and bearing his name is today the best known multicultural meeting-place in Budapest.

I formally call on Babeş to say who is the bad Romanian that is usually selected by the House for committees, while the good Romanian is not. I declare that although I no longer have the good fortune to be selected for any very important committee I still do not wish to bring upon myself the title of bad Romanian: because I declare before the whole world that there is not on the whole globe of Earth a better Romanian and a better Hungarian patriot than myself. It is true that we tread different paths to ensure the happiness of the Romanian people, divergent paths: and I promise that I shall never go by his path, but I wish and pray to God that he may go by mine. Let anyone glance at the map and they will see that the Romanian who incites the Romanian nation to constant hostility to the Hungarian is the Romanian people's greatest enemy; they may be convinced, if they have a little experience of life and the world, that conflict with one another will only shorten the life of both: because if the Hungarian is destroyed today, the Romanian will be destroyed tomorrow.

Manó Gozsdu,
Speech in Parliament
Minutes of the Upper House,
6 April 1861

Nyom Bettfenstein és Rusch Bécsben 1867.

GANZ ÁBRAHÁM.

Kiadta: Sarkady István a „Hajnal" Szerkesztője.

The Swiss immigrant established one of the
fastest-growing iron-works in Europe. Ábrahám Ganz in 1867.

Ábrahám Ganz

In 1843 a young skilled worker was almost killed in an accident in the foundry of the Pest steam-mill. The twenty-nine year-old ironmaster Ábrahám Ganz was experimenting with new technology when liquid iron splashed into his eyes. It was only his good reflexes that prevented the molten metal from covering his entire face. For days it seemed that he would lose his sight completely, but in the end he escaped with just the loss of his right eye. When, shortly afterwards, he went back to the foundry, all that he said was *One eye's finished, but the pouring worked*. And with that he went on experimenting. The ambitious young man caught the attention of the leaders of Hungarian industrialisation, and soon István Széchenyi himself and Lajos Kossuth became involved in an argument over him. Thanks to his amazing capacity for work, his fanaticism and persistence, twenty years later he had risen from a manual worker to the biggest industrialist in the country, the creator of the engineering industry in Hungary. In the course of his career he came near to ruin more than once, but was always capable of making a fresh start and so emerged from the crises stronger than before.

Ábrahám Ganz was the eldest of the nine children of a Calvinist cantor and schoolmaster in the Swiss village of Unter-Embrach. He lost his mother at an early age. His father intended him to go into the Church, but as a teenager he was more interested in what went on in the village locksmith's workshop, and at the age of fifteen was apprenticed to an iron-founder in Zürich. As was the custom of the time, after serving his apprenticeship he became an itinerant craftsman, looking for a position, and for years drifted around the towns of Switzerland, France and Italy, working in a variety of foundries. During his years of wandering he not only mastered his trade but also acquired from his employers the ins and outs of getting work and of selling at market. He shared with no one his secret plan that one day he would set up his own foundry and so raise his father and brothers from poverty. There was no prospect of his achieving his dream without capital, and after almost ten years of wandering he was materially no better off than when he had started. He happened to be working in Vienna when because of his poverty his father tried to call him home by letter. In his reply he spoke of his plans for the first time, and said that he felt that he had sufficient patience, courage and persistence to wait for the right moment to open his own foundry. *Anyone that has no hope in his future is to be pitied.*

In 1841 the right moment came. In Vienna he heard for the first time that skilled workers were needed in Pest to build and maintain the machinery of a new sort of steam-mill. The Hengermalom (Rolling mill) Company had been formed, on the initiative of István Széchenyi, for the purpose of exporting Hungarian wheat in milled form, as flour. Ganz packed up the documents proving his professional training and applied for work to the manager of the mill, a Swiss like himself. He was a talented young man and in a few months' time had made good the several years' backwardness in his progress. He soon became an iron-founder in the rolling-mill, and then was put in charge of the repair workshop of the whole foundry. *Now I'm in Pest*, he wrote proudly home to Switzerland, *and I've carried out the first pouring of iron into a mould in this town (…), and it seems that things aren't going to go too badly, so I'm going to stay here for a few years and I hope that I'll be able to save some mon-*

ey. The workshop of which he was in charge had originally been opened only for maintaining the machinery in the mill, but Ganz saw that the spare capacity could be put to other use. He began to make and sell agricultural machines, scales, printing presses and iron decorations for buildings. His products were even shown at the 1842 industrial exhibition, and an enthusiastic account of them appeared in the newspaper *Pesti Hirlap* – written by the editor himself, Lajos Kossuth. The foundry was soon making a lot of money and Ganz did his best to fulfil every special order. It was while he was trying out new manufacturing processes that the almost fatal accident happened. Although by 1844 the number of his workers had exceeded 100 he still complained in letters to the family about the amount he had to do and how tired he became. The directors of the company tried to motivate him, as he had become irreplaceable: they gave him a new contract, and he received a percentage of the revenue. In the autumn of 1844, however, he realised that he was receiving less money than he ought. He made a complaint, but when it was rejected he resigned his position.

Perhaps he had actually been waiting for that moment, as in four years he had spent hardly any of his high earnings and so had been able to amass a significant amount, 6,000 forints. He bought a house and land in Buda, near the Danube, for 4,500 and spent the remainder on machinery. The engineers working on the Chain Bridge – then under construction – and the management of the Óbuda Shipyard – also founded by Széchenyi – placed orders with him, and so after obtaining licences he had taken on seven workers when there came an unexpected turn of events: first the deliveries of anthracite for the furnaces failed to arrive, then the orders too ceased. It soon emerged that it had been Széchenyi himself, at the request of the manager of the Hengermalom, that had banned the delivery of coal and iron to his competitor, and the placing of orders with him.

We know what came next from a laconic entry in Széchenyi's diary: *Ganz the ironmaster came to see me saying that Majson would not let him have any coal because I had forbidden it*. The Count dismissed Ganz, saying that he should return to working with Hengermalom as he was about to ruin the rival foundry. Embittered, Ganz turned to the man whose name he knew only from the newspaper article that had praised his work: Lajos Kossuth. He had no idea at all that the rivalry between the two statesmen would settle his destiny too. Kossuth wrote to Széchenyi saying that he could not believe what he had heard *from the man of Swiss birth*, that the great figure of industry *should wish to bankrupt a competing private initiative*. He informed him that he would make the matter public knowledge, but that he would delay doing so for a week so that *His Honour the Count would be so kind as to act in the way that his liberal principles and philanthropic feelings would recommend*. Széchenyi dismissed it as blackmail in a furious letter, but Kossuth persisted. In his answer he asked Széchenyi, as deputy chairman of the Society of Founders of Factories, to reconsider his decision. Whether for that reason or some other we do not know, but in any case the first delivery of coal arrived at Ganz's foundry a few days later, and he also received an order from the builders of the Chain Bridge.

INDUSTRIAL DEVELOPMENT IN THE REFORM PERIOD. Boosting the national economy occupied an important place among the Hungarian ambitions for reform in the first half of the nineeenth century. In addition to the imposition of taxes on the nobility and the creation of a modern credit system under the programme which Count István Széchenyi proclaimed in the 1830s, great importance was attached to the introduction of industrial technology that had been successful abroad and the development of infrastructure. For this, however, there was also need of foreign-trained skilled workers, and they were welcomed in the newly built factories and in such construction projects as the Széchenyi Chain Bridge, the first permanent bridge on the Danube in Budapest. Széchenyi, the more conservative in political questions, adopted Anglo-Saxon free market principles in the economic sphere, while Lajos Kossuth, of more radical political tendencies, had a preference rather for protectionist policies that shielded Hungarian industry. In this spirit there grew up the *Védegylet* (Defence Association), a society the members of which agreed only to buy Hungarian goods and never to buy foreign manufactured items when Hungarian-made were available. Kossuth's paper *Pesti Hirlap* became an important forum for Hungarian industrial development. The two great reforming politicians clashed frequently on this question.

The obstruction had been removed, and a year later twenty-two workers were employed in the constantly expanding business. Kossuth felt something of the effects of Ganz's success in his own affairs too, and in the course of a year wrote an article in his paper that amounted to an advertisement. Ganz's iron columns, balcony railings and cast-iron stoves were in constant demand for building work in the rapidly developing city. Business was going so well that the ironmaster called for two of his brothers to come from Switzerland to Buda: Henrik helped in administration and Konrad became a foundry apprentice. Ábrahám took discipline at work seriously, and once wrote in a letter *Konrad is a brilliant foundryman, but he chatters a lot and so I have dismissed him.* Later, of course, he took him back, but from then on his employees did not slack while at work. The greatest pitfall in the building industry almost ruined Ganz too: the chain of debt. *Everyone demands what they're owed on the one hand, and on the other hand they're never prepared to pay what they owe. (...) Three smeltings a week, and yet we're getting nowhere,* he remarked to one of his brothers.

The year 1848 brought a new turn to Ganz's life. He had by then been living in Buda for eight years, but there is no indication that he had learnt Hungarian. With his brothers and immediate colleagues he spoke German, but from the year of the revolution he called himself a Hungarian. It would have been much easier for him to identify himself with the German population of Buda, who cheered the Austrian soldiers when they occupied the city during the Freedom War. He, however, did not forget what he owed to Kossuth, and he supported the independent Hungarian state unreservedly. In 1849 the Ganz factory began to make gun-barrels for the Hungarian *honvéd* army as it fought for liberty. As they left the factory he inscribed them with *Ne bántsd a magyart* – Hands off the Hungarians! He also abandoned his plan of finding a wife in Switzerland; in the year before the revolution he met Jozefa, the sixteen-year-old daughter of Lőrinc Heiss the dyer, and in 1849 they married. An end soon came to months of happiness, however, as not long afterwards Ganz was brought before the Austrian military court and sentenced to six years imprisonment. A few days later, however, he was released on the intervention of a Swiss officer.

He had to start almost everything afresh. Of his supporters Kossuth was in exile, Széchenyi in a lunatic asylum, and privately-owned Hungarian manufacturing was in crisis. Ganz now had sufficient money to be able to set up again in Switzerland or some other more fortunate country, but he wanted to remain in Hungary. He knew that he could only stay on his feet if he could make a product for which there was also great demand abroad. At the time the railway network was growing explosively in Europe, and broken wheels were often brought into Ganz's works. He realised that old-fashioned spoked wheels could not stand the strain, but discovered that in America hard-wearing moulded wheels were used. After two years of experimentation to develop the required technology, he began to manufacture his own wheels. He went to Vienna, knocked on the doors of several railway companies, and made them an astonishingly daring offer: the use of his wheels free of charge for two years, undertaking to repair any damage that might occur, on condition that if the wheels stood the test they would be bought. He showed his invention at the 1855 exhibition in Paris too, where he was awarded a medal, which persuaded railway companies all over the world to make enquiries about the unknown East-European foundry. Ganz ploughed all his money back into the business, and himself lived with his wife in a simple three-room flat on the factory premises. That was where he received surprised foreign clients, who had expected to see a wealthy industrialist. By this time there were not just the two of them: as they had had no children of their own they had adopted two little girls. In addition to bringing them up Mrs Ganz also assisted in the works, washing overalls herself in the factory yard. In this way they were almost ruined again, as the wheels that were delivered free yielded no income for a further two years. There were times when the workers' wages could only be paid late, on credit, but the employees made no fuss as they were confident that together they would succeed.

After the lean years the first harvests began to come in. By the end of the 1850s the sometime foundry apprentice had realised his dream. By that time he was selling wheels to fifty-nine railway companies in Europe, his workforce was five times greater and his earnings ten times more. He knew that success did not merely require constant development of technology, but also one had to build a team. He invited to Buda the best trained technical experts of the age: the engineers Antal Eichleiter and András Mechwart, who soon became key men in the factory and introduced new products; thus at the start of the 1860s the Ganz works was considered one of the most up-to-date in Europe. The two engineers were given not only good salaries but also a share of the profits. Ganz demanded quality from his workers, but did his best to keep good experienced men. Not only did he offer the best wages in the capital but also – a rarity even in Western countries – sick pay and retirement pensions. He put a lot of money into schemes for 'poverty-relief', that is, support for hospitals and orphanages.

By then Ganz was one of the richest men in Hungary, though few were aware of it. A lot of people were amazed when in 1862 he had a Danube-side mansion built near the Chain-Bridge as a worthy centre for an international firm. He took only one flat in the building for his family and used the rest for stores and business premises. Before the Compromise the authorities too began to cultivate his friendship. He was awarded a gold service cross by the Viennese court and had the entrée to the most distinguished circles. Franz Joseph himself visited the world-famous factory, which by then occupied whole city blocks. Ganz did not feel comfortable at receptions and formal occasions, could not fit in and did not even wish to. In 1866 he and his wife and daughters paid a visit home to his native village so that they should never forget where he had come from. He had close ties with his family, and so took it very hard when his brother Konrad died of an inherited nervous disorder. From then on he was certain that a similar end was in store for himself, and he suffered from continual headaches, which he thought were early signs of the trouble.

On 23 November 1867 the Ganz factory produced its 100,000th railway wheel. His colleagues marked the occasion with a big celebration to cheer up their chief: eight hundred people gathered, including members of his family. As if about to take his leave, Ganz gave all his workers a commemorative medal. Three weeks later the family were sitting at lunch when Ganz excused himself and left the table. He went into the next room to see his daughter who was sick in bed, stroked her head, then threw himself from an upstairs window into the yard, dying instantly. He did not leave a farewell letter, and everyone was baffled as to why he had done such a thing when at the pinnacle of success. From his will, written not long before, it emerged that it was his most important aim that his work, the most successful industrial enterprise in Hungary, should continue to operate after his death. His heirs had to undertake to keep the firm intact – the board of directors that he had appointed did so for a further ten years – and the engineers were given part-ownership. The workers at the factory had to be kept on, and their wages guaranteed. His brothers, his wife and their adoptive daughters, as well as sixty-four god-children – children of his workers – also received substantial legacies.

Ganz had planned everything to do with the future of the factory, and so his firm functioned in accordance with his principles even after he was gone. When eventually an investment company bought the family members' share András Mechwart was chosen as managing director and remained at the head of the company for twenty-five years. The Ganz works remained one of the most significant commercial groups in Hungary, and by now has survived by a century and a half the impoverished Swiss cantor's son who thought that anyone who had no daring dreams was only to be pitied.

You ask why I do not intend to come home? At that word I pause and think: would I have a secure living back at home, one that would satisfy my needs? So many plans are going round in my head, but for their accomplishment I need time and suitable circumstances. Since it is my decision and I was born not only to seek my own happiness but in order to promote your happiness and that of my siblings, and having lived through the quickly passing years of my youth I cannot look into the future with such indifference, because my plans are serious, and believe me, if one sets about something and does not succeed he must not despair; patience, courage and persistence are mighty aids to a man's achievement of happiness, and anyone that has no hope in his future is to be pitied.

Ábrahám Ganz,
a letter to his parents from Vienna
26 November 1840

The "Rabbi in boots" some time in the 1870s, shortly before his death.

Lipót Löw

On Sunday 3 June 1849 the declaration of Hungarian independence was celebrated in Veszprém. The west-Hungarian town had not long before been retaken from the imperial forces by the Hungarian army, and the county authorities, although rather after the event, wanted formally to celebrate the dethronement of the Habsburgs, which had occurred in April. For the ceremonial speech they called on a speaker of renown whose patriotic convictions were well known and who had himself fought with the army in the war. Nevertheless, the choice was an unusual one: the speaker was none other than the Chief Rabbi of Pápa, the thirty-eight-year-old Lipót Löw. By their selection of place and time the county authorities also gave a lesson to the faithful of both religions: the Christians had to enter a synagogue for the first time in their lives, and the Jews had to listen to the rabbi in their company, and on a Sunday into the bargain. But only the most conservative in both camps were scandalised, and on that day patriotic fervour prevailed over every custom.

The citizens of Veszprém and the surrounding villages, Hungarian- and German-speaking alike, Catholics, Protestants and Jews filled the synagogue, and the leaders of the county were present to a man. When Lipót Löw went into the pulpit to proclaim Hungarian independence the representatives of the county authorities and the Christian citizens of the town raised their hats to him in token of respect. At this sign of honour for their rabbi the Jews present too uncovered, which on any other occasion would have been considered sacrilege. One man, a Veszprém barber who until then had had little time for Jews, was deeply moved by the inspiring words and by the fact that the rabbi, who had learnt Hungarian as an adult, *delivered his speech in such a pure Hungarian spirit, it was as if he were of the greatest Hungarian stock.* Under the influence of the speech wealthy Christians and Jews alike offered significant sums *to the altar of the fatherland.* A *honvéd* captain personally took the rabbi's speech to Artúr Görgey, the commander-in-chief, who even decided to invite Lipót Löw to be Chief Rabbi of his army. This never came about. A few months later the Freedom War ended in disaster, and Rabbi Löw was imprisoned on a charge of treason. Even after his release he remained the most important leader of Hungarian Jewry; the widespread use of Hungarian in synagogue sermons was due to his influence, as was the creation of the first Hungarian-language Jewish periodical; he also had a hand in the foundation of libraries, museums and industrial concerns.

Löw was born on 22 May 1811 in the small Moravian village of Černa Hora, a late child of the well-known Prague rabbi Judah Löw ben Bezalel (credited with the making of the Golem). They were the only Jewish family in the village, and so young Leipold Loew (Judah Leib Löw) soon added Czech and German to his mother-tongue Yiddish and the Hebrew of the Bible. His second mother-tongue, however, was music, and he was an excellent violinist, pianist and flautist. His father intended him for the rabbinate, and so at the age of thirteen he left the family home and studied the Torah and Talmud in a number of *yeshiva*s in Moravia. In the course of his travels he went to Kismarton in Hungary when he was eighteen, and there encountered Hungarian for the first time. He was less and less restricted to Jewish subjects, and also studied linguistics, aesthetics and history, in addition to translating Schiller from German into Hebrew. The Chief Rabbi of

Moravia noticed the talented young man, but by no means approved of him. He publicly criticised him for concerning himself with worldly affairs – he had corresponded with the Chief Rabbi of Arad, Áron Chorin, who was active in the reform of Judaism and therefore was regarded as a renegade. Instead of bowing to the wishes of his superior, however, Leipold Loew decided that after ordination as a rabbi he would leave Hungary and continue his studies at a regular university.

As he had only attended religious schools he had to matriculate at a traditional school too in order to enter university. Because of his age he did not want to pass through the classes from the beginning, and so between 1835 and 1841 he completed the courses at Pozsony Evangelical Lyceum and at Vienna University, and the teacher-training course at the Vienna Catholic High School; he also took lessons in Classical Greek at Pest University. At Pozsony, in addition to Latin, the Christian religion and natural science, he studied Hungarian. By so doing, however, he aroused the anger of the Pozsony Orthodox Jewish community, who saw in the young rabbi a betrayer of tradition. In 1840 the Hungarian Parliament removed the obstacles to the free settlement of Jews. Leipold Loew promptly Magyarised his name as Lipót Löw and chose to make Hungary his new country. In 1841 he accepted the invitation of the Jewish community of the small west-Hungarian town of Nagykanizsa. In his new post as assistant rabbi he studied Hungarian with exceptional thoroughness, beginning his every day at three in the morning with language lessons. He took this so seriously that three years after his arrival he was preaching in Hungarian and teaching Hungarian in the community's school. He also began the first Hungarian-language Jewish periodical, but this survived only a single issue for lack of subscribers.

Löw believed firmly that the Jews of Hungary had to be Hungarian-speaking and patriotic in order to obtain equal rights. His conviction was not shared by all: some anti-Semites were opposed to the emancipation of the Jews and conservative Jews were afraid of assimilation. When in 1843 the lower house of Parliament voted for rights of citizenship for Jews the Orthodox Jews of Pozsony petitioned the *helytartótanács* with an objection, and eventually the upper house rejected the proposal. By contrast, Löw became one of the leaders of the Jewish movement that urged deliberate assimilation. This did not mean that he had given way to anyone in religious questions. When Lajos Kossuth wrote in his paper that the Jews ought to give up certain externals in return for equal rights Löw replied in an open letter. He said that religious rules did not prevent Jews from doing their duty to the country; anyone could be a good patriot even if he happened not to eat pork. On the basis of the rabbi's arguments Kossuth partly revised his position. The politicians of the Reform Period, however, began to take notice of Löw, who by then had been elected Chief Rabbi of Nagykanizsa; for example, members of the liberal noble opposition in Zala county went to hear his preaching, delivered in faultless Hungarian.

THE JEWS IN HISTORICAL HUNGARY. Even as early as when the nomad Magyar tribes settled the Carpathian basin there were Jews living in Hungary, whose rights were sometimes extended, sometimes restricted by the medieval kings. Although Emperor Joseph II of Austria compelled the Jews in Hungary to adopt German surnames the majority of them were assimilated step by step into the Hungarian way of life. In the first half of the nineteenth century law after law made possible the free movement of the Jews and their economic activity, which rendered the country attractive to immigrant Jewish merchants and manufacturers. In addition to the well-to-do urban Jewish population, open to modernisation, more and more poor Eastern-European Jews arrived who clung to their traditional culture. Jews participated in the revolution of 1848 and the ensuing Freedom War in a proportion far in excess of their actual numbers. Even though pogroms did take place in a number of towns, the Hungarian political and cultural élite always sided with the Jews in these clashes. With the Compromise, the emancipation of the Jews was put on a legal footing and complete equality of rights was achieved. By the end of the nineteenth century the most assimilated Jewish minority in Europe was that in Hungary; the majority of the urban Jewish population considered themselves Hungarians of Israelite religion, and in numerous 'nationality' areas they tipped the balance of numbers in favour of the Hungarians. The greater part of the communities abandoned the Orthodox religious restraints and joined the 'modernising' tendency that practised Judaism in the reformed style.

He was thirty-one when he married Leontin, daughter of the Chief Rabbi of Pest, Arszlán Schwab Löw – like himself, a supporter of assimilation. She – cultivated, sensitive and famously beautiful – bore him three children in four years, and the rapidly growing family quickly outgrew the rabbi's lodging in Nagykanizsa, where for lack of a yard they had to keep the chickens in the kitchen. In 1846 Löw applied for the post of Chief Rabbi in Pápa. As one of the biggest Jewish communities in Hungary lived in this small west-Hungarian town those in distant parts too watched to see who would move to its head. The very influential conservative Jews of Pozsony launched a veritable campaign against Löw being selected: their open letters branded him a "destroyer of Israel" on account of his reformist principles. He had influential partisans too, however, and even Ferenc Deák supported his move to Pápa. In the end the adherents of Hungarianisation were in the majority, Löw was elected, and a year later was able to consecrate the classical synagogue in Pápa – it is still standing – together with the organ which scandalised the Orthodox. From the start he worked to bring Christian and Jewish townspeople closer together. He taught Hebrew in the Calvinist college and Hungarian in the Jewish school, at one time also undertook the teaching of French to the young Calvinists. He launched the paper named *Magyar Zsinagóga* (Hungarian Synagogue), the aims of which were the dissemination of *enlightened religiousness, pure morality and keen patriot-*

ism. He published the almanac *Magyarító egylet* (Hungarianising association), which is considered the first appearance of the Jewish element in Hungarian literature.

News of the March revolution reached Löw in Pápa. An enthusiast for the Hungarian cause, he was soon to be disappointed – first when reports of pogroms arrived, then when the authorities suspended recruitment of Jewish patriots into the National Guard because of the tensions. Despite the prohibition a Jewish National Guard regiment was raised, led by the left-wing politician Mihály Táncsics in protest against the decision. As the armed struggle widened and the government once more permitted Jews to take up arms in defence of the country Rabbi Löw at once began to recruit from his pulpit. Such was the effect of his preaching that eighty-seven Jewish men volunteered for the Pápa National Guard – a far greater proportion of their number than came from the other denominations in the town. Their rabbi went with them too as chaplain, and the rousing speech that he gave in camp at Sellye was distributed in printed form. It is no surprise that when Pápa fell into Austrian hands again in December 1848 Löw was immediately arrested for *preaching in support of Kossuth and against the Emperor.* He was released after being questioned, but there were a number of Jews in Pápa that would have liked to be rid of the rabbi with the modern ideas. *If the people in government were Hungarians they handed over their rabbi to Hungarians, and if they were Austrians, depend on it, the Jews were the first to complain* … was the reminiscence of the local Catholic chapter. But there were also many Christians who were not pleased at a Jewish rabbi being held up to the nation at large as an example of Hungarian patriotism.

Perhaps the liberal leaders of Veszprém county, who took a symbolic decision that was considered unprecedented, had a message for them too. When the town and region once more changed hands they invited Lipót Löw to proclaim the independence of Hungary in a celebratory oration to the faithful of all denominations. As a result there took place in Veszprém synagogue the first ecumenical ceremony in the history of Hungary with Jews and Christians alike taking part. The speech gained the rabbi nationwide recognition – perhaps his wife was the only one to feel that the celebrating would not last for ever, and she hid her husband's writings under a box of potatoes for future use. Two months later Löw saw the fulfilment of his old almanac: the Parliament, sitting in Szeged, voted unanimously for complete emancipation of the Jews. He wrote in his diary: *It has come late, but come it has.* He was not able to rejoice for long: the Freedom War ended in disaster, and the law never came into force.

In October 1849 Löw was sick in bed at home when the Austrian authorities came for him. He was arrested for treason and rebellion and taken to the Újépület prison in Pest. On the same day his father-in-law, the Chief Rabbi in Pest, was also imprisoned. It became clear that two Othodox Jews in Pápa had denounced him, but other incriminating statements too confirmed that he had called for armed opposition to the imperial forces and fostered the republic. In the course of the proceedings witnesses for the defence too appeared from the community, who helped their rabbi with what is now known to be false evidence, saying that Löw had always been loyal to the imperial authorities. The mayor of Pápa gave evidence on his behalf, as did the Catholic parish priest and the local landowner. While he was detained Löw tried to spend the time usefully; for example, he gave lessons to the prison governor's young son. *I am allowed to walk in the corridor from seven until nine in the morning. After that I read and write and teach little Hassenteuffel*, he wrote in his diary, which he kept in German. On 14 December 1849 the door of his cell was opened in an unexpected way – he was released through the intervention of Széchenyi's friend Baron György Sina.

He returned to Pápa, but felt little disposed to remain in the town where his own people had betrayed him. He accepted the invitation of the south-Hungarian city of Szeged, which was without a rabbi, and moved there. The imperial police kept him under scrutiny for years, but that did not trouble him greatly. During that time, when even to wear a beard reminiscent of Kossuth's invited punishment, Löw conducted services in braided Hungarian formal dress (normally worn by the Hungarian nobility) and welted top-boots, for which reason the people of Szeged quickly dubbed him the "rabbi in boots". When in 1851 he was ordered to show his sermons to the censor in advance he put the text of the Old Testament on the astounded official's desk. He was jailed for impudence, but would not retract. In that year his wife was sick and died, and he was left alone with already seven children. Two years later he remarried; his new wife was Babette Redlich, widow of a Jewish *honvéd* who had died in the Freedom War, who also presented him with seven children.

When a number of Orthodox rabbis engineered the suspension of Hungarian-language services in synagogues, Löw delivered from the Szeged pulpit a eulogy that he had written on the death of István Széchenyi – naturally, in Hungarian. In 1865 he returned to Veszprém, the scene of his famous speech, where he courageously spoke of the memory of the revolution at the consecration of a new synagogue. It is no surprise that after the Compromise the Parliament obeyed his words in formulating Law 1867/IX, which consisted of a total of two clauses: *§1 The Israelite inhabitants of Hungary are declared entitled to the exercise of the same civil and political rights as the Christian population. §2 All laws, customs or ordinances contrary to this are hereby revoked.*

In practice, of course, not everything changed at a stroke, and the "Jewish oath" of medieval origin, for example, which prescribed a humiliating ceremony, was abolished later in courts of law when Löw objected to it. He was involved in public life at both national and local levels, and together with the city clerk of Szeged drew up the regulations for the city library; together they also took the initiative in the foundation of Szeged Museum. At the same time Löw also remained a greatly respected religious thinker. He made Szeged an international centre of Jewish studies for ten years, and manuscripts came from Paris, Dresden, London and even New York to his judaistic periodical *Ben Chanan*. Although he was reckoned one of the intellectual forerunners of the religious Reform Movement, he felt it a personal disaster that at the national congress of 1868/69 Hungarian Judaism split into three camps. He himself did not join any religious tendency, and until his death regarded the creation of unity as his aim.

He was proud that his children were successfully integrated into Hungarian society. He even lived to see his son Tóbiás at the age of twenty-six be appointed deputy public prosecutor, the first Jew to hold such a post. His son Vilmos married in America, and there translated Hungarian folksongs into English, together with works by Petőfi and Madách. Immanuel, born in 1855, followed his father into the rabbinate, and was a respected leader of the Jewish community in Szeged for almost seventy years. Only on one occasion, however, did Lipót Löw hear him preach – on the occasion of his ordination as rabbi.

The patriotic rabbi of the Freedom War died after a brief illness on 13 October 1875. Among the first expressions of sympathy to reach the family were those of Lajos Kossuth, then in exile, and Emperor Franz Joseph. From newspaper accounts it is known that so many attended his funeral that there was not a cab nor a private car to be had. Not long afterwards the famous writer Kálmán Mikszáth wrote about the Jews of Szeged who followed Lipót Löw's principles in answer to an anti-Semitic newspaper article: *If they cannot surpass us in patriotism neither do they lag behind us. Preaching in Hungarian resounds in synagogues (…), the young girl in love bemoans her grief in a Hungarian melody, and the family preserves from the dust in the house the portrait of the late old rabbi, bedecked with national colours.*

A street in Szeged bore the name of Lipót Löw from 1912 until 1941, as long as it could. Not long afterwards his son Immanuel,

53

The imposing Szeged synagogue where Lipót Löw preached in Hungarian.

freeman of the city, member of the upper house of Parliament, a brave man in his father's mould, cursed Hitler from the pulpit. In the summer of 1944, at the age of ninety, he was loaded into a cattle-truck. There has not been a street named after Lipót Löw in Szeged for a long time.

Fervent patriots esteem human dignity, civic liberty and national independence more highly than repose, comfort and pleasure. Their guiding principle is: The word of the fatherland is the word of God: and at the sound of that word they are at any moment on their feet in patriotic fervour, blazing in readiness to act. And with such spirit you too have blazed forth, highly esteemed National Guardsmen. Just as God called on Moses from the midst of the fire, so the fatherland has called on you from the midst of the flames that engulf it, and you have been ready in burning love to answer that call, ready to be torn from the arms of those dear to you. Husband has left wife, father has left children, the worker his workplace, the farmer his harvesting. You have said with one heart and mind: We shall not bend like reeds, but are steadfastly purposed for any sacrifice that we may defend the integrity of our beloved fatherland, protect our hard-won liberties, lay a sound foundation for the future happiness of our children. (...) The Hungarian won the fatherland a thousand years ago by strength of arms and by shedding his blood; other than here he has nowhere. And after a thousand years the Hungarian has achieved the transformation of this fatherland by strength of spirit: this land has been born anew. And almighty God, who establishes the boundaries of countries, has designated this land that on it the Hungarian nation may blossom forth and the Hungarian name be glorified. But the judgements of God shall stand for ever, his decree endure from generation unto generation. And henceforth Trouble not the Hungarian! *is the law of divine providence.*

Lipót Löw,
God is with us!
Speech in camp at Sellye
July 1848

Pasteur's discoveries vindicated the "saviour of mothers".
The last photograph of Semmelweis, 1864.

Ignác Semmelweis

On 31 July 1867 the forty-seven year-old Professor of Medicine, together with his wife and child, visited the clinic of a dermatologist friend in Vienna. During the coach journey from Pest the doctor played and sang songs with his daughter. The long journey tired him, and so he gladly accepted a guest-room that he was offered in the clinic to take a rest. When he woke again and wanted to find his family nurses barred his way at the door. They informed him that he was in an institution for nervous disorders, to which he had been admitted as a lunatic. He tried to resist and to break out of the room, but there were six of them opposing him. When, after a lengthy time, the straitjacket was taken off him he tried to escape through the window. He was beaten severely, several bones were broken and his chest was perforated. Injured from head to foot he wept for nights on end, tied down. His wife and friends did not visit him. For lack of medical attention his wounds festered and he developed septicaemia. His agony went on for days, but no priest was summoned to him so that no one should witness what had been done to him. After terrible suffering he died, two weeks after his arrival.

Finally, the entry in the register of deaths was falsified; according to the official account septicaemia resulting from a previous injury had been the cause of death. Only after his funeral was his death announced, and the papers printed brief obituaries to him. In his native country he had not been considered a particularly important person, and *Pesti Napló* (Pest Diary) only wrote: *Doctor Semmelweis, teacher at Pest University, as we learn through private channels, died yesterday morning in Vienna. May his remains rest in peace.* It was many years before he began to be called world-wide the saviour of mothers. Ignác Semmelweis had not been mad, but had only clung passionately to the truth. He was an unpleasant man because he proclaimed teachings that were unpalatable to the world of medicine. His family and friends let him down, and his posterity kept the story of his life and death a secret for more than another century.

He was born in 1818, fifth child of a German merchant family that had migrated from Austria to Buda. Although his mother-tongue was German he called himself a Hungarian from his schooldays, and later made a show of his nationality at every opportunity. His father intended him to become a military lawyer, and so at the age of nineteen he was sent to the law faculty of Vienna University. He was not, however, interested in a legal career, and after his first year transferred to the medical school. To punish him for this his father called him home to Pest, but he could not be dissuaded from a medical career. Eventually he returned to Vienna and there completed his studies. He would have liked to be a specialist in internal diseases, but could not find a vacancy and so took a course in obstetrics, and at the age of twenty-six was able to work as an unpaid resident at Professor Klein's famous No. 1 maternity clinic. In 1846 he was made an assistant lecturer, and his work consisted of dissecting patients who had died. In his new sphere of work the most noticeable problem in the clinic stuck him at once. One mother in ten died of puerperal fever, and in some years even more. The young doctor began to investigate the connection between the deaths and circumstances at the clinic.

GERMANS IN HISTORICAL HUNGARY. Germans have lived in the Carpathian basin for more than a thousand years, and by the Middle Ages the Transylvanian Saxons had established some significant autonomous towns. In the eighteenth century, to replace the population lost during the Turkish wars, landowners and the Habsburg rulers systematically settled three waves of immigrant Germans on the Alföld and in southern Hungary. The Germans of Hungary even today are known as Swabians in common parlance, but only a small minority came from Swabia and the remainder from Bavaria, Austria, Pfalz, Hessen, the Netherlands and Alsace. Immigrant families were given tax-exemption, land, and the animals and equipment needed for farming. A wave of systematic immigration of such proportions is only to be found a century later, in that going to America. In the early nineteenth century German was the mother-tongue not only of the Swabian villages but also of a significant part of the urban population too. German was the language of the capital, Pozsony, and of the majority in the rapidly developing Pest and Buda, later to become the capital. The majority regarded themselves as *Ungarndeutsch*. The German nationality was rapidly assimilated in the second half of the nineteenth century, and Magyarisation of surnames too was common practice.

According to accepted theory the deadly infection was caused by some cosmic force, while others blamed lack of ventilation or, indeed, too much of it. Some maintained that the small bell carried by the priest administering extreme unction inspired such fear in expectant mothers that they died in the days following the delivery. *As a doctor I could not visualise how fear, that state of mind, could lead to such material changes as puerperal fever did*, Semmelweis wrote later. Nevertheless he carried out an experiment: the priest was admitted to the building in secret, without a bell, but incidence of puerperal fever – naturally – remained at the same level. It occurred to him that expectant mothers who did not enter the clinic but gave birth at home or in the street never died. He also observed that in the maternity clinic where midwives were trained, where circumstances were in principle similar, there were half as many cases of puerperal fever as in the University clinic where he worked. There was one essential difference between the two maternity units: in the medical department clinic dissections for educational purposes were also regularly performed. Semmelweis sensed that the problem had something to do with these autopsies. He confirmed that the number of cases always decreased when there were no medical students on the premises. By then he was accumulating statistical links, but his theory had not yet been formed. In the spring of 1847 he went on a trip to Venice, to have time to think over his findings in peace and quiet. On returning home he was informed that a young pathologist colleague had died after cutting his finger with a dissecting knife while carrying out an autopsy. The answer came in a flash: *I was shocked in my entire being, and I was thinking about it with unaccustomed passion in an agitated frame of mind when suddenly a thought brought me up short – puerperal fever and Kolletschka's illness were one and the same.* The discovery was not at all self-explanatory: medical science was not yet aware of the existence of bacteria and other living pathogens. Semmelweis therefore formulated his theory that the cause of puerperal fever was nothing other than ptomaine.

He had, with his own hands, handled decomposing organic matter, and realised at once that he himself and his colleagues had been directly responsible for the flood of deaths of women that had recently given birth. The solution to the problem seemed clear: *However painful, however overwhelming such a recognition is, countermeasures are not to be found in denial; and if we do not wish this misfortune to persist the truth has to be brought to the knowledge of all concerned.* He immediately introduced in the maternity unit the washing of hands in bleach to prevent doctors being able to carry ptomaine to patients. Later he ordered that doctors and nursing staff must wash their hands between inspections of patients. The result spoke for itself: in May 1847 thirty-six new mothers died in the clinic, in June only six, and in July only three. Semmelweis thought that the discovery was so unequivocal that it was enough to obey the rules logically and other clinics would follow the example of Vienna. He was to be disappointed. By autumn the incidence of puerperal fever was rising again because doctors had begun to take the instruction less than seriously. It seemed excessively simple and at the same time scandalous that they themselves were responsible for the spread of disease. Nor was it easy to accept spiritually. One of the best known obstetricians, who had accepted his Hungarian colleague's theory, realised that he himself had caused the death of his niece. He fell into depression as a result and not long afterwards threw himself under a train. It is not surprising that despite the favourable results the majority were reluctant to take cognisance of the discovery. Semmelweis was in despair at the scornful dismissal. *All this aroused in me such an unhappy state of mind that did not make life enviable in the least. Everything was in doubt, everything remained unexplained, there was room for doubt in everything and the only indisputable reality was the great number of dead.* His supporters, a dermatologist and an internist, made known the significance of the discovery in brief communications, but the break-through did not come. Obstetricians working elsewhere did not believe the favourable clinical results and simply thought that Semmelweis was a fool.

During the events of 1848 Semmelweis remained in Vienna, and although he joined the National Guard he was mainly involved with his private revolution. That was, however, on the brink of failure. Although the proportion of deaths had fallen to 1.3% Semmelweis irritated Professor Klein by harping on the same subject, and so in 1849 he dismissed him from the clinic. He was unemployed for eighteen months, after which he decided to try his luck in Pest. He took a post as an unpaid consultant in the maternity department of the Rókus Hospital, and also – to keep himself alive – opened a private practice. He was friendly with his medical colleagues, was often in society and even went dancing. He was delighted to be back among Hungarians, though it was typical of him that unlike his brothers he refused to Magyarise his name. It seemed that his career was shaping up in promising fashion. When he arrived in Pest the proportion of new mothers dying of puerperal fever in the hospital maternity department was very high. He introduced the rules of hygiene that he had developed in Vienna and in a short time brought it down to 0.85%. Not only were the results similar to those achieved in Vienna, however, but so was their reception. Hungarian doctors too were reluctant to concede that it was they that were causing the deaths of their patients. When in 1855 Semmelweis applied for the professorship of the maternity department his colleagues expressed a preference for a candidate who could not even speak Hungarian, and the Ministry in Vienna decided to appoint the latter.

Semmelweis was thirty-nine and a lecturer at the University when he married Mária Weidenhoffer, the twenty-year-old daughter of a German merchant family in Pest. They loved being together, and it was noted of them that she even accompanied him on visits to patients, waiting for him in the carriage. They had five children, but they also had to suffer loss: one boy and one girl died in infancy.

Despite the further professional setbacks Semmelweis decided to publish a study underpinned by scientific evidence. He felt that if he failed to shake up the medical fraternity he himself would be responsible for further deaths. *The knowledge lived in me* – he wrote – *that since 1847 thousand after thousand of deaths by puerperal fever and of infants had occurred that could have been avoided had I duly repudiated every false opinion that is expressed concerning puerperal fever.* First he published professional articles in Hungarian in a medical weekly, then wrote a five-hundred-page book in German. He used statistics from London, Dublin and Paris, as well as those from Vienna and Pest, to prove that there was a close connection between the number of autopsies, disinfection of hands, and cases of fever. He also sent copies to the best known professors of obstetrics in Europe. Apart from a few scornful hostile opinions he obtained no reaction to it. One critic called the book the *Koran of ptomaine poi-*

soning, the deluded author of which *calls us to arms to convert the infidel by fire and sword.* Semmelweis was embittered by the renewed rejection and continued to blame himself for the lack of success: *God alone knows the number who have gone to the grave before their time because of me.* He thought that he had chosen the wrong medium, and addressed acerbic open letters to his most reputable colleagues. For example, he addressed the director of the Viennese clinic, under whom the death rate had risen back to 13%, as follows: *You too have had a hand in this butchery, Professor. The murdering must stop, and in order for it to stop I shall stand guard, and if any one dare proclaim dangerous teachings concerning puerperal fever he will find in me a worthy opponent. There is, in my opinion, no other means of putting an end to the murdering than the remorseless exposure of my opponents.* The passionate tone of the leaflets turned his colleagues in Pest against him too, as they felt that he was also bringing disgrace upon the Hungarian experts. Connection was even broken off with his wife's relations, and from that point he was simply called Náci the fool by the family.

Nowadays the state of mind into which Semmelweis must have lapsed at this time would be diagnosed as manic depression. According to his wife he became excitable, would often walk up and down the room all night, and outbursts of temper were frequent. There is nothing, however, to suggest that he was mentally ill. In addition to his healing work he also filled the post of financial director of the medical staff, published normal scientific articles on a variety of subjects and acted as an examiner. According to a story that arose later about his sick mental condition, at a staff meeting he took from his pocket the text of the midwife's oath and read it aloud without any preliminaries. After that his colleagues held a quick conclave, reached agreement with the family and took a decision: *Dr. Ignác Semmelweis has for the past three weeks suffered from mental disturbance of such an order as makes it necessary that he be on the one hand removed from his usual surroundings and office, and on the other hand [receive] the appropriate supervision and medical treatment that a mental institution will provide for him.* The minute-book of the staff committee has

He blamed himself as well as his colleagues for mothers' death.
A photograph at age 43.

since been made public, there is no reference in it to the midwife's
oath, and Semmelweis only complained of the delay in receipt of
an increase of salary in a quite normal voice. After the meeting his
wife told him that they were going for a spa cure and that on the
way they would call at their dermatologist friend's new clinic in Vienna. That was how Semmelweis came to be in the Lower Austria
National Mental Institution, where, in fact, the staff murdered him.
Neither his wife nor his colleagues from Pest attended his funeral.

Obviously, his death was not their intention, only that the in-
creasingly troublesome man be taken out of circulation. The Viennese institute falsified the documents proving its responsibility
and kept them locked away for a century. The doctors that took
part in the conclave put it about that their colleague had cut his
hand in the course of an operation, thus developing septicaemia.

No one had a good word for the late doctor after his death. When the death-rate from puerperal fever rose again, no one pointed out that Semmelweis had been right. His wife changed her name and became a morphine addict, and his son Béla committed suicide at the age of twenty-three. Ten years after the publication of Semmelweis's book which had met with no response Louis Pasteur discovered bacterial pathogens, thus proving the correctness of his theory. Later experiments also showed the importance of the disinfection of the hands. Some years later – outside Hungary – Semmelweis began to be called the saviour of mothers, and more years still later, in his native land too. Streets and hospitals have been named after him, and his sanitised life-story is found in school-books. Nowadays we do not care to confront his life, full as it was of needless battles, and his tragic death.

By nature I abhor all polemics, sufficient proof of which is that I did not respond to all those attacks; I thought that I could rely on the passage of time for the truth to burst forth of itself: but my hope of this has not, in thirteen years, come to fruition, not to the extent that would have been desirable for the benefit of mankind. (...) Fate has become the trustee of the truths which this book contains. It is my ineluctable duty to stand up for them. I have abandoned hope that the important and true nature of the matter would render the struggle superfluous. It is no longer a question of my inclinations, all that counts is the lives of those who have no part in the struggle over whether I or my opponents are right. I must overcome my nature and step forth into the public gaze, because silence will turn out badly; the many bitter hours that have already weighed me down on this account are no enticement; I have cried out and endured them; consolation for those that yet await me is extended by the knowledge that what I have said stems from my conviction.

Ignác Semmelweis,
The aetiology, contraction and prevention of puerperal fever
Vienna, 1860

Gregersen in 1910, relaxing in the garden of his country house.

Gudbrand Gregersen

If a young Norwegian carpenter's luggage had not been plundered on Austrian railways the Parliament in Budapest would look quite different today, as would the Keleti and Nyugati stations, the Mátyás church, and sundry bridges and public buildings throughout Hungary. Aged twenty-three, Gregersen had been drifting through the towns and cities of Central Europe in search of lucrative building work, and in the spring of 1847 set out on foot from Prague for Vienna, from where he meant to go on to Munich. He had no money for a ticket, but sent his luggage by train. His battered chest contained spare clothing, underwear, "good Norwegian woollen stockings" and a few personal items from home. On arrival in Vienna he went straight to the customs office for his luggage. When he opened the chest, instead of his belongings he found a few bricks, some rags and a quantity of straw. Gregersen was very cross at being robbed. His friends had gone to the imperial city to enjoy themselves, but he did not want to go with them in the shabby working clothes that he was wearing. He heard from a Hungarian master builder of the building that was taking place in Buda and Pest and decided to try his luck in the unfamiliar Danube-side town, to earn enough to replace his clothes. He said goodbye to his friends, promising to meet them in six months' time in Munich. In the end he spent sixty-three years in Hungary, where he became a *honvéd* officer during the Freedom

War and then the biggest building contractor in the country, with a hand in almost every significant building project in the Age of Dualism. On one occasion he went bankrupt, at other times fire destroyed all that he had, but he got back up and started again. He died a Hungarian nobleman and the biggest tax-payer in Budapest, and his honesty was legendary at a time when the building industry was rife with corruption and scandal.

He was born in 1824 into a peasant family in Modum, in the south of Norway. He grew up with twelve siblings in a farmhouse outside the village. The end of an idyllic childhood, full of skiing and skating in addition to work around the house, ended with the death of his mother. His father remarried, but the fourteen-year-old Gudbrand no longer felt at home. H went as an apprentice to a local stonemasonry firm, then moved to Christiania,[5] the capital, where he obtained practical and theoretical instruction from the best master builder. *Once I had attained an excellent proficiency (…) I obtained a letter of commendation and (…) in March 1842 went to Copenhagen by steamer* – he reminisced at the end of his life about the beginning of his years of wandering. He worked for a German carpenter, then produced his masterpiece, one of the richly decorated windows of Copenhagen city hall. *I became an upright, worthy assistant carpenter, full of vain hopes,* and these hopes he wanted to realise in the rapidly developing towns of Central Europe. After five years of wandering Gregersen – GG, as his friends called him – reached Hungary, where there was a burning need of skilled builders. In the end he found employment not as a builder in Pest, as he had planned, but in extending the first railway line in Hungary. In the autumn of 1847 he was working in Upper Hungary, now Slovakia, and was soon given his first independent commission, the construction of a smallish wooden bridge. From then on his professional career was inseparably linked to the great railway building in Hungary, in which he would not have become involved by choice. At that time the press often had occasion to write about swindles in the railway, but in contrast the name of Gergersen is always found as synonymous with the honest contractor.

We do not know what persuaded the Norwegian expert, who originally spoke no Hungarian and who was much more at home among the Austrian-German community, to support the rebellious Hungarians in 1848. At all events, Gregersen volunteered for the *honvéd* army and served as a pioneer officer in an engineer unit. He demonstrated both his expertise and devotion at the same time by constructing the pontoon bridge at Paks, indispensable for operations in the Dunántúl, the territory west of the Danube, in a day and a half, which was considered record time. After the Freedom War ended in defeat he thought it best to flee the country and went to Italy, where he worked on building a bridge over the Piave. He could have stayed or moved on, but he wanted to settle in Hungary. After returning he helped in building the Esztergom–Párkány railway, and in so doing discovered Szob, not far from Pest, where he bought land and built a house. No doubt he did this from practical considerations, as he could go from there by train both to Pest and to the sites where he was working in Upper Hungary. Before long a closer bond too kept him there: in 1852 he met and married Alojzia Sümeg, daughter of the local master butcher.

Although she was a Catholic, as was the majority of the village, they married in a Lutheran church. Gregersen clung so fiercely to his Protestant faith that years later he would not allow even his grandchildren to be christened in any other. At home he and his wife spoke German, a language that was adequate for work too. Nevertheless he felt it important to learn Hungarian as well, and every day wrote down designated Hungarian words on a chit so that he would be able to look at them as he went about his business. This was the one thing in which he did not succeed: all his life he spoke the language of his adopted country less than well and with a strong accent. Not so his children, who learnt Hungarian while still little, as well as Norwegian and German. Hungarian was therefore more and more frequently to be heard in the

Gregersen house: beginning in 1854 they had nineteen children, of whom twelve survived to adulthood. Not long after it was built the house in Szob had to be extended with a second storey so that there would be room for the growing family.

Gregersen took as a pattern the well-to-do, easy-going peasant life to which he had been accustomed in Norway. After a while he took on staff, later even kept a servant, but the family took their share in the work on the land, in laundry and housework, which he believed to be of educational value. The traditional Norwegian extended family was his model, and so when he felt that his roots had been put down permanently in Hungary he lured his siblings there too. At first they all worked in building, then a family firm was established which obtained commissions as a sub-contractor. The first big independent job that Gregersen Bros. undertook was the construction of the railway bridge at Szolnok which linked Pest and the eastern part of the country. Built in 1857, 500 metres in length and spanning a number of stream-beds and water-meadows, it was reckoned the biggest wooden viaduct in Hungary. Gudbrand himself oversaw the whole project, and his brothers worked as foremen. In a letter to Norway he wrote that with the building of the bridge he would make a real name for himself. He was right. The Norwegian master-builder and his brothers, who worked quickly, accurately and economically, were called on to build a dozen railway lines, more than thirty viaducts, a couple of tunnels and several stations. His use of compressed air in laying the foundations of the bridge at Szeged in waterlogged soil – the first such use in Central Europe – was viewed as a technical miracle. It was with the same bravura that he bored the railway tunnel to the south of Déli (Southern) station in Buda, which is still taking the strain today.

Gregersen was still not reckoned a really rich man when he felt that he had in some way to express his gratitude to Hungary for having accepted him. In 1860 his name too is to be found on the roll of aristocrats and bankers who contributed to the building of the Hungarian Academy of Sciences. Later too he donated biggish sums to charitable purposes. When he had amassed sufficient capital he set up his own firm. He bought a plot on the outskirts of Pest where there had previously been a wood-yard, a furniture factory and a sawmill. The business went so well that he took part in the construction of the first railway line in Transylvania as not only a contractor but also as a shareholder in the investment company. In the same year, 1868, he also became a partner in a steam-ship company. And then – all in the same year – he became bankrupt in a matter of days. As the result of a stock-market crash building work was halted and so he too became insolvent. As he did not want to be in debt to subcontractors almost all his wealth slipped away. It seemed that he was going to have to abandon his dreams of having his own company. However, he called on his former associates and instead of going to the banks obtained a number of small loans from them in order to stay in business. As his honesty was legendary they were happy to lend to him, and in a few years' time he had repaid them in full. He had just recovered, when in 1870 his entire wood-yard was destroyed in the biggest fire in the city. His property suffered greater damage than had previously been recorded in a fire in Pest. He rebuilt everything, and it was all burnt down again in 1875. Anyone else would have given up long before, but he recovered from this too.

THE BIRTH OF BUDAPEST. By mid-nineteenth century the two towns on the Danube, Buda and Pest, had developed politically, economically and culturally into the most important centre of population in Hungary. In 1838 the medieval and Baroque centre of Pest was destroyed by flood, which made it possible to rebuild the centre in Classical style. The first to suggest the union of the two towns was the great reformer Count István Széchenyi, whose name is linked to the building (between 1839–49) of the first cast iron bridge on the Danube, the Chain Bridge. Formal union had to wait until 1872. Pest, Buda and Óbuda – a market town mainly inhabited by Serbs – united to form the most rapidly developing city in the Europe of the time: Budapest. Immigrants arrived from every corner of the Austro-Hungarian Monarchy by the hundred thousand – Slovaks, South Slavs, Romanians and Jews – and the population rose to two hundred thousand by the turn of the century. Not long before, Budapest had been mainly German-speaking, but within a generation it became a Hungarian-speaking, multiracial city. The municipal leaders laid out the scheme of the new capital on Parisian lines, with radial arteries and boulevards, which encouraged the opening of coffee houses, theatres and places of amusement. When in 1896 the Millennium Exhibition was staged in Budapest to celebrate the thousand years since the *honfoglalás* – the traditional date of the entry of the Magyars to Hungary in 896 AD – many of the familiar landmarks of today were in place: the bridges, baths, the Fishermen's Bastion and the first underground sewer system in the Continent.

After the fever of railway building, decades of development in Budapest followed, and Gregersen took part in that too with some world-class work. He helped to realise the plans of the greatest architects, taking part in – among others – work on the Mátyás church, the Fine Art Museum and the Opera House. When a new radial avenue was built in Budapest at the proposal of Prime Minister Gyula Andrássy, those living in the mansions along it did not want to be disturbed by the noise of horse-drawn traffic on the stone of the road. As a solution Gregersen produced tens of thousands of wooden cubes and used them to surface what is now Andrássy út. The firm then collaborated in the construction of the Nyugati (Western) station in Pest, to the design of the Eiffel office in Paris, and of the National Theatre. It was for the latter that Gregersen was given his first official recognition, the Knight's Cross of the Order of Franz Joseph. By this time he was recognised in a wide circle of people, and had accordingly to keep up appearances. In 1875 he built the family's mansion in Lónyay utca, near his factory. Decorated with frescoes, the equipment in the two-storey neo-Renaissance build-

A Gregersen-bridge under construction in the Carpathians in 1894.

ing was twenty or thirty years before its time: bathrooms, flushing toilets and dumbwaiters added to the comfort of the occupants. From this point the Gregersens lived a double life: in Pest, an upper-middle-class life with servants, cooks and governesses, giving banquets and going to the Opera – but whenever the chance arose they would withdraw to Szob, where they spent their rural time much more privately, often filling their days with manual work.

Gregersen did not spend all his income from the business, and because of his bad experiences did not invest it in the stock exchange: with the profits he bought land on the outskirts of Budapest. Over a few years he acquired a considerable part of the Danube-side suburbs, and with the growth of the city the value of his land soared. His mighty wealth and his honesty are both demonstrated by the fact that as early as 1873 he was the biggest *virilista*, that is, tax-payer in the capital, and according to a later compilation he was the third largest landowner in Budapest. In the building work undertaken by him several thousand, sometimes tens of thousands, of workers were employed at one time. It is typical of his attitude to business that in all probability he did not make a *fillér* from the job that made him famous throughout Hungary. On 11 March 1879 the river Tisza, swollen by rain, flooded the southern city of Szeged, a very large number were killed and almost all the houses in the centre were destroyed. Gregersen immediately offered his experience in under-water building for rescue work. First he built temporary wooden houses for the families rendered homeless by the flood, then with his specialised pumps he pumped out the inundated city centre. He employed three thousand men, and they filled 160 horse-drawn carts and eighty-four railway trucks daily with soil, with which the low-lying parts were raised and dykes erected around the city. He made one of his brothers and his son move to Szeged, but he himself too was present until almost the end of the operation. The work took three years and the Gregersens exceeded the estimated cost, thus ending the installations with a loss. In one of his articles the writer Kálmán Mikszáth, who at the time was working as a journalist in Szeged, quoted 'Gudbrand Gregersen', who had come from far away, as an example contrasting with the local entrepreneurs, who were always on the make and playing tricks. Recognition came from somewhere else too, however: in recognition of his works in Hungary, but chiefly his flood defence works in Szeged, Franz Joseph bestowed Hungarian nobility on the son of a Norwegian peasant. On learning of the Austro-Hungarian distinction his native land too honoured Gregersen, and he was awarded the highest Norwegian decoration, the Order of St Olav.

The building of Keleti (Eastern) station in Pest too was a great success for the firm. The site was a former peat-bog, and the new station was built on piles; only after work had begun did it emerge that the soil conditions were even worse than anticipated. Piles had therefore to be driven to a depth of fifteen metres rather than eleven, which significantly increased the cost and jeopardised the prospect of completion to schedule. The Gregersens – or as they now called themselves, G. Gregersen and Sons, Building Contractors – felled three thousand cedars in the Carpathians and drove them into the ground in record time. It speaks volumes for their professionalism that when recently the foundations were exposed again in the construction of the new metro line the piles were found to be intact. The Elizabeth Bridge at Komárom and the funicular mountain railway in the Carpathians were also reckoned similar examples of technical bravura. The ornate doors and windows installed in the new Parliament building, however, deserved notice for their traditional forms. If, before the turn of the century, anyone wanted to boast of the achievements of the Hungarian building industry they usually listed what the Gregersens had done. Thus it was possible for them to produce a significant part of the pavilions at the 1885 Industrial Exhibition in addition to the central hall. The firm also had its own pavilion at the Exhibition, which astonished the public and the press. It was a Gothic wooden building, in which a huge map showed what the firm had built in Hungary and where. *A markedly foreign name, but long a household one*, wrote the *Vasárnapi Újság* (Sunday News). *Such entrepreneurs as this show that the success of our exhibition is not a matter of chance, but the coordination of existing strengths.*

By this time the company was working in the farthest corners of the Monarchy: In Fiume (today Rijeka, Croatia) it built what was at the time the largest wooden harbour in the world, but it was also commissioned to work in Przemyśl (today in Poland), Prague, on the Bay of Cattaro (today Kotor, Montenegro) and in Bosnia. For this it became necessary to create subsidiaries, but even then Gregersen controlled the company in the traditional way, like a sort of patriarch. At festival times he listened to concerts by the band consisting of workers in the factory, and at Christmas the workers received presents from him. As he grew older he went back more and more often to the land of his birth, where he had also bought an estate and a farmhouse. He is reckoned one of the founders of higher technical education in Norway, and donated huge sums to that purpose. He was received several times by the king and prime minister of Norway – which had become independent from Sweden at the turn of the century – and talked with them in the peasant dialect of his village. He was always capable of blending his Norwegian and Hungarian qualities, being at the same time multinational big businessman, Hungarian nobleman and Norwegian peasant. He took it as a compliment if he was praised in the papers for adopting Hungarian ways, but in his final years even in Hungary he liked to speak only Norwegian, and even engaged a Norwegian servant, who remained with him until his death. He never retired: even when over eighty he frequently went out to all the sites in the provinces to see for himself how the work was progressing.

He sent his six sons to the best European universities: three became architects, one a bridge-building engineer, one a forestry engineer and one a lawyer, and so Gregersen could be sure that he would leave behind a prospering family business. The boys did indeed go into the company, but the future did not turn out as he had dreamed. The eldest son, György, was a talented engineer like his father, and even worked on the building of the Suez Canal as well as in numerous projects in Hungary, but died of pneumonia before he could take the company over. His brother Hugó developed a steadily deteriorating mental condition as the result of infectious encephalitis. One night he climbed the pillar of the Elizabeth Bridge in Budapest – then under construction – in his nightshirt, was diagnosed irrational and went into the institute for nervous diseases at Lipótmező. Ödön was in charge of the Prague subsidiary and among other things was involved in the renovation of the Charles Bridge. He died in Prague of a sudden illness, after which his father wound up the subsidiary. Endre, the lawyer, as a young man led a dissolute life and took no interest in the business later either, but he established the first Norwegian diplomatic post in the family house in Lónyay utca and remained its consul-general all his life. The forestry engineer, Béla, was in fact in charge of the company's sawmill in Bosnia, but felt most at home in nature as an amateur botanist and had no taste for managerial duties. Finally, Nils, born in 1857, took over the operative direction, and became managing director of the business even while his father was still alive. Of the six only three married, and of them only Hugó, the invalid, had sons who would have been able to go into the company when they grew up. The eldest Gregersen did his utmost for this to happen: he had a long legal battle with his daughter-in-law so that he should be able to supervise his two grandsons' education. After the turn of the century, however, it became clear that the now gigantic firm was not going to be able to continue as the family business of which its founder had dreamed.

On Christmas Eve 1910 Gudbrand Gregersen, then eighty-seven, gave presents to members of the family and employees as usual, recited a Christmas poem to them in Norwegian, had cake and wine taken to the policeman on duty at the corner, then went to his room to rest. He had every reason to be proud of changing the face of his adopted country over sixty years with his own two hands and his talents. He went to sleep for ever, mentally alert and physically healthy. For a little while after his death it seemed that the firm that he had left to his family would forge further ahead: a commission had been received from the government of

The Gregersen family outside their house in 1888.

Turkey for the modernisation of the harbour of Constantinople. The work could not be completed because the world war broke out, and building work for peaceful purposes was soon at a standstill everywhere. In the economic crisis which followed the war the building industry too was badly affected, and furthermore the firm's Transylvanian, Upper Hungarian and Bosnian sources of timber were now in foreign countries. And as there was no one that felt disposed to start again amid the problems, in 1921 the proprietors of G. Gregersen and Sons, Building Contractors, decided to wind up the company. This took years, and the family lived on the income from the vast real estate and the gradual sale of it. Even in 1951 they retained property that could be confiscated, and from which the wandering Norwegian carpenter's last surviving daughter and grandchild could be deported.

We Franz Joseph the First … cause it to be remembered and by these presents made known to all whom it may concern that by virtue of the submission of the Hungarian ministers about our person it has been brought to our gracious consideration and regard that Gudbrand Gregersen, entrepreneur of Budapest, has at various times and occasions rendered outstanding services to our faith, our majesty and our majestic ruling house, and likewise to the common good of our Hungary and its fraternal countries, in that for 38 years he has worked in Hungary and striven zealously in the uplifting and development of domestic industry, he furthermore carried out a great part of the construction works necessary on the occasion of the building up anew of the free royal town of Szeged, devastated by the overflowing waters of the river Tisza (…). Finally seeing that over and above this he has also made huge sacrifices for the advancement of the common good we have by our royal decree dated this 13th day of the month of October in the year 1883 deemed the said Gudbrand Gregersen and (…) his progeny and posterity of both sexes to be elevated among and into the ranks of the real, true, ancient and undoubted nobility of Hungary and its fraternal countries and in further evidence of our royal grace and favour towards him we further grant him the use of the style Saági,[6] so that henceforth for all time the said Gudbrand Gregersen and all his legitimate progeny and posterity of both sexes in addition to the use of the style Saági may be able to enjoy and possess all the rights which the real, true, ancient and undoubted nobility of our said Hungary and its fraternal countries have heretofore in any way enjoyed and possessed or do enjoy and possess in accordance with law or ancient custom.

Gudbrand Gregersen's letters patent of nobility, 1883

The highest-ranking soldier of Arab extraction in the West.
Fadlallah in about 1910.

Mihály Fadlallah el Hedad

The fourteen-year-old Syrian immigrant, sword at his side, glared at His Majesty Franz Joseph I, Emperor of Austria and King of Hungary. It was July 1857, and the emperor had come to the military riding-school near the harbour of Trieste to inspect the Arab thoroughbreds that had come from distant lands. The expedition led by Col. Rudolf von Brudermann, however, had brought back not only horses from Damascus but also a young boy. Fadlallah el Hedad had been known in his village as *Nekhle* (Palm-tree) because of his height. His family had fled their native soil because of the wars of religion, and his parents were dead. As he was good with horses it had not taken much to persuade the soldiers from far away to take him home with them. Arab stallions had been bought to improve the blood-line at the stud-farm at Bábolna, and he had taken care of them on the long voyage home. He had been given the frogged uniform of a Hungarian groom, and allowed to wear a sword at his side. The king had waxed so enthusiastic over the splendid horses that, ignoring the rules of protocol, he had begun to chat with the soldiers. He beckoned to the groom too, laid his hand on the boy's sword, and asked him who he was and how he came to be there. Nekhle could not understand a word that Franz Joseph said, but what he was doing was more than enough for him. It is a deadly insult to a free Arab if a stranger touches his weapon, and so the boy crossly grabbed His Majesty's hand.

The atmosphere froze: everyone was paralysed at the treasonable act. The emperor, however, was pleased at the young Arab's nerve. He gave orders that the boy was to be sent to officer cadet school at Treasury expense, and if his nature was so fiery be trained as an army officer. There is no proof of whether the grabbing of the hand actually occurred – it may be merely anecdotal – but what is a fact is that the boy did come from Syria with von Brudermann's expedition, he was present at Franz Joseph's inspection, went to officer cadet school on a scholarship, and became an officer in the Hungarian army by the name of Mihály Fadlallah el Hedad. He spent more than sixty years at Bábolna, as its commanding officer made it internationally famous, indeed, made it the best horse-breeding establishment in the world at the time. He considered himself a Hungarian, but never denied his Arab origins and kept his Arabic language to the end of his life. He ended his career as the highest-ranking soldier of Arab birth in the Western world.

HUNGARIAN HORSE-BREEDING. Thanks to their horses, the nomadic Magyars carried out successful campaigns in the tenth century in what are now Germany, Switzerland and Lombardy, and horse-breeding remained the principal form of animal husbandry for a long time after the occupation of Hungary by the Magyars. The ancient Hungarian horse was an undemanding, small and hardy creature, and in the Middle Ages was bred without the introduction of any alien blood. In the Turkish period the Hungarians became acquainted with the conspicuously faster Arab breeds, with which they improved their stock. The culture of high-quality horse-breeding made the light cavalry called *hussars* the most important army of the Hungarian military; armies in all European countries and beyond developed similar units. The Habsburg rulers soon recognised that within the empire Hungary was the region best equipped by nature to provide the horses needed by the armies, but was not able to produce them in sufficient quantity. In 1784 Emperor Joseph II charged József Csekonics, a captain in his

bodyguard, with creating a state reserve, and thus founded the famous stud-farm at Mezőhegyes in Békés, south-east Hungary. After this satisfied expectations, in 1790 an Arab farm was opened at
Bábolna in western Hungary. Not long afterwards Count István
Széchenyi introduced the breeding of English thoroughbreds too,
and so dominated horse-racing in Hungary.

He had been born in 1843 in Labenon, at the time part of Syria.
His ancestors had been Maronite Christian Arabs, and had probably been metal-workers by trade, as that is what the Arabic word
hedad means. In mid-nineteenth century first the Druzes, then the
Shi'a Moslem extremists made bloody onslaughts on the Christians, and the family had been forced to flee from them into Beirut. National frontiers counted for little, as every country and territory around was part of the Ottoman Empire. We do not know
how Nekhle's parents met their deaths, but in any case he was an
orphan in his early teens. He had to work with his relations, who –
like a lot of Maronite families – made a living by cultivating silk-
worms and producing silk thread. It was considered natural for the
teenagers to work alongside the adults. *The Maronite community,* he
later wrote, *is one of the most industrious in the world. There is not a foot
of land that they do not cultivate with care and great labour.* One day his
relatives sent him with a caravan to Damascus to collect the money
for silk that the family had sold to merchants in Syria. He probably
failed in this, as he remained in the Syrian capital and was roaming the streets when he met Col. von Brudermann and his expedition. He liked the look of the soldiers, with their strange uniforms,
that were transporting the selected horses and asked if he might
go with them. The Imperial and Royal officers must have thought
that horses from the desert, which had never seen a stable, would
be happier if handled by an Arab groom, and so they agreed. The
ship docked in Trieste on 22 July 1857, and a few weeks later the
herd of Arab horses, together with the cadet from Syria who had
found favour with the emperor, arrived at Bábolna.

The boy spoke nothing but Arabic, and Ferenc Kozma, an officer of the horse-breeding corps and an apostle of Hungarian horse-breeding, took him under his wing, and soon regarded him as an adopted son. Nekhle quickly picked up Hungarian and converted from the Maronite faith to the Roman Catholic. Soon everyone was calling him Mihály (or Misi for short), the Hungarian name that he was given in baptism. At first he had difficulty with the strict military discipline, but when in 1865 he swore allegiance as an officer no one would have said that he was not a Hungarian nobleman in uniform. The young Lieutenant remained at Bábolna as an officer in the horse-breeding corps.

Emperor Joseph II bought the estate at Bábolna for a new imperial stud. From 1816 on exclusively Arab horses were bred there, and every ten or fifteen years stallions were brought in from Arabia to improve the blood-line. Rudolf von Brudermann's expedition was the third since the foundation, but was reckoned the best selection of stock until then. The blood-line of the horses brought in by him determined the composition of the stud for long years to come. The commanders of the stud maintained that the secret of success was that he had managed to purchase the carefully bred horses of Bedouin tribes in the desert. It was obvious that if an Arabic-speaking officer who knew the region took part in the next purchasing journey it would be able to return to Bábolna with stallions of outstanding quality. For this, however, there had to be a long wait: either the money was not available, or the authorities could not agree. Meanwhile Mihály Fadlallah el Hedad was promoted First Lieutenant and posted to a depot in the country to set up a stud-farm to supply the hussar regiments there. The tall, good-looking officer did not marry: the girl that he courted did not dare to marry him because she was afraid that he would take her with him to distant Arabia. That they were close, however, is proved by the fact that descendants of that nervous girl are still alive and claim that Mihály Fadlallah el Hedad was their great-great-grandfather.

In Western dress among desert nomads.

He went on his first buying journey at the age of thirty-three and on that occasion had to go only as far as Constantinople, where he bought ten stallions from the stud of the recently deceased Sultan Abdul Aziz. That was enough to refresh the blood-line, but the young officer yearned for real desert horses. He knew that it was not enough to buy horses in Damascus or other big towns, it was necessary to go out to the remotest Bedouin encampments and there to make offers for such thoroughbreds as their owners would not even wish to sell. He was certain that, contrary to the practice of previous years, it was not enough to concentrate on stallions but that mares too of excellent lineage were needed to re-invigorate the Bábolna stud. Although at the time he was only in charge of a rural stud-farm he saw it as his principal aim to perfect the stock at Bábolna, and made no secret of the fact that he would create the world's best stud-farm in his chosen country. An opportunity came for him to tell Rudolf, the heir to the throne, of his plans: he received Fadlallah, now a captain, in the interval of a performance in the Burg Theatre in Vienna. That conversation may have been the reason why the government agreed to fund the purchase of real Arab horses. The expedition was accompanied by a representative of the Ministry of Agriculture, which was financing the journey, perhaps so that there should be someone holding the purse-strings in case Fadlallah wanted to give too much for each fine animal. He was twenty-eight when he first stepped onto his native soil again. *Inquisitive Arabs came in droves from far and wide,* said a later newspaper article about it, *strewed flowers in the path of the gold-braided Hungarian army officer and escorted him with banners into the presence of imams, who welcomed the celebrated son of their land with great ceremony.* His local knowledge really counted for a lot. He returned to Hungary with four Bedouin stallions and five mares – one of them the black stallion who became Bábolna's number one stud, whose blood-line continues to this day.

The ever nobler blood-line of the stud attracted more and more the attention of breeders outside Hungary, and it became customary for rulers and heads of state visiting Hungary to put Bábolna on their itinerary. *The armies of Italy, Greece, Romania, the Balkan countries and even Turkey buy most of their horses in Hungary,* announced a German book on the subject. *Two English cavalry regiments recruited their stock in Hungary, and performed with excellent results in the campaign in Egypt. Saxony and Bavaria, where there is only a little horse-breeding, are using more and more Hungarian horses. It is no* surprise that in recognition of his deserts Mihály Fadlallah el Hedad was awarded the Order of Franz Joseph. Thanks to his professionalism and his knowledge of the language and the region a series of further expeditions were able to acquire better and better horses. In 1899 he was promoted Lieutenant-Colonel on appointment to the command of Bábolna. No one was troubled by his Arab origins, and Hungarian and Austrian officers alike looked on him as a Hungarian.

His greatest professional success came in the last World Exhibition of the century. The international horse show was held in the setting of the Paris Expo of 1900, with 1,717 horses on display from some hundreds of studs. Every day tens of thousands queued to see the finest horses in the world: it was Europe's farewell to the centuries-old way of life in which the horse had played a pivotal role in military affairs, transport and sport alike. Bábolna exhibited eight horses, winning four gold medals and two silver, together with two international championships. The stud itself won the gold medal. One of the Bábolna Arab thoroughbreds was considered so outstandingly fine that a special 'prize of prizes' was instituted for it. In the words of a French paper: *This wonderful stallion unites in itself both the perfect type of the noble Arab – very beautiful, rounded, muscular form – (...) and poised, dynamic gait, and so the jury that judged the top stallion class were unanimous in seeing the need to create a special prize for 'Grand Champion'.* Everyone in Paris talked about the overall winner at the horse-show, the Bábolna stud in Hungary and its experts. Mihály Fadlallah el Hedad was able proudly to send home a report of his experiences: *Such are the purchases of horses, likewise the outcome of careful and expert rearing and training, that the richest and most carefully preserved in purity of breed of the Arab studs in Europe is at Bábolna, and I can safely say that even in the East I have never seen such valuable, pure and rich breeding material as that at Bábolna.*

Now promoted Colonel he made use of his unexpected popularity to realise his dream: to organise an expedition and bring horses to Hungary from a corner of the desert where no European had ever been. In October 1901 a brief notice in the leading Hungarian weekly *Vasárnapi Újság* (Sunday News) stated that *Col. Mihály Fadlallah el Hedad of the horse-breeding corps left yesterday for Arabia to procure, on the commission of the Minister for Agriculture, breeding material for the Bábolna stud. He will go first to Beirut in Syria, then into Mesopotamia as far as Baghdad.* The fifty-strong group rode a total of 3,600 Km in eighty-five days in search of the stud-farms of nomadic Arabs who had had no contact with Western civilisation. The colonel examined 4,000 horses and from them chose the thirteen that he eventually purchased. The trading was by no means an equine beauty-competition. Only the vendors and Fadlallah were aware that the world's best horses were being bargained for. *The European has no conception* – he wrote later – *of the condition that these much sought-after horses were in. Those scraggy nags with their ribs protruding that come from the villages to the weekly market in Debrecen are incomparably better looking, more fit to be seen, than the horses which we bought for bright gold. (...) The weary look of misery and exhaustion blinked in the horses' eyes. Their coats were long and tangled. All their lives they had chewed, at best, on stems of thorn-bushes and were quite unused to regular food. (...) If an uninitiated person saw my state horse-purchases in that lamentable condition, I would scarcely have avoided a sharp rebuke. On the first day we could not even feed our poor horses properly for fear that the new ration would damage their stomachs, so accustomed were they to deprivation.*

In looking for these animals he sometimes risked his life. Even the Turkish soldiers escorting the Hungarians dared not set foot in the territories defended by the nomadic tribes. He visited Bedouin tribes that were at war with one another, and could not know whether the horse that he bought in one oasis had not been stolen in the course of conflict from the tribe at the next stopping-place, for which death would have awaited him. On one occasion they rode over the desert with no water for two days, and then waded belly-deep in the mud of a swamp, and every night they had to endure sandstorms or the attacks of armed robbers.

When, months after their departure, they returned from the desert to Damascus, the Governor of Syria declared that never had such fine Arabs gone to Europe all at once. In Beirut Fadlallah also called on his relatives. *Everyone must have felt that spiritual softening, the sense of unaccustomed warmth of heart that fills one's whole being when one sees the house where one was born, one's native land, after a long time*, he wrote emotionally. The army officer, now a Hungarian and Catholic, held the new-born child of a relative under the water of baptism according to the Maronite ceremony. The Hungarian papers gave a detailed account of their journey, and they were fêted nation-wide on their return. The disciplined army officer had a second opportunity in a short while for expressing his sentiments: *Everywhere on the way home to Bábolna we were met by welcomers small and great, who greeted the homecomers with smiling faces. I cannot deny it: so many signs of affection bathed me, I was moved. I was home! Back among the hills and valleys of Bábolna, where Divine Providence had led me forty-five years before.*

The horses purchased by the expedition made it possible to guarantee for a long time more the position of Bábolna as leading stud in Europe. Fadlallah wrote of his experience on the journey in a book which not only preserves the memory of the greatest Hungarian expert on horse-breeding, but also, with its detailed ethnological observation and lively style, makes excellent reading. On the fiftieth anniversary of his military service the commandant of the stud was awarded the Commander's Cross of the Order of Franz Joseph and great festivity took place at Bábolna in his honour. A fellow officer greeted him on the double occasion: *If I could speak your language I would, Fadlallah, in order the better to come closer to your heart! But there is an ancient proverb, that he that does not know Arabic should not speak Arabic.[7] This way too you will understand, because even then I would only say may Allah and the great God of the Hungarians grant you long life!* Nor did public opinion of the time dispute his rightful glory, and in 1909, for example, a newspaper article put it thus: *Now too the Arab stud at Bábolna is a precious*

The blood-line from Arabia is still preserved at Bábolna.

national treasure, in a class by itself. But that it has risen from mediocrity so comparatively quickly to the present high level, so to speak, is solely and exclusively to the credit of the present commandant, Col. Fadlallah el Hedad, who not only runs the stud expertly but also knows its every unit, and cherishes and cares for them with kindness and affection.

Having raised the Bábolna stud to world level, Lieutenant General Fadlallah retired in 1913 at the age of seventy. After relinquishing command he remained at Bábolna, moving to a little two-room flat in the officers' mess. He was very helpful to his successor in the selection of Arab horses for breeding purposes. He was a bachelor, but even in his last years did not live a lonely life. He used to enjoy telling the children of Bábolna tales of his native land – they nicknamed the old man with the strange name 'Uncle Paddler'. He died in 1924 at the age of eighty-one, but the descendants of the Arab horses that he bought live to this day at Bábolna. The former Syrian immigrant lies in Bábolna cemetery, not far from the main road down which not long ago his refugee compatriots were passing westwards in search of a better life.

On the third day the tribes that were encamped farther away still came with their horses. On that day a grey stallion was brought, two and half years old and 149 cm in height, and although the horse was tiny I thought it suitable and worth buying. I offered fifty Turkish pieces of gold for it. The owner was unwilling to sell it. I said to the Bedouin too, who would not part with his horse for a tent-full of gold, had he not thought it over? "Why would you wish to exchange your body for your soul?" said he, looking at his horse with fanatical love, and withdrew sadly into his tent. And certainly that night the Bedouin had a sorrowful leave-taking with his horse, because after all he had taken all things into account and thought it over and two days later I bought Em Tiur from him for 130 Turkish pieces of gold. The Arabic name means 'Mother of birds'. (…) That noble animal could indeed be the mother of swift-winged birds that cleave the air. And though the 130 gleaming pieces of gold did much to soothe the Bedouin's pain, it was touching to see the way that he looked at his horse for the last time … That evening the spirit was on the banks of the Tigris; the body, that is, Em Tiur's grieving master, was perhaps clinking his gold …

Mihály Fadlallah el Hedad,
My travels in Mesopotamia and Iraqi Arabia 1901–1902
Budapest, 1904

Turkish dervish, Hungarian scholar, British spy.
Ármin Vámbéry in the 1860s.

Ármin Vámbéry

Queen Victoria of England invited people whom she esteemed highly to record their birth-dates in a book at Windsor Castle, so that she would be able to send them personal greetings every year. On 5 May 1889 the Lord Steward of the Household knocked at the door of the room in which an honorary member of the Royal Society, the leading expert in Great Britain on Central Asia, was staying. Under his arm he carried the *royal birthday book*, the pages of which bore the birth-dates and signatures of crowned heads, military leaders, world-famous artists and scientists. The guest turned the pages in some embarrassment, and then confided shamefacedly in the Lord Steward that unfortunately he did not know the date of his birth. Back home in Hungary no one had thought such a thing so much as worth recording about a fatherless, sickly, penniless Jewish child who had been born at the height of a cholera epidemic: there was little chance of his surviving to adulthood. "Don't worry about that", came the reply. "Her Majesty attaches far more importance to her guests' achievements and merit than to their origins." So it was that Ármin Vámbéry's birthday became the date that he, despite his confusion, dictated for the queen's records: 12 March 1832. He had risen from the ranks of beggary until later monarchs sought his company and asked his advice. He was crippled in one leg, but had traversed half a continent on foot. His dozen books and some hundreds of articles had appeared all over Europe. He spoke sixteen languages. He was the best known and most respected Hungarian of his time in the Anglo-Saxon world. Yet back home in Hungary he was considered an upstart, a vagabond and a charlatan.

He had first seen the light as Hermann Wamberger, in the north Hungarian town of Szentgyörgy, now in Slovakia. His father was a pious Jewish businessman, who read the Talmud all day rather than ledgers, with the result that his children were brought up with a love of letters and accustomed to privation. The last great cholera epidemic carried him off, and his son Hermann was born a few days later. At the age of twenty-two, his widow was burdened not only with supporting her family but also had an invalid son on her hands: he suffered from luxation of the hip, and although doctors submitted him to painful treatments all were futile, and he could walk only on crutches. His mother soon remarried and the family moved to the small town of Dunaszerdahely, where the majority of the inhabitants were Jewish, and lived by gathering leeches. Hermann went to the local Jewish school, but his mother had a feeling that her lame son was meant for something better. She intended him to become a doctor and transferred him to the Protestant elementary school, after which he went to the Piarist grammar school in Szentgyörgy. This move was considered a shocking scandal in the Orthodox Jewish community, but his mother stuck to her plan. In his schools Hermann was teased both for his crutches and for being Jewish. The first he could change: he discarded his crutches and with astonishing persistence learnt to walk with a stick. His birth, however, still isolated him and so he read and dreamed a very great deal. Even at the age of ten he had to work in order to earn his school fees. The puny little boy was of little use for physical work, but he was a success in tutoring his contemporaries at home. It soon became evident that he had a remarkable gift for languages. After Hungarian, German and Hebrew, he studied Latin as a child. He taught himself French because he read somewhere that "anyone that does not know French cannot claim to be a cultured man". By this time young Hermann was very much aware that only education could offer the chance of breaking out of poverty.

It often seemed that he was not going to succeed. After the sixth class he had to abandon his studies for lack of funds, and from then on was completely self-taught.

At the age of twenty he went to Pest, by then also able to read Swedish, Spanish and English. He was so poor that he could not afford to rent a room, but shared a bed with an apprentice tailor in a slum. In the hope of finding a place as a language teacher he spent all day standing outside the Orczy coffee-house in the crowd of those seeking work. Eventually a Jewish family from Slavonia entrusted him with teaching their daughter, but he soon had to leave that comfortable position because "an arousal of quite a different sort" came over him in addition to enthusiasm for study, and he fell in love with his pupil. He worked as tutor in a variety of families for a total of six years, and during that time learnt from books the three most important Middle Eastern languages: Turkish, Persian and Arabic. By then he was certain that if he had money he would not go to medical school but meant to make a living from languages and study.

When he returned to Pest he went into the University Library reading-room to study. There he read from morning to night and attracted the attention of the librarian, the poet János Garay, who introduced him to his friends. The Hungarian intelligentsia of the period of Absolutism saw in the talented young Jewish man an example of successful assimilation, and heard from him that his great ambition was to travel to Turkey, as the Oriental roots of the Hungarian language intrigued him. On their recommendation he went along, just as he was with holes in his shoes, to call on Baron József Eötvös, the most receptive spirit of the age, in his home and ask for his assistance in realising his goals. He was not disappointed: Eötvös arranged for the Academy to bear part of the expenses of the journey, and gave the man some money, a pair of trousers and a shirt. It was thanks to him that in February 1857 a brief notice could appear in *Pesti Napló* (Pest Journal): *A young son of Hungary is leaving shortly for Constantinople to study Oriental languages, principally Turkish language and literature. His name is Ármin Vámberger.*

The young man, who from then on used the Hungarian form of his first name, spent years in Turkey, where he lived at first among Hungarian refugees from 1848. It saddened him that most of his compatriots failed to fit in on Turkish soil, and many of them idled their time away as beggars or became addicted to hashish. He decided that he was not going to end up like them and did his best to integrate into Turkish society. As he knew all the important languages of Europe he soon became indispensable at the Turkish court and translated for ambassadors and ministers. In Istanbul he was known to all as Reşid efendi, and even sent his articles to *Pesti Napló* in that name. He made such progress in Turkish that in 1858 he edited a German-Turkish dictionary. That was his first book: the authorial name that he had chosen appeared on the title-page: Ármin Vámbéry. He felt it important to demonstrate his Hungarian origins in this way. His new-found Turkish friends had known nothing about that, and only saw in him a Westerner that had converted to Islam. One influential supporter of his even took him to the *medrese*, the Moslem religious school, where he was the first European to be able to take part in debates with the theologians. *The Turkish clothes that I had put on, my outwardly Oriental presence and my knowledge were merely an exterior,* he recalled later. He was very impressed to find that in Turkish society there was no hereditary nobility, and everyone could advance by his own powers, but he could not accept Oriental despotism. *It became clear to me that a life worthy of man is only to be found in a setting of Western aspirations.*

Four years after leaving Hungary he was elected a corresponding member of the Hungarian Academy of Sciences – a young man who had completed only six years of schooling. He did not spend long in Hungary. He persuaded the president of the scientific body to support him on a journey to Central Asia, in the course of which he would be able to look for the Oriental relations of the Hungarian language. Although several in the meeting objected to a lame man receiving money for a journey, in the end he was sent on his way with a thousand forints and a letter of introduction in Latin, addressed to "All Sultans, Khans and Begs in Tartary". This latter Vámbéry did not take with him, realising that if it had been found on him on his journey he would likely have been executed as a Christian spy. He eventually obtained a usable document in Constantinople which referred to him as a dervish of the true faith under the defence of the Sultan. Turkish friends actually tried to dissuade him from risking his life on such a journey. He felt that there was nothing to be lost. *What could have happened to me, what privations could there have been that the bitter fate of my young days had spared me? I had seen enough starvation by the time that I was eighteen; lack of clothing was a daily occurrence in my early youth and from early childhood I had my share of derision and contempt for being a Jew.*

He set off in 1882. First he spent almost a year in the Ottoman embassy in Teheran, unable to go further because of warfare in the region. Eventually he was able to join a party of pilgrims returning from Mecca to Samarkand. *Tomorrow I leave in the strictest disguise of a dervish, as an absolute beggar. If my journey is a success – no European has gone that far before me – if I am not found out, I shall make a name for myself and the Academy in the eyes of all Europe. Long live our dear fatherland! Vámbéry.* Indeed, he went to countries where no European had been since Marco Polo, for an inquisitive unbeliever could easily fall into the hands of an executioner. Thanks to his perfect command of languages, it was believed everywhere that a begging dervish of the true faith had come among them. He walked halfway across the continent, from Persia to the frontier of China, leaning on a Hungarian *fokos*, a walking-stick with a small axe-blade for a handle. His life was frequently in danger, but thanks to his quick wits and gentle manner he always escaped. Although he did not find any Oriental relations of Hungarian he did map unknown peoples, religions and customs. So as not to be discovered he made his notes in Arabic script but Hungarian language. His method of scientific description was a forerunner of the "participating observation" of modern cultural anthropology; the group accepted him as a member, and he openly but critically surveyed the world of Islam.

In May 1864 he returned eagerly to Hungary, with a mass of notes and a Tartar secretary accompanying him voluntarily. *As I stepped onto the shore of the Pest landing-stage, next to the Chain-Bridge, and hurried to the near-by Europa Hotel with my secretary, the living witness of my journey to Khiva, I thought that I would not be able to contain my delight. (…) The gloomy moment of my arrival – completely unnoticed – and the hurtful indifference of my compatriots fell all the more painfully on my heart. No one came to call on me, no one took any notice of me, with the exception of my sole faithful well-wisher, Baron József Eötvös.* Regarded as an eccentric, the scholar became resigned to Hungarian indifference. After a month he went on to London, where he was received as a world-famous explorer and was entertained in stately houses. *My present journey in England is a triumph such as Kossuth is the only foreigner to have seen,* he wrote in one of his letters, and he was not exaggerating in the least. From British politicians with interests in Asia, through aristocrats eager for the exotic to men of learning, everyone asked questions about the unfamiliar countries. The Queen received him personally and he became friendly with the Prince of Wales. At first details of his journey appeared only in periodicals, and later his memoirs were published in book form.

For half a century after 1864 he was reckoned the most influential Hungarian personality in England. That was the age of great discoveries, and the great Hungarian scientist fitted in well with the series of Livingstone, Burton and other celebrated travellers. Among the English the *self-made man*, who had raised himself from lowly societal degree, had his own standing, and Vámbéry was a perfect example. Furthermore, it was his book that first drew attention to the Russians' steady acquisition of territory in Central

Asia. His readers at first saw in it the excessive anxiety of a patriotic Hungarian's hatred for Russia, but when the first reports arrived of Russian invasion of Turkmenistan speeches in Parliament, quoting Vámbéry and calling for intervention, increased in frequency. Finally Lord Palmerston, the Prime Minister, himself sought his opinion on the political relationships of the various emirates and khanates.

If he had stayed in England the former Hungarian pauper might well have been knighted, but he chose to return home. *Even if I loathed the slothfulness, negligence and blind fanaticism of the Asiatic, the precise opposite to all these here affected me no less unpleasantly. And as I sought the golden mean I yearned to back in Hungary, where – on the fringe of both worlds – I hoped to find happiness.* In 1865 he went home to become principal of the Oriental Languages department of the University of Pest. One condition for holding this position was that he be baptised, which he satisfied. He did not, however, obtain the position, although no one else applied for it. The University was under the influence of the Catholic clergy, and it was taken amiss that Vámbéry had become a Calvinist. In the end, his appointment was due to the fact that Franz Joseph I received him in Vienna because of the report of his popularity in England. At the emperor's request the University appointed him lecturer in Oriental languages – though not actually professor. When he took up office the Rector greeted him with *Do not think that we are unaware of your double nature. We know very well that your knowledge of Oriental languages is weak and your appointment to the department very dubious. But we are reluctant to oppose His Majesty's order, and you have only that our hands are tied to thank for your position.*

THE JEWS OF HUNGARY AT THE TURN OF THE CENTURY. In 1867, the year of the Compromise, the Hungarian Parliament passed a law enabling the emancipation of the Jews, thereby also speeding their assimilation. A numerous social stratum formed, educated, enterprising and mercantile, which felt that Hungary was its fatherland, and successfully blended its Hungarian and Jewish qualities. One of the leading protagonists of the movement was the liberal politician Baron József Eötvös, Minister of Education. The Jews of Hungary played a distinguished part in the extraordinarily rapid economic development of the period, and quickly rose to important positions in business, manufacturing and financial services. The successful assimilation of the wealthy Jews is shown by the great number that were granted nobility, several of them even the title of Baron. Politicians of Jewish origin obtained positions in several governments at the turn of the nineteenth-twentieth centuries. At the same time, by the 1880s political anti-Semitism had appeared in Hungary, and the National Anti-Semitic Party won seats in Parliament, but was marginalised by the political élite. The trial at Tiszaeszlár (…) was a powerful symbol; Jews in that village were accused of carrying out a ritual murder, but were acquitted. Numerous Jewish intelligentsia were also catalysts of cultural and academic life in Budapest. Theodor Herzl and the founders of the international Zionist movement too were born in Budapest. The 1910 census recorded approximately a million Jews living in Hungary.

Despite the disappointig reception he still wanted to settle in Pest. A number of his colleagues persisted in doubting whether he really did know Persian, and were convinced only when the Shah came to visit. Because of his lowly birth he did not receive an invitation to a reception for the Prince of Wales, but the heir to the British throne took his friend in and sat him at his side.

His academic work also earned a lot of criticism because of the part that he played in debates on Magyar prehistory. Vámbéry was, that is, one of the most important supporters of the theory that the Hungarian language was not of Finno-Ugrian origin but Turkic. By the end of the "Ugor-Turkic war" he recognised that Finno-Ugrian elements are dominant in Hungarian, but at the same time maintained that the ancient Magyars had been of Turkic ethnic descent. He was one of the first to state by this that in the case of a people language and ethnicity are not necessarily identical in origin. While many praised him for his original error in casting doubt on the Finno-Ugrian relationship, all the more attacked him when he wrote that the Magyar stock had been blended over the centuries from numerous ethnicities, and in *the veins of today's generation not a droplet of ancient Magyar blood remains.* When he was dubbed a charlatan on that account the most respected politician of his time, Ferenc Deák, defended him: *Leave Vámbéry alone! This man has got farther on one leg than very many have on two!*

RESEARCH INTO MAGYAR PREHISTORY. Medieval tradition held that the Magyars that entered Hungary in the late ninth century were relatives of the Huns or the Scythians. In the eighteenth century scientific methods too began to be used to prove or disprove their Oriental, Asiatic origins. Modern linguistics have proved the Finno-Ugrian origin of the language, but because of the Romantic national consciousness of the nineteenth century many people rejected the "fish-oily northern kinsfolk" and referred to other linguistic evidence that demonstrated similarity of vocabulary with Turkic. By mid-century numerous intellectuals of the time were engaged in what became known as the "Ugor-Turkic war". Nowadays the accepted academic position is that the Hungarian language is Finno-Ugrian in origin, but that in the course of migration was enriched from the vocabularies of other Oriental languages, including Turkic. That, however, does not prove that in the anthropological or genetic sense the Hungarians that entered Hungary were mainly of Finno-Ugrian descent, and this continues to be a topic of scientific debate both serious and frivolous.

A pupil wrote of him: *A gentleman with a limp, leaning on a thick stick, would appear outside the gate of his house at precisely three in the afternoon. (...) Shopkeepers and those working on the Danube embankment would correct their watches (...) and there was a time when England set its political watch-hands by this modest little man, with his pleasant smile, steely will and inexhaustible energy.* In reality, all his life Vámbéry was a frequent visitor in the most important British circles. Dickens took pleasure in hearing accounts of his experiences, while it was he that first told Bram Stoker about Vlad Tepeş Drakuleă, the Romanian warlord in Transylvania, better known as Dracula thanks to Stoker's famous novel. (Some even maintain that Stoker derived the word *vampire* from Vámbéry's name.) He gave the elderly Queen Victoria lessons in Hindi, and frequently met with Europe's first Jewish Prime Minister, Benjamin Disraeli. Now we know: the latter was interested in what he had to say not merely out of friendship. At the end of his life it was made known of Vámbéry – chiefly by his Russian opponents – that the scholar had all along been an English spy. From secret documents that have since been made public all that can be conjectured is rather that from the 1870s on he prepared geopolitical analyses for the British Secret Service, but that during his Asian travels he was not even in touch with it. The question of espionage could not have arisen, as Vámbéry never made a secret of his friendship with Britain and Turkey. Before the turn of the century he resumed contact with the Sultan's court and with Sultan Abdul Hamid II, who did not always know how to choose between Westernising reforms and despotic governance. He intervened in numerous diplomatic affairs, and assisted in improving Turco-British and Austro-Hungarian relationships. Although the truth was revealed after his books were published in the Islamic world, many Turks believed that even at the end of his life Vámbéry was a real dervish who had pretended to be a European so as to serve the interests of the faithful. He himself, however, considered himself a free-thinker and treated all organised religions critically while respecting the faiths of their adherents.

From his memoir *My Struggles*, written in middle age, it may appear that he never abandoned his optimism and believed unreservedly that more and more channels of advancement would soon open in Hungary for capable, up-and-coming young people like himself. It was only after his death in 1914 that it became evident from his single work of literature that doubts actually tormented him. His fictive biographical novel *A Tartar's Memories* is, in the last analysis, a criticism of a frequently hypocritical Western culture, and in it he writes of constantly rising anti-Semitism too. The lame dervish died in Budapest at the age of eighty-one. When the best known Hungarian writer of the day, Mór Jókai, was asked what had been the most important reading experiences in his life he replied the Bible, Shakespeare and Vámbéry.

I burned with enthusiasm when in my childhood I learned of the lives of the Hungarian national heroes. The heroic age of 1848 filled my young heart with pride; but later too, on the way back from Constantinople on the Danube steamer, when my foot first touched the soil of Hungary at Mohács I fell to my knees and kissed the ground in genuine rapture. I was infinitely happy and truly immersed in a sea of delight; but I soon had to appreciate that many, indeed most, did not regard my Hungarian patriotism as sincere, but belittled and derided it because, as the saying was, a Jew could not be a Hungarian, only a Jew. (…) Everywhere and on all occasions I was met with that endless snobbery, the equivocal shrug, indifference, and the silence which is more deadly than the most elaborate rhetoric. (…) I have always drawn courage and consolation from the thought that the shortsightedness of society could not deprive me of my natural right to my native soil. The land on which I saw God's daylight, on which my cradle rocked and on which I lived the golden days of my youth, that land is my fatherland and such it will remain. This is my native land, I bear in my heart its joys and sorrows, and have always been happy if, in one way or another, I could be of use to Hungary.

Ármin Vámbéry,
My Struggles, 1905

The countess in 1879.

Vilma Hugonnai

On 14 May 1897 doctoral diplomas were being handed out at Budapest University in the usual manner. On this occasion, however, the graduation ceremony was considered special, and the hall was packed with journalists. They were interested in the seventh doctor-to-be who stood beside the six young men in their black tail suits – fifty years of age, dressed in grey silk, and, what was more, a woman. Vilma Hugonnai read out the doctoral oath in a firm voice. The first Hungarian female doctor of medicine had struggled for twenty years for women to be allowed to graduate in Hungary. At first she had been derided, attempts had been made to prove that women were unsuited to a scientific career, and finally bureaucratic obstacles had been put in her way. She had not given up, but with head held high had complied with the humiliating procedures simply in order to be permitted to heal. In the process she had become a dedicated spokeswoman for the rights of women. Every Hungarian woman that has completed a university course has her to thank for her degree.

She was born the fifth child of an impoverished aristocratic family. Her first education came from a governess in the family mansion near the capital, and later she went to a girls' boarding school in Pest. She left there when she was sixteen, having attained the highest educational qualifications that a woman could attain in the Hungary of the time. The young countess, however, was very interested in the world around her, especially in the rapidly developing field of natural science. Unfortunately, an aristocratic young lady of limited wealth could not dream too long in those days, and she was married off at the age of eighteen to György Szilassy, a landowner. She became pregnant almost at once, and gave birth to a son in her husband's family *kúria* at Pánd, to the south-east of Pest. It did not trouble her husband that she read a lot, but he was not pleased that she read books on medicine. He recommended novels suitable for upper-class ladies, but she would not choose her reading material as was expected. *I didn't read novels, although novels old and new were available to me in the library, but I dealt with serious scientific books,* she recalled later. Not only at home were her interests considered a dangerous craze. At roughly that time, in 1864, the famous Hungarian dramatist Imre Madách declared in his inaugural lecture at the Academy that the principle of a woman's life was dependence on her husband: *A woman develops at a younger age, but never attains the full maturity of a man: she learns and grasps things quite easily, but lacks the genius of creativity. She remains a dilettante, and never advances art and science.*

She was twenty-five and self-educated when her husband read out to her a newspaper article about women even being allowed to study medicine at the university of Zürich. Vilma sighed: *Lucky things!,* at which her husband burst out irritably *If you think that studying is such happiness go and study, I won't stand in your way.* His wife packed her bag that very day. She would not have been able even to obtain a passport without her husband's consent, but he kept his word, and in 1872 Vilma Hugonnai enrolled in the medical faculty at Zürich University. She was not allowed to take her six-year-old son with her, and neither her husband nor her father gave her any material support. The countess therefore had to work as well as study, and became a midwife and nurse in the university clinic. She only saw her son in vacation time. She graduated with distinction on 3 February 1879, practised medicine in the surgical department of a Zürich hospital, and was at once offered a post in a charity hospital. She would have had rapid career advancement in Switzerland, but she wanted to go home to her son – by then in his teens. In February 1880 she returned to Hungary.

In Hungary her Swiss degree was not valid, and so she applied to the teaching staff of the medical faculty of Budapest University to have it registered. The university realised that this procedure would set a precedent, and that if the request were acceded to a career in medicine would be open to women. The professors requested guidance from the government. In his letter to the University Ágoston Trefort, Minister for Religion and Public Education, summed up the problem thus: *It is a question of principle: is it permissible for women to practise medicine at all in Hungary, whether on the basis of the registration of a licence to practise medicine obtained abroad or on the basis of one obtained by following a course of study here?* And he quickly swept the question off his desk. Naturally, everyone referred to the laws then in force. Firstly, Vilma Hugonnai had no secondary education, only a degree. In response she took the school leaving examination – at the age of thirty-four, only the second woman ever to do so in Hungary. When she requested the recognition of her medical degree a second time a committee of professors decided by a majority vote that women must be incapable of performing medical tasks, and so the request could not be granted. The Minister then referred to the fact that there was no legal possibility of co-education in higher education: *Much though I desire to encourage the education of women – universities cannot be opened to women.* This refusal did not deter Vilma. She twice requested an audience with Trefort, to try to persuade him personally. The Minister's argument was that women that embarked on a scientific career would subvert the state and cause turmoil in academic life. She refuted this piece of imagination in a letter, quoting examples from other countries, to which Trefort offered her a backdoor entrance: let her train as a midwife, and then begin to practise medicine without registering a foreign licence, no one would

Vilma Hugonnai's licence as a military doctor (1915).

punish her for that. She, however, was reluctant to be an exception in a system that was unacceptable to her. She did indeed enrol and train as a midwife, but after obtaining her licence only acted as a midwife.

Her husband was not pleased that his wife had started to work, especially as she had an independent income. Their disagreements became more frequent, and so eventually in 1884 they divorced under the new law on civil marriage. By that time Vilma was considered a spokeswoman for women's rights. In her essay *Women's sphere of work* she called for reform of the schools, for which reason many made fun of her. Despite the atmosphere of rejection that surrounded her she was not long without a companion. She was surprised herself when a man called at her midwifery clinic. Vince Wartha was a professor of chemistry, forty years of age, and asked advice on a particular disease. He himself had qualified in Switzerland and had confidence in her expertise. He was a very big man, and suffered from a constant tremor as the result of excessively rapid growth in his youth. Vilma evidently succeeded in doing more than cure his medical problems, as he decided that he would like to spend the rest of his life with her.

The wedding took place in 1887. Wartha was one of the most multi-faceted Hungarian academics: he made significant advances in industrial chemistry, in electronics, in ceramics and in wine-making, in addition to which he played chess and was a photographer. He had a hand in the development of the eosin glaze at the Zsolnay ceramic works in Pécs. It pleased him greatly that his wife too had chosen a scientific career and that they could be intellectual equals as partners. He persuaded Vilma to abandon her midwife practice, but for a reason quite different from her first husband's: he wanted her to be able to devote all her time to science and the women's movement. Late-coming love inspired her too, and in a letter to a woman friend she told of her happiness with her greatly cultured husband: *Good married couples form the basis of the blossoming of family and state. Living together in a good relationship, each partner has twice as much capacity for work, and work is the mainstay of good health and the creator of material wellbeing.* They had not been living together long in their one-storey house near the Népliget when Vilma – once again with complete disregard for social convention – at the age of forty gave birth to a little girl.

Vilma became leader of the Hungarian Midwives' Association, and took part in the establishment of the National Association for Women's Education. Furthermore, she did not abandon the registration of her medical licence, which was by then regarded more and more as a matter of symbolic importance in Hungary. Oddly enough, the international political situation came to her assistance. The Austro-Hungarian Monarchy annexed Bosnia, where the Moslem women were disinclined to present themselves to male doctors, and fearing an epidemic the authorities looked for women doctors. In 1894, therefore the new Minister of Culture asked the medical faculty for a fresh assessment of the situation. The professors – at once and unanimously – voted to open the professions of medicine and pharmacy to women, with the proviso that every female candidate had to be examined individually and might only be accepted with special ministerial permission. On this basis the government promulgated an order for the training of women in the Arts, Medicine and Pharmacy, which was signed by Franz Joseph in 1895. Vilma once more applied for her Zürich licence to be recognised. Again she had to wait and a lengthy procedure began, in the course of which three strict conditions were prescribed for her. These too she humbly met, but there was still symbolic objection to her. In the examination on internal medicine, for example, the world-famous pulmonologist Professor Frigyes Korányi carried on a conspicuously friendly conversation with his female colleague instead of an examination. And in 1897, almost twenty years after obtaining her Swiss degree, Vilma Hugonnai was admitted as a doctor of medicine.

She immediately opened her own practice, where she mainly received women and the poor. Although she had believed that with the obtaining of her Hungarian licence the matter would be ended, she was mistaken. Attacks were launched on women proposing a scientific career sometimes by members of Parliament, sometimes by university staff, but she always responded to the accusations with detailed arguments. She was asked to write an article on the emancipation of women for a lexicon that was being prepared, but in the end instead of the text that she submitted there appeared an article questioning the equal rights of women, which stated: *There is no doubt that the physical constitution of women is weaker than that of men, while their spiritual functioning displays differences from the psychic activity of men such as cannot be called favourable to their emancipation.* This moved Vilma to write her essay *The Women's Movement in Hungary*, in which she produced detailed arguments against the opponents of emancipation. She had to endure much further humiliation for speaking out. When her supporters proposed her as a member of the council at the annual general meeting of the Medical Association, the majority rejected the proposal on the grounds that, unfortunately, the constitution of the Association made possible the election of only 'an irreproachable man'. And although her persistence had opened the universities to women, there too change proceeded very slowly. In the autumn of 1900 there were thirty-one female students at Budapest University, and they might only hear lectures separated from the men and accompanied by chaperones, and after receiving their degrees there was little chance of their finding employment. It took years more for the state health authority to appoint a woman doctor, and then only in a poor-house where no male doctor was willing to work. It was with the intention of shaping attitudes that in 1907 Vilma wrote her book *Women as General Practitioners*, translating and expanding a German professional work.

She had to wait right until the war for opposition to cease, because then everyone was needed to attend to the wounded. So it was that in 1914 at the age of sixty-seven Vilma qualified as a military doctor and called on other women doctors to follow her example. A total of eighty-four women doctors came forward, almost all of those that had qualified in Hungary by that time. By the time that she had reached her goal of seeing women doctors accepted by society she was alone again. First, her teenage daughter had died of a serious illness, then in 1914 she lost her husband too. *I count myself blessed to have been the helpmate of Vince Wartha,* she announced to a newspaper. *My husband lived for his family and for science. Our home was a museum in which we served science together.*

HUNGARY IN THE FIRST WORLD WAR AND THE COL-
LAPSE OF THE MONARCHY. The Kingdom of Hungary took
part in the 'Great War' on the side of the Central Powers as part of
the Austro-Hungarian Monarchy. One of the immediate preliminaries of the war was the international rivalry for influence over
the Balkans, in the course of which in 1908 the Monarchy, referring
to the historical rights of the Kingdom of Hungary, annexed Bos-
nia-Herzegovina. This dispute led to the assassination in Sarajevo,
the declaration of war on Serbia, and the mobilisation of the other
countries in Europe. As the war spread the Monarchy was forced to
fight on more than one extended front, and Hungarian soldiers were
involved in the Balkans, Galicia and Italy. In 1916 the sixty-sev-
en-year reign of Franz Joseph ended with his death, and his successor Charles IV tried in vain to reorganise the Monarchy on a feder-
alist basis, and the nationalities that had been living together in one
mass wished everywhere – with the support of the *entente* powers –
to secede. The former Habsburg Empire suffered a grievous defeat
in the war and collapsed into its parts, as did the Kingdom of Hungary. In 1918 left-wing revolutions swept the country, after the failure of which the king tried to resume the throne, but this even the
conservative élite would not support. Hungary remained a kingdom until 1944, but no further kings sat on the throne.

The struggle that Vilma Hugonnai had waged to obtain her
qualifications and practise her profession was by then a symbol of
her life. In 1918 the writer Gyula Krúdy drew one of his female
characters thus: *The poor thing would have liked to study, like Vilma
Hugonnai, who was the role-model of every young girl*. At the end of her
life, however, the role-model of young girls that wished to study
had to face the fact that under the *numerus clausus* law that governed admission to the universities the higher education of wom-
en, like that of Jews and other minorities, was severely restricted.
When in 1922 the first Hungarian woman doctor died, the medical journals – which published notices of the deaths of all known
members of the profession – did not carry a single obituary of her.

"A role-model for all young girls."

In both the audiences that I had with His Excellency, he emphasised that *"Women would subvert the state were they to be given equal rights with men"*, and quoted as an example Russia (...) That enlightenment would cause more disturbance than ignorance is disproved by Switzerland, the first country where the universities were opened to women. Why women trained for professions should do more harm than those who, without thorough knowledge, are allowed to exercise their influence in everything in which they wish to be involved, I do not know. The more knowledgeable women are, the more beneficial will be their influence. And on what kind of a footing rests the state that a few intelligent women might overthrow? I'd be ashamed to be the child of such a state.

Mrs György Szilassy, *née* Countess Vilma Hugonnai,
letter to Ágost Trefort, Minister for Religion and Public Education,
1881

Rátz's portrait on Jenő Wigner's desk in Princeton.

László Rátz

One Saturday morning in 1913 Jenő Wigner, aged eleven, a second-year grammar school pupil, was going down a broad avenue in Budapest that led to the Városliget, on his way to call on his maths teacher. No other teacher ever invited him to his home, such a thing was not customary in those days, but this was not the first time that László Rátz had expected him for coffee. The nervous, dreamy boy had been missing school for months because of illness, and it seemed that he would have to repeat the year. He was going to have to take an extra examination at Rátz's – he was a teacher in the Budapest Lutheran Grammar School, and had immediately noticed Jenő's ability in maths. He had lent him books from his own library so that he could teach himself, given him intriguing problems from Secondary School Maths Pages – of which he was the editor – and in general talked about mathematical problems with him as if he were a colleague. He also often invited him to talks in which he debated the latest scientific questions with university teachers. That morning Rátz talked to his pupil about the need always to be clear about one's capabilities; therefore it would do no harm for him to know that Jancsi Neumann, aged ten, was even cleverer than him at maths. That upset little Jenő, but he very soon realised that his teacher was right. Many years later, now Nobel Laureate in Physics, he still relaxed in his study at Princeton by solving the problems in Secondary School Maths Pages beneath a photograph of Rátz, and like him a number of world-famous mathematicians, physicists, engineers and economists too have been unable to forget the influence of that outstanding teacher. László Rátz's life was not in the least adventurous, he did no spectacularly heroic deeds, and yet he was a hero, a hero of teaching and the nurturing of talent, who through his pupils transformed the natural sciences of the whole twentieth century. Since then the answer to the secret of his effectiveness as a teacher has been the subject of study.

He was born in Sopron in 1863, just at the time when that west-Hungarian town with its German population was beginning to be Magyarised at great speed. His father, August Rátz, registered his son as Ladislaus Wilhelm Rátz, and his primary schooling was in German. He must have studied Hungarian at high school, and in the Hungarian literary circle he wrote prose and verse under the name of László Rátz and took part in reciting competitions. Before taking his school-leaving examination he attended the famous Lutheran lyceum in Sopron where the most dread teacher in the school, the maths and physics teacher known by the pupils as 'Old Zero', realised that his pupil showed exceptional talent in the sciences.

It was thanks to his teacher too that young Wigner fell in love with maths, and after leaving school enrolled in the science faculty of Budapest University. It is typical of the breadth of Rátz's interests that he took a year off from his studies for a course in philosophy at the university of Berlin, and spent another year in the Maths and Physics faculty at Strasbourg. In 1890 he obtained his certificate as a teacher and immediately went to Budapest Lutheran High School as an assistant teacher. For thirty-five years he taught nowhere else; the school became the most important place in his life and teaching and his pupils its most important elements. He lived a few blocks away from the school on Lövölde tér – architecturally little changed today – and rarely left the district. His friends describe his appearance as 'teacher-ish': he was tall, became bald at an early age, and sported an imposing moustache in the style of the time. He was never without his bowler hat, starched collar and black overcoat. His friends too he found among his colleagues and – like his pupils – always addressed them in the polite form. All that did not mean that he was a dry old stick, old before his time: he loved a joke, and to a ripe old age spoke in class with youthful enthusiasm.

The Budapest Lutheran Grammar School was one of the most famous educational establishments not only in Hungary but in all Europe. The extremely modern school offered the best of conditions to children and teachers like. The latter were paid salaries fifty per cent above the norm, and received housing subsidies and retirement pensions. Rátz's remaining there was not at all exceptional, as most of the teachers spent their entire careers there. Most of them had studied abroad, trained themselves continuously, and were considered well-known experts in their fields. Jenő Wigner later wrote of this: *Those great teacher-characters adored teaching, and were exceptionally successful in motivating students to study. Not only were their commitment to their calling and their factual knowledge impressive: they also succeeded in imparting respect for knowledge and love of it.* Lofty ideals, a caring atmosphere and tolerance characterised the school. Despite its connection to the Church it often took in talented Jewish pupils – no attempt was made to force them to attend lessons on the Lutheran faith. A lively student life was encouraged, and students had a range of artistic, sporting and academic societies to choose from. The school was fee-paying but offered a wide range of scholarships, so that even less well-to-do families might enrol their sons. But there was no discrimination: while exceptionally great energy was put into the special training of talented pupils, Jenő Wigner for one failed in physical education and János Neumann in singing.

From the outset László Rátz was reckoned a teacher-character most representative of the spirit of the school. It was said of him that he constructed his every lesson carefully, and at the same time was mindful both of bringing out the best in the talented and of helping the weaker to keep up. In the words of one colleague: *He did not present maths to his pupils as an abstract theoretical science but pointed out incrementally its close connection with everyday life. (...) By systematic preparatory work he made sure that mathematical truths appeared to his pupils almost by their own volition. By this method of teaching he raised mathematics from the difficult subject that it is often held to be into one studied with love and interest.* He adored teaching and was well aware of how to motivate his pupils. *Being examined by Mr Rátz was positively enjoyable,* Wigner reminisced. *He asked a lot of questions, but kindly. It was immediately obvious how passionately he loved mathematics.* It is no surprise that to his pupil, the courses in mathematics that he took at the universities of Budapest and Berlin seemed little more than repetition.

SCIENTISTS OF HUNGARIAN ORIGIN: THE MARTIANS. Many, from Enrico Fermi to Albert Einstein, have remarked on the high proportion of their fellow scientists living in America that were of Hungarian origin. Among them were such distinguished men as the Nobel Laureate atomic physicist Eugène Paul Wigner (originally Jenő Pál Wigner); Theodore von Karman (Tódor Kármán), who developed supersonic flight; Edward Teller (Ede Teller), known as the father of the hydrogen bomb; Leo Szilard (Leó Szilárd), one of the principal physicists of the Manhattan Project; Dennis Gabor (Dénes Gábor), Nobel Laureate inventor of the hologram; or John von Neumann (János Neumann), who worked out the theory of the internal organisation of the computer. All of these started out from the Budapest of the turn of the century, where there was a network of some of the world's best secondary schools. The secret of success lay in the multicultural environment that integrated students of Jewish and German origins alike, and in the teaching of contemporary science at the highest level. The members of the Hungarian scientific generation that began in the early twentieth century mostly began their research in German universities, and during the 1930s moved from there to the USA. They spoke English with a distinctive accent, and their colleagues often jokingly called them 'Martians'.

László Rátz was a deeply religious man, but he in no way forced his religion on his pupils. At the same time, his personality surely had something to do with the fact that while still at the grammar school the Jewish Jenő Wigner adopted the Lutheran faith. His talented pupils waited all week for the coffee sessions with Rátz on Saturdays, when they could talk informally about intriguing mathematical problems. Such a thing was unusual not only in a secondary school but even in a university. When he recognised the exceptional mathematical intelligence of the unusual, introverted Jancsi Neumann he gave him private tuition for a while and then made it possible for him to be three years ahead of his class in maths. Neumann's father was a wealthy banker, but Rátz took no money for the private tuition. He recognised with his keen teacherly sense that the precocious boy was a future mathematical genius, and so when he felt that there was nothing more that he could teach him he asked university teachers to take him on. To the less able Jenő Wigner he gave not private tuition but books, so that he could discover scientific connections for himself. In addition to teaching them mathematics his relationship with his pupils was close: he was president of the Youth Song and Music Association, and so often sang with them. He also organised a number of study trips to the Adriatic, the Lower Danube and Venice, and on one occasion he sailed round the Balaton with a group of thirty-four. He himself rated these expeditions the greatest experiences of his life, and even recorded them in his professional biography.

His attitude to teaching figures large in his career as headmaster. In 1909, experienced and active in the public life of the school, he was elected headmaster by the staff. At the time this was considered the acme of a teaching career, and furthermore the position brought with it a very good salary. Rátz held the post for five years, and then made an unusual announcement to his colleagues. He said that the duties of headmaster took too much of his energies away from teaching, and therefore he wished to be relieved. The staff were horrified and tried to dissuade him, as resignation was considered a loss of prestige. Rátz, however, was determined once more to devote his life entirely to the classroom. After standing down he was appointed honorary headmaster. As his physicist colleague Sándor Mikola put it: *He might have ceased to be headmaster, but he was still our leader.* Rátz did not, however, only exercise enormous influence on modern science through his school pupils: his greatest intellectual contribution was as editor of Secondary School Maths Pages. He edited the publication alone for twenty years, and not only received no payment for it but also devoted money to its publication and distribution. He saw it as the aim of the paper to develop students' capacity for problem-solving, and so in every number he offered a competition. After a while entries came from all over the country, but the reward was only that the names of the best appeared in the paper. Twenty years later someone noticed that the very best mathematicians in Hungary – such as Tódor Kármán, the father of aerodynamics, designer of the jet-propelled aircraft – had all been named in Rátz's paper as distinguished students.

After the turn of the century Rátz and his colleague Sándor Mikola – based on their own experience – worked out the methodology of secondary school teaching of mathematics. In the introduction to the book they summed up their aims as follows: *We want the pupil leaving secondary school to take into life a scientific mathematical schooling; it is our hope that in this way thinking in mathematical fashion will have an effect on public life. The student must see how many strands connect mathematics with practical life, with the sciences and with our entire concept of the world. (…) The revision of teaching in this direction is necessary in order that the principal features of modern culture could be understood.* The new method gradually came into the official national curriculum and contributed greatly over the next seventy years to the world-wide fame of Hungarian mathematical education. As a result Rátz was frequently invited to address conferences abroad and was awarded a high distinction by a government – true, only that of France.

According to his colleagues Rátz taught with youthful vigour in his later years too. Finally, after thirty-five years' teaching he retired at his own request. Even after that he regularly went into his workplace and took part in the training of young teachers. He remained in constant touch with his former pupils and was proud to hear of the first serious international successes of Wigner and Neumann. In 1930 he was travelling home from taking the waters in Karlsbad when he suffered a cerebral haemorrhage. He was admitted to a sanatorium in Városliget, not far from the school where he had spent his whole life, and there he died at the age of sixty-eight. At his funeral in Sopron his friend and colleague Sándor Mikola said farewell in these words: *The real teacher is not a functionary who carries out his official duties but also a spiritual pastor, whom everyone expects to care for the souls committed to his charge, to work voluntarily and free of charge for the advancement of culture, and finally to be an artist who will have ideas all the time. That's the sort of real teacher that László Rátz was.*

Of my former teachers, I feel the greatest gratitude and affection towards László Rátz. I feel more deeply now than before what a rare thing it is that one should resign from a senior position – in his case, the direction of a school – and take one more modest. He loved to teach, loved to see the way in which understanding affected pupils' knowledge, the way in which they realised how marvellous it is that the human mind is capable of linking one thought to another, capable of creating a wonderful structure – a strong structure – by logical processes. Many great scientists have expressed their amazement at these capacities of ours, but he loved seeing and feeling the marvel. László Rátz – I have his picture in my study at the university – did not only teach in school. He gave private tuition to János Neumann, whose almost unique talent he recognised in embryo, and to me he gave several valuable books to read, from which I not only studied mathematics but also acquired a sense of wonder at the marvellously clever way in which inferences weave themselves together. I understood very early that that is the essence of mathematics, that is the art and privilege of the mathematician.

Jenő Wigner,
letter from Princeton, 1973

"Is society fair about the rights of women?"
Rózsa Bédy-Schwimmer in the 1890s.

Rózsa Bédy-Schwimmer

On 5 December 1915 fifteen thousand people watched as the Peace
Ship with 148 passengers on board sailed from New Jersey harbour and set course for Europe. Politicians and personalities in public life – among them the inventor Thomas Alva Edison – waved
the Swedish ship good-bye. All were confident that the travellers
would perform their mission and succeed in bringing to a peaceful
settlement the powers that had for eighteen months been waging
the First World War. The delegation was led by two very different
persons: Henry Ford, the motor manufacturer, and the journalist
Rózsa Bédy-Schwimmer, president of the Hungarian Association
of Feminists. Their plan, for which they had gained the support
in principle of President Wilson, was to convene a high-powered
peace conference at The Hague with the involvement of six neutral nations, at which the conditions of a peace agreement would
be worked out, after which the warring countries too would be
brought to the discussion-table. *The slogan, Out of the Trenches by
Christmas! is not pompous, empty words,* said Ford to the journalists on
board, *but a prayer in which all humanity will join*. It had not been Ford,
however, but Bédy-Schwimmer that had had the idea of the Peace
Ship some months earlier.

An internationally familiar activist for women's rights, she differed from the English and American suffragettes in rejecting all

forms of violence, and was a convinced pacifist. She thought that if a meritorious proposal of peace were to come from the United States (at the time, still neutral) the parties exhausted in the war would find it hard to reject, especially as public opinion in Europe was for it. She had won the flamboyant industrialist to her cause: not long before he had announced that he would not sell cars for military purposes to any country. In the end the civilian peace-delegation's voyage did not result in peace; some said that the action had come too late, others that it was too soon. The Dutch government – fearing that it would bring upon itself the wrath of some warring power – would not even allow them to go to The Hague, and in America too the war party politicians got the better of the pacifists. Although it failed, the Hungarian woman's initiative was the greatest large-scale attempt at ending the war. Bédy-Schwimmer was always motivated by the attainment of seemingly idealistic great purposes: the struggle for women's right to vote or the creation of an international organisation on the lines of UNO. She was the world's first woman ambassador, later a candidate for the Nobel Peace Prize, and yet she died stateless because she would not relinquish her pacifist principles.

She was born in 1877 in Budapest into a well-to-do family, but spent her childhood in the south Hungarian town of Temesvár (today Timişoara, Romania), where her father dealt in grain. There she attended the public school for girls, which at the time offered the highest education available to girls. Her great-uncle Lipót Katscher, the journalist that founded the Hungarian Peace Society, had a great influence on her. From him she learnt that it was possible to fight for really important goals without violence and gently. She succeeded at the age of sixteen in gaining admission to evening classes at a commercial school for boys. She learnt to sing and to play the piano, and then, equipped with a certificate in commercial subjects, tried to find employment. At the time women were occasionally employed in the Civil Service, for example as post-girls or clerks. Rózsa found a position as book-keeper and commercial correspondent, but was forced to discover that as a woman she was worse treated than men and worked for a lower salary. She gave an account of this unjust situation and her experiences in that connection in newspaper articles. She was twenty when she joined a newly formed protective organisation, the National Association of Women Civil Servants. In this she worked so effectively for the benefit of the women working in the Civil Service that in 1900 she was elected president of it. At about that time she married, but the marriage did not last long; only her husband's surname Schwimmer reminds us of him.

At that time she did not merely read about the operations of international women's rights organisations but also had first-hand experience. In those days the feminist movement was especially strong in Great Britain, where activists fighting for equal rights for women did not even refrain from acts of violence, broke the windows of political party offices, and on occasion used incendiary bombs. Rózsa sympathised with the goals of feminism but deplored the use of violence. In 1904 she went to Berlin with her colleague Vilma Glücklich to attend the congress of the International Woman Suffrage Alliance, which preferred peaceful methods. There the idea came to them that representation of female civil servants was not enough; an organisation was called for that would speak up for the rights of all Hungarian women. On returning home – in cooperation with two hundred women and fifty men – they established the Association of Feminists, of which Rózsa Bédy-Schwimmer became the first president.

They considered their most significant goal to be the winning of the right of women to vote, but the matter of secondary school and university education for women was also important. At this time – thanks to Vilma Hugonnai – the universities had been opened to women in principle, but all manner of regulations prevented their enjoying this in appropriate numbers. Thus, for example, in 1904 the rule was brought in that only women with exceptional results in matriculation could be accepted for university, while for men 'satisfactory' was good enough. The Feminists' Association spoke out about every injustice, from women's limited rights of inheritance to regulations affecting marriage. The Association was not organised on a class basis: working-class women and aristocrats alike became members. By this it aroused the wrath not only of conservatives but also of social democrats. *A few toothless, over-made-up wealthy ladies, who have outlived every adventure and love affair, have plotted with a couple of typists who have experienced nothing because they are so ugly that even dogs won't look at them, and formed the feminist movement in Hungary* – so scoffed a left-wing newspaper. In 1905, when they circularised the parliamentary parties on the subject of female suffrage, István Tisza, the liberal Prime Minister, said in his statement: *I am a confirmed opponent of the right of women to vote in parliamentary elections. I shudder at the thought of our wives becoming so many fellow-citizens. (…) We poor men would be the losers by this reform, but I believe that in the final analysis so would the women too.* A few politicians did in fact support the introduction of female suffrage, but most of them added that the question was not timely, there were more important things to be dealt with first.

Cartoons ridiculing the feminists began to appear in the papers as did articles twisting their words. In response, in 1905 the Association decided to set up a paper themselves so that their views should go to their supporters undistorted. As editor-in-chief of *Woman and Society*, Rózsa commented in her article outlining their policy: *We shall discuss everything that concerns women as people, wives, mothers and citizens. (…) We mean to judge every manifestation of contemporary life from the point of view of whether society assesses the rights of women justly. Not for the sake of women as such, but for the good of the body of society that we have always seen as unitary, we mean to demolish a dreadful lie: in half of itself, humanity calls knowledge shame and sin; ignorance it calls innocence; spiritual darkness it calls feminine charm (…) interest in social work it calls a modern whim.* One of the most modern public papers in Hungary was founded, and meanwhile they attacked misogynistic institutions in vitriolic articles, compiled guides for girls on choice of careers, gave useful advice on the protection of children's health, housekeeping and legal questions, and drew attention to the lack of hostels for working women and the consequences of the backwardness of sexual enlightenment.

They became known nation-wide in connection with the so-called Kmetty affair. Károly Kmetty, professor at the law school and member of Parliament, first initiated *numerus clausus* admission to the universities on the basis of sex, not race. To the noisy acclaim of several members of Parliament he called girls that obtained degrees 'female monsters', and women that acquired knowledge 'family-wrecking bombs'. The speech exalted the uneducated state of women into a national virtue, and Rózsa responded in an outspoken article. The paper had an even greater effect than her arguments, however, when it was discovered that Kmetty's own wife was a 'female monster' with a degree and a teaching certificate. The national press printed a full account of the dispute, giving space to the feminists' arguments too.

Rózsa did not only make herself heard on national questions. She also spoke up when the bank workers' newspaper declared war on the employment of women. *Nowadays there is scarcely a financial institution in which women have not ousted qualified men from at least a few positions*, wrote the paper, supporting its fears of redundancy with moral arguments: *How can one imagine that the place where men, smoking cigarettes and cigars, do their highly responsible work in an atmosphere of the confidentiality of colleagues, often with talk of lively flirtations, would be the place to cultivate the unsullied morals of that delicate flower, a young girl?* Bédy-Schwimmer made the National Union of Office Workers investigate and reject the proposal for the exclusion of women. The Social Democrats accused her, because of similar actions, of representing the interests of only women from wealthy, good families. They were also angry with her because in 1912, after a workers' demonstration had been broken up by police, she had not only spoken out against police brutality but also criticised the Social Democrat demonstrators: they had demonstrated only for the extension of men's voting rights, and had acted violently, taking up cobble-stones and tram lines.

The Association of Feminists was criticised after this from two directions as a body of bored housewives who only talked but were incapable of any worthwhile action. In response Bédy-Schwimmer and her organisation arranged for the biggest international event of the time, the congress of the International Woman Suffrage Alliance, to take place in Budapest. Three thousand delegates came to the conference, some even from South Africa and China. It took place in the Great Hall of the Music Academy, and speeches were interpreted into fourteen languages. The participants not only spoke of the right to vote and the situation of women in society, but also protested against arming for war and restraint of freedom of speech. The conference was reported by 230 foreign journalists, and its organisation convinced many sceptics in Hungary too. Rózsa wrote about it as follows: *The wonderful disciplined behaviour of the huge crowd disarmed those who could only imagine the parliament of women as a caricature of the conditions in our unruly Parliament. (…) The organisers also took the foreign visitors to the provinces: in Debrecen, Szeged and Nagyvárad, and in smaller places too the feminists were well received, so different were they from the stereotypes of the cartoonists.*

After the extraordinarily successful event Bédy-Schwimmer changed the principal organ of the movement. From then on the feminists' paper appeared as *The Woman*, and the wife of the aristocrat Count Sándor Teleki joined the editorial board. She believed that opportunities should be found to collaborate with every political party, and established connections with people, from the left-wing opposition through the bourgeois liberals up to the government party, who might be expected to agree to the right of women to vote. After a while she could only make her contribution from abroad: in 1914 she was elected press secretary of the International Woman Suffrage Alliance, and so moved to

London. There she was caught by the outbreak of war, and so as the citizen of a hostile country could not return to Hungary. She obtained a visa for the neutral United States, where she attempted to organise an international peace conference. She was received by President Wilson and other influential politicians, and made the acquaintance of Henry Ford, whom she won round to her idea for the Peace Ship. The millionaire was prepared to devote all his wealth to the creation of peace, but from the outset the idea was mocked by the faction urging America to join in the war; they called the organisers either highbrows or soft in the head. The international press therefore regarded the peace delegation as a piece of eccentricity, and first Holland, then, fearing for their neutrality, Norway, Sweden and Denmark would not permit conferences to be held on their territory. On the ship, furthermore, an influenza epidemic broke out, resulting in a death. After a while the peace delegates blamed one another for the failure, and so the mission was soon abandoned. The action did, however, bring Henry Ford an extraordinary amount of attention, some of which went to Rózsa Bédy-Schwimmer too.

Even during the war Rózsa returned to Hungary, and wherever she could she spoke out for peace. She wrote in her characteristic style: *Where governments, to the irremediable harm of peoples, strike poses and pontificate 'We shall never die' under the compulsion of the false situation that they have themselves brought about, (…) honest men, in whom there still remains the power to express their opinion, may continue with the greatest vigour the organisation of pressure to be brought on their governments.* She prevailed on everyone who believed in peace and equal rights for women to write in her paper. Endre Ady, best known of modern poets, stated: *The legal dominance of men has become bankrupt, and after so many sins of selfishness, lovelessness and despotism it would be very much in the interests of humanity for them to be made to attempt appeasement and the realisation of the human ideal with those whose hands are still clean: women!* After the left-wing revolution the Association of Feminists joined the coalition that supported Mihály Károlyi, the republican Prime Minister. This had two political consequences. The government tabled a motion proposing women's suffrage, and Rózsa – as she was so well known internationally – was appointed Hungarian ambassador to Switzerland.

THE REVOLUTIONS OF 1918–19. In the autumn of 1918, because of the prolongation of the war and the economic crisis, demonstrations and strikes broke out in Budapest and other large towns. The soldiers took the imperial monogram off their caps and replaced it with an aster, which became the symbol of the movement. With the victory of the Aster Revolution Hungary seceded from the Austro-Hungarian Monarchy. Count Mihály Károlyi, an aristocrat of left-wing views, became President of the first Hungarian republic. Six months later his authority was usurped by the communists led by Béla Kun, who intended to install a proletarian dictatorship. The Republic of Councils, modelled on Soviet Russian lines, lasted 133 days. Numerous moderate left-wing intelligentsia supported its programme, which declared social equality. At the same time many of the civilian population fell victims to the 'Red Terror'. In the autumn of 1919 counter-revolutionary forces, supported by the Entente Powers which invaded Hungary brought the Soviet Republic down. As many of the communist People's Commissars had been of Jewish origin, the so-called 'White Terror' retribution had an anti-Semitic thrust.

THE PEACE OF TRIANON. The representatives of Hungary, no longer in the Austro-Hungarian Monarchy, signed the treaty ending the First World War in the Petit Trianon palace at Versailles on 4 June 1920. Of the defeated countries, Turkey and Hungary suffered the greatest losses. Hungary's 282,000 square kilometres shrank to a mere 93,000, and her population from 18.2 million to 7.6 million. Transylvania and the adjacent area went to Romania, the northern part known as Upper Hungary (essentially identical with modern Slovakia) to the re-created Czechoslovakia, and the southerly parts to the new South Slav state of Yugoslavia; Austria, Italy and Poland also received pieces of historical Hungary. Two-thirds of the occupants of the territories detached had previous-ly belonged to ethnic minorities and now became citizens of their own states; one third, roughly 3.2 million people, were ethnic Magyars, and thus became minorities in the lands of their birth. Refugees flooded Budapest and the large towns, and every politi-cal party saw it as its goal to re-establish the frontiers. As there was scarcely a citizen of Hungary whose relatives were not cut off be-yond the frontier the Peace of Trianon caused social trauma to the generations that spanned it.

In the alpine country, where it took until 1971 for women to be given the right to vote, people were not very pleased at the world's first female ambassador. Rózsa Bédy-Schwimmer's accreditation was not accepted, and so in 1919 she resigned. She had courageous-ly spoken out against the Red Terror under the Soviet-style Re-public of Councils and did the same a few months later during the counter-revolutionary White Terror too. It comes as no surprise that after that she had to flee Hungary– first going to Vienna, then emigrating to the USA. Some years later she applied for American citizenship but her application was rejected: as a confirmed pacifist she was not willing to speak the sentence in the oath of citizenship according to which, if need be, she was prepared to take up arms in defence of her new country. The case dragged on for several years, and in 1929 went as far as the Supreme Court. In the case of *US state contra Rosika Schwimmer* the judges decided that the plaintiff could not be granted citizenship. As she had had to resign her Hungar-ian citizenship during the process, from the age of fifty-two she was left stateless. This meant that she could no longer travel, as she could neither be certain that any country would allow her to enter, nor that she would be allowed back into America. She suffered her new situation with head held high, and on several occasions signed her letters 'Madame Schwimmer – without a country'.

There was no reduction in her activity in public life at an intellectual level. She spoke out on women's rights and on the creation of international peace. She was one of the first to recognise the dangers inherent in Nazism and fascism. After Mussolini's movement had gained ground she wrote to Vittore Emanuele, King of Italy, asking him to have the fascist politician declared mentally ill, otherwise he would sweep the country into a war. In one of her radio talks she compared the world to a china shop in which three or four bulls were on the rampage: she was watching helplessly the destruction of a hundred million people. She proposed that democratic states set up a world organisation that could act as a matter of principle against dictators that created the risk of war. She was also one of the first to conceive of the creation of what later became the International Court of Justice at The Hague. Many still thought her a naive dreamer, but some went even farther: she was variously accused of being a Bolshevik functionary and a German spy. She did not let such accusations pass unnoticed, took legal action, and was awarded a total of $17,000 in damages. Naturally, she also found supporters. In 1937 an international committee, of which Albert Einstein, Selma Lagerlöf and Stefan Zweig were members, awarded her the World Peace Prize. After the Second World War broke out she was again suspected by the American authorities. Her home was watched, her mail often arrived opened, and she had increasing difficulty in obtaining a residence permit. At this time she tried mainly to assist Europeans fleeing Nazism and created the international archive of the feminist movement.

In 1946 she lived to see the Supreme Court overrule the decision refusing her nationality in the case of another immigrant, but did not re-open proceedings on her own account. She continued to live as a stateless person and, having no retirement pension, kept herself by teaching the piano. In 1948 her admirers proposed her for the Nobel Peace Prize, and support came from Great Britain, Hungary, Sweden, France and Italy. We do not know what chance she had of being awarded the prize: that same year the founder of the Hungarian feminist movement contracted pneumonia, and at the age of seventy-one died of complications in her New York home. Almost at the same time the communist authorities in Hungary banned the organisation that she had created. The archives on feminism in New York City Library and the universities of Northampton and Stanford are today named in her memory.

Kmetty is asking for the establishment of numerus clausus: he is against women studying at university. Bánffy goes further and believes that in the question of "woman-training" the Minister must position himself for limitation not only in the universities but at secondary schools too. If discussion of the budget were not so urgent, every friend of darkness that exalts the ignorance of women as a national virtue might well come up with a proposition about elementary education or children's nurseries as well. And every reactionary demand is brought up in the name of woman's sacred, natural duty, family happiness. (…) Has not every Hungarian woman blushed deeply at the reckless statement that education makes women into monsters? There we could sit in the gallery and listen, ablaze with shame, at the defamation and diminution of our sex. (…) Just let them go on with such a rumpus! Perhaps this uncouth howling will awaken those women too that hitherto have believed that they are the worshipped idols of the family. Their awakening will lead them to join the women's movement, which aims to achieve national advantage and domestic ties by means quite other than those of the Kmettys, Bánffys and Béla Tóths. Is feminism gaining ground? Already? There has not yet been a women's movement in Hungary, but as God is just there's going to be one!

Rózsa Bédy-Schwimmer,
Female monsters
in *Woman and Society*, 1907

Everyone's Uncle Robert giving out soup. Budapest, 1927.

Róbert Feinsilber

In early 1925 long queues stood in vain outside the soup-kitchens that had been providing hot food for the poor of Budapest: the city authorities had closed them. Social tensions threatened to explode, as every day sixty or seventy thousand had been receiving a free meal. In the nick of time Jenő Sipőcz, the deputy mayor, heard that a private businessman had offered to set up a free 'people's kitchen' instead of the city. This stocky, bearded elderly man – a citizen of Turkey with property in Holland and who dressed in Russian fashion – took the city's disused field catering equipment and before long the down-and-outs of Budapest were queuing at his soup-kitchen in the Belváros. Róbert Feinsilber – or as he quickly became known, Uncle Róbert – soon made himself an indispensable social institution. The press described him as an apostle of charity until in 1930 he was expelled from Hungary for fraud. From then on they called him a swindler who had enriched himself through the soup-kitchens, and many must have had their consciences allayed on seeing it proved that there is no such thing as an unselfish helper. Was he a generous friend of the people or a cheating adventurer? The indications are that he was both, in his way a Hungarian Robin Hood. A millionaire turned organiser of assistance, he took care of tens of thousands when the state failed in its duty, and in the end he died a beggar in a mental clinic.

Even his childhood was a series of adventures. He was born in a Jewish goldsmith family in 1865 in Yemen, then part of the Ottoman Empire. His mother was twelve when she fell pregnant by a boy of thirteen. The two youngsters had decided to run away from home and were rowing out to a steamer bound for Jaffa when the girl went into labour and their son was born in the rowing-boat. If little Róbert had been born a few hours later in international waters he would probably not have acquired the Turkish citizenship that later saved his life. The parents worked in Jaffa as jewellers, than moved to Holland, where in keeping with their occupation the mother took the name Feingold and the father that of Feinsilber. The family began dealing with diamond-traders in Amsterdam and Constantinople, and quickly amassed a sizeable fortune themselves. Young Róbert had no taste for goldsmithing, preferring the life of the gilded youth, and so travelled the world on his parents' money. His destiny was sealed by his journey to Russia, where he visited Lev Tolstoy's estate at Yasnaya Polyana and fell completely under the writer's influence. He exchanged his European clothes for Russian, and his Jewish faith for a sort of Tolstoyan Christianity. He decided to devote his life to supporting the poor and distributed the money that came to him from home among the needy.

He first turned up in Budapest at the turn of the century, or at least a missionary named Róbert Feinsilber is listed in the Budapest address-list for 1906. He came to public attention during the First World War. He is said to have started doing rescue work: the chief of the Budapest police used him to dissuade intending suicides from carrying out their plans. By 1916 he had opened his own hostel for women that had survived suicide attempts. After the war he was busy looking for Hungarian prisoners of war that had been sent to Siberia. At first he sent them letters, news of Hungary, and later took steps to bring them home. According to some sources, he was the model for the Englishman in Tolstoy's *Resurrection*, who followed prisoner convoys distributing bibles. His most adventurous case was his search for a young man who had enlisted while still a university student and been captured by the Russians. The prisoner had spent three and a half years in Siberia, then made a daring escape and made his way to China. Feinsilber learnt from a traveller's letter about the fate of a young Hungarian who was wasting away in Shanghai, and managed to organise his return to Hungary.

The financial crisis of the twenties brought much unemployment and poverty to all parts of the country. The needy flocked mainly to Budapest and long queues snaked every day outside the capital's soup-kitchens. When in 1925 the city authorities announced that they could no longer afford to distribute food Feinsilber told Jenő Sipőcz, the deputy mayor, that he was willing to take over the soup-kitchens. The latter jumped at the offer, because the developing situation threatened to be a famine. He immediately summoned a press conference, at which, according to an article, he introduced Feinsilber as follows: *He speaks German, English, Russian, French, Spanish and of course Turkish, furthermore he is a widower, a man of independent means, and has done six years in school. This last, however, does not preclude him from being a highly cultured man of great wealth, which he would like to put to the public good. Gentlemen of the press, kindly make it publicly known that Mr Feinsilber is taking over the soup-kitchens. (…) We call on the gentle public of Budapest for their moral and material support for this generous undertaking to improve the lot of the people!* The city did not fund the action, but gave permission for charitable donations to be collected.

THE HORTHY PERIOD. In the chaotic political situation following the fall of the Republic of Councils the victorious powers supported the coming to power of an anglophile, conservative naval officer, Miklós Horthy. In 1919 he entered Budapest at the head of an army, mounted on a white horse, and the following year was elected Regent. In the twenty-four-year period that bears his name Parliamentary elections were held regularly, but the activity of the left-wing parties was restricted, and so right-wing governments followed one another, sometimes orientated towards the English-speaking world, sometimes towards Italy or Germany. The stability of the regime ensured that the economy, which had collapsed during the war and the revolutions, was consolidated – but there were enormous social differences. Although Horthy himself was overtly anti-Semitic, industrialists of Jewish origin (with whom he even cultivated warm personal relationships) supported the regime, as did the leaders of the Churches and the big landowners. At the centre of his policies was the revision of the Treaty of Trianon and the recovery of the parts of the country that had been lost. The leaders of the country tended to hope for this only from Nazi Germany, which was preparing for war, and so Hungary was sucked into the Second World War on the side of Germany. Horthy did not personally sympathise with Hitler, did not stand trial as a war criminal and died in exile.

Feinsilber set up his soup-kitchen in Kálvin tér, later in the Városliget. Although he was a man of brusque manners, quick to anger, who would soon raise his voice if something failed to please him, the poor quickly came to love him. After a few months everyone called him Uncle Róbert – not only the paupers in the queue but also the crowd in the popular New York coffee house where he would regularly drop in of an evening and mingle with the journalists and literary figures that spent their time there. From the outset he displayed a genius for organisation. He arranged with a series of stall-holders in the Budapest markets and with restaurants owners to collect anything that was unsold when they closed and would go bad. Later he also had left-over food delivered from barracks. He hired two big storage premises where the food was collected and sorted before being taken to the distribution points. He picked well-spoken young men from the queue and trained them to record what was collected. They went for assistance to the rich people on Uncle Róbert's list of addresses with a pre-planned strategy. When the Regent's wife donated a thousand *pengős* the clerks immediately called on the aristocrats with the news, and they all tried to out-do her. When a factory owner reached deep into his pocket he set off a competition in giving among the wealthy bourgeoisie. Feinsilber promised restaurateurs and businessmen – who were not too keen to be charitable but were snobbish – that he would see to it that their names were inscribed in the Golden Book of Budapest. At first he had twenty-five people going round the city with contribution lists, later four hundred, and the most important possible supporters he approached himself.

Uncle Róbert was soon dispensing hot food in four places, and a few years later he started a new charitable programme: in his house he created the Office Rescuing Suicides to Life. After a while the police took intending suicides – alive – from the top of the Chain Bridge, or after they had had their stomachs washed out, to Uncle Róbert's 'dissuasion office', where his ten people talked to them and offered them advice. He did not ask for money from those that were helped, but it could be known that donations were accepted from their relatives. In the 1920s everyone in Budapest knew the tubby old gentleman with a goatee. It is said that trams would stop if he waved to them, and the passengers were quick to greet him. The press too adored him, and one daily paper called him *the rare good madman of the city*, and his biography was published too. He had a feeling for the media, and was always ready to make statements to journalists that asked him questions. If donations were coming in more slowly he would give an interview and say something like *Nobody's supporting me, only the market women. Yes, they do, they give (…) But I've got very great difficulties to overcome, because the poor are always here waiting, and I've still got to give them lunch even if I don't get any support from anybody. I've run up six hundred and fifty million koronas worth of debt so far, but it hasn't once happened that there's been no lunch (…) People have no heart and don't give!* At such times the consciences of the richer bourgeoisie would trouble them again, and they would open their purses once more. He managed to persuade Horthy's wife herself to stand in the street with a box when there was a special collection in the Belváros, and to help encourage people to donate. In his statements Uncle Róbert also spoke of his further plans: at one time he dreamt of a network of mobile soup-kitchens, at another time of the creation of free hostels for the homeless.

For years no one asked on what he maintained the office, paid the cooks, van-drivers and food-dispensers, nor how he afforded regular journeys abroad and a four-room flat in the luxurious New York mansion, the present Boscolo hotel. The scandal broke out in 1930, when a brother and sister in business complained about Uncle Róbert because he had given them large amounts of credit at usurious rates of interest. According to this, Feinsilber had lent them 25,000 *pengő*s at 25% in the name of his daughter, who lived in London by teaching the piano. When they fell behind in repayment he had their apartment house in Klauzál tér auctioned. Although the rate of interest was not outrageously high, it turned out in the light of the complaint that the benefactor of the poor was not at all tender hearted towards the less poor. He had regularly given quite large loans, and had become so rich from the prohibited credit activity that, according to a property review in 1930, he owned seven apartment houses and two private houses in Budapest, in addition to deposits of 150,000 *pengő*s in Vienna and a million in London. The detective work was conducted with the greatest discretion, because no wealthy debtor was anxious to appear in the papers. The gossip began as follows: some said that the restaurateurs bought some of the fresh food that was offered as donations, and many complained that Uncle Róbert had deceived them over the Golden Book of Budapest and other favours. Those that breathed sighs of relief at the rumours, as they freed them from remorse concerning the poor, also began to spread lies about the 'swindling soup-distributor'. For example, that he had tricked money out of actors, or that he had valuable paintings and pieces of jewellery in his home. It

The poor of Budapest having lunch.

is merely probable that after sharing out his own wealth Uncle Róbert had not been particular about the means if he wanted to make money: he had loaned out money received as donations at high rates of interest, bought real estate and deceived people with non-existent benefits.

Under the influence of the complaint Feinsilber was investigated on suspicion of fraud, but eventually the affair ended without charges being brought. Decades later a journalist found on the report of the investigation a two-line manuscript note: *Close the case, we are not going to defy Róbert Feinsilber's paupers. What's done is done, expel him.* In fact it would not have been in anyone's interests to put in the dock the man who had fed tens of thousands, a man very popular with the poor, and to whose charitable work the Regent's wife herself had given her name. In the end, therefore, by the tortuous reasoning that as a Turkish national Róbert Feinsilber could not be held to account, he was simply disposed of: he was expelled from Hungary. The poor remained, the 'apostle of the poor' departed. Uncle Róbert did not, however, go far, but settled in Vienna. Under the name of Onkel Robert he soon opened an office for the assistance of the suicidal, and the Austrian police too collaborated with him. There too scandal broke out after a while: it turned out that he was offering credit at high rates of interest to cash-strapped businessmen. At the time he made a statement about his years in Hungary to the Hungarian journalists that were following the scandal and called on him: *I did not steal from the poor, because I always gave them what they needed, I was merely a careful steward of the crumbs that the rich sent …*

We know little of Uncle Róbert's later life. His Turkish citizenship helped him to survive the persecution of the Jews, but by then nothing remained of his erstwhile wealth. Whether he had obtained it as an honest businessman, or whether by fraud, there is every likelihood that he once again distributed all that he had. After 1945 he was looking for accommodation as a homeless person, and finally found himself a little room in a Viennese woman's house. In the fifties, when his name cropped up again in the Hungarian press as a symbol of 'mindless charity', a journalist actually called on him in his room and asked him what was the truth about his making millions by running a charity. Uncle Róbert denied it angrily: *Slander! I was a rich man even before that, and I gave away a lot of what was mine. My father was a millionaire in Constantinople.* That was his final word. He lived on for a few years in complete solitude, slowly losing all connection with the outside world. The swindling apostle of the destitute died at the age of ninety-two in a mental home. He could not know that the poor of Budapest, whom he had once fed, still spoke of their benefactor long afterwards.

I have been in Hungary for thirty-nine years. What remained of my wealth I devoted to the assistance of suicides and those that had fallen on hard times. I shall continue with that work as long there is breath left in me. My wealth is actually now for the most part used up, but today those people are helping me whom I saved, whom I restored to life. I have friends among the traders in the Market Hall, and everywhere assistance comes to me, so that I feel it the greatest joy if I can ease the sufferings of others. For me the purpose and meaning of life is charity. If I still have any property at the time of my death I shall leave it all to the last fillér to the poor. It is my wish that when I die I be buried in the simplest wooden coffin, and that the fillérs saved at the funeral service too be given to the starving and the fallen. One last thing: I am not ashamed of having been a Jew. After all, the twelve apostles too were Jews.

Róbert Feinsilber,
Autobiography in *Magyarság*
18 July 1929

*Richter in 1939, the year when he resigned after creating
the Hungarian company best known world-wide.*

Gedeon Richter

His staff said a tearful farewell to the founder of the Hungarian company that was the best known in the world as he left for Switzerland. It was not the first time that Gedeon Richter and his wife had been to Switzerland: his firm had interests there and in fifty other countries. This time, however, the couple were making no ordinary journey. In the summer of 1944 Richter, aged seventy-one, had only been able to go back onto the premises of his factory a few months previously; before then even that had been denied him. He had had to leave the position of managing director years earlier, and for a long time had only been given permission to enter the factory that he had established as an unpaid adviser. By that time the authorities enforcing the Jewish laws must have realised that without Richter's expert knowledge Hungary's most important revenue from export would dry up. Perhaps they also were aware that even in the most unpromising personal situation the world-famous research chemist and businessman was going to do all that he could for the pharmaceutical works to operate successfully. His friends and foreign customers had tried for years to persuade him to emigrate and lead his manufacturing empire from Switzerland. Again and again he had refused, he could not live without his homeland and his factory.

In June 1944 he finally accepted a Swiss safe conduct from the Red Cross, and so went to the factory in Kőbánya to say good-bye. The management and staff were in tears, but were relieved that Mr Richter, for whom they had the warmest regard, was going to a place of safety. A few weeks later they were horrified to see him – in his threadbare coat with its yellow star – coming through the gate once more. *Couldn't get a sleeper to Bern,* said he with a melancholy smile, *and I can't subject my wife to a journey like that.* Not long afterwards the father of Kalmopyrin and many other medicines left his home without a murmur, and weeks later walked, head held high, in a column heading for the Danube embankment. Perhaps he did not want to see what he had built up becoming someone else's, and perhaps he no longer saw any value in anything.

Gedeon Richter's ancestors had been merchants who emigrated from Bohemia to Hungary, and his parents in their time were landowners. Gedeon was born in 1872, and it is highly likely that he too would have lived on his land had his life not begun with a tragedy. His mother died of complications at his birth, and a year later his father was carried off in a cholera epidemic. The five children that they left were taken in by their maternal grandparents. Although they inherited substantial wealth they had no access to it until they came of age, and so grew up in straitened circumstances. It shows that the Jewish family had become assimilated, that after primary school Gedeon's grandparents sent him to the highly reputable Franciscan grammar school. His school reports do not show him as a particularly good student, but he was rather keen on visiting the school library and immersing himself in books on medical subjects. The practical side of the subject appealed to him also: at the age of fifteen he found a job in a chemist's shop.

After leaving school he knew exactly what career to choose, and at university studied to be a pharmacist. In 1895 he needed a further two years' practice to be able to open his own business. The profession of pharmacist was going through an enormous change at the time. By the end of the nineteenth century it was usual for there to be a chemist's in every biggish place, and the pharmacist was a respected member of the local intelligentsia. There were few pharmaceutical factories to be found in Europe, and in the main pharmacists made their own tablets and serums. Everyone had their own secret formulae, and ambitious assistants could learn these from them. Richter therefore served his apprenticeship in more than one town in Hungary. After that he could have settled down, but he meant to be the best in his profession, and to the surprise of those around him spent a further four years as a pharmacist's assistant abroad: first he spent a year in German towns, and England, France and Italy followed. In addition to routine work he found a way to visit a few of the innovative pharmaceutical factories of Europe and in 1901 returned to Hungary as one of the best-trained pharmacists of his time, able to speak and read five languages.

The slender young man, losing his hair early but sporting a moustache in the fashion of the day, was reckoned almost too old when he finally decided to use what remained of his inheritance to buy a little chemist's shop in Pest. He received permission on 12 January 1902, and that date may be considered to mark the birth of Richter Pharmaceuticals, or of the manufacture of pharmaceuticals in Hungary. Richter knew precisely what experiments he meant to carry out in the laboratory in the cellar: on his travels abroad a new method of healing, 'organ therapy', had aroused his interest; that is, 'the healing of people with animal fluids'. At that time science everywhere was familiar with the workings of the endocrine glands and hormones, but no one except Richter thought of making medicines from them in large quantities. Adrenalin, for example, had been isolated from the adrenal gland by a Japanese scientist in 1901, but production of Tonogen, the first adrenalin preparation that had the effect of raising the blood-pressure, was begun by Richter's staff in 1902. In the same year he brought out two other hormonal preparations: Thyrecide, which contained

The Sas (Eagle) pharmacy. One of the biggest pharmaceutical factories in Europe was founded in the basement.

the active ingredient of the thyroid gland, and the drug Ovarium, extracted from the fallopian tube of the pig. He obtained the necessary animal parts from slaughterhouses, initially causing no little consternation by so doing. After a while he allotted an expert to each slaughterhouse, who collected the basic material in airtight porcelain containers and sent it to the laboratory post haste. The Latin name of every new product was followed by that of Richter:

he was confident that his name would soon become a guarantee of the purchaser's trust. He was at the same time a scientist familiar with the latest international scientific discoveries and a business-man who could assess demands with lightning speed.

It was only after his first professional successes that he was able to begin building in his private life too. The *Pharmacists' Gazette* of February 1902 was delighted to announce that *Our colleague Gede-on Richter, new proprietor of the Eagle pharmacy in Üllői út, Budapest, has become engaged to Annushka Winkler, daughter of Bernát Winkler, industrialist of Szeged.* This was no sudden flaring of love, because as was the way in those days the engagement followed discussions with the Winkler parents and Miss Annushka – or as everyone called her, Auntie Nina, or Mina – was Richter's faithful and de-voted companion for more than forty years. The former orphan boy had finally come into harbour at the age of thirty-one; in 1903 their only child, László, was born.

In a few years' time the demand for Richter's new medicines had become so great that the underground laboratory could no longer cope. In 1906 he bought land on the outskirts of Pest and a year later a smallish, purpose-built factory stood there. The Gedeon Richter Chemical Factory, or 'chemist-factory', as the lo-cal people called it, went into production in September 1907. In an article written at the time he set out the aims of the new factory: *to produce medicines that medical science would recognise as apposite for the healing of patients*; furthermore, he meant his preparations to com-pete with 'the powerful similar enterprises outside Hungary'. He was successful. In record time a modern business, capable of com-peting on an international footing, had been built up.

The laboratory meant everything to him. The day did not go by when he did not personally take part in the latest experiments. First, he made oxytocin, which stimulated birth pains, and was the factory's first internationally successful product. In 1911 he took further the development of Bayer's popular *Aspirin*: Rich-ter's *Kalmopyrin* was, unlike its competitor, water-soluble, and had far fewer side-effects. Italian, French and English chemistry technicians also worked for Richter, and he spoke with them all in their native languages. He tried to bind to the factory for life anyone that he employed, and indeed to employ their family members as well. As director of the factory he established a creative community, modern in spirit, in which everyone knew what the rest were doing. Management, researchers and technicians met at the lunch-table every day and discussed problems; manual workers could take part in training courses, and everyone took home far better pay than was usual at the time. Richter was not only *au fait* with international research but also kept a close eye at all times on the influence of politics on the market. After the outbreak of the world war he realised that army hospitals were going to require antiseptics, and produced great quantities. Because his preparation Hyperol was a solid it was easily transported, and the Hungarian army ordered it in bulk. Because of similar innovations the factory developed steadily during the war years, yet Richter cannot be seen as profiteering. He had his own conception of business integrity: when a number of foreign competing products did not reach Hungarian chemists' shops during the war he too cut back on manufacture. When he was asked why he did not take advantage of the difficult situation all he said was: *I consider it unfair to compete in a market where there is no competition.*

By the end of the war the Richter Chemical Factory was considered the biggest pharmaceutical enterprise in Central Europe; its main competitors were the German factories. In 1919 politics interrupted the development of the firm for the first time. Under the Republic of Councils the authorities appropriated the factory and appointed a commissar in charge of it. Richter did all that he could to delay the actual handing over of the business, and so a people's commissar summoned him and ordered him to cooperate. Thugs gave greater emphasis to his words. For the first time in his life, Richter had to leave his factory, and until the commune collapsed took refuge at his father-in-law's in the country.

The Treaty of Trianon meant a blow for the factory too: half of the domestic market was lost. Richter saw that remaining in business meant expansion abroad. Even before the war he had started to build a European network, but from now on he regarded international presence as a matter of priority. For an enterprise in a country that had been defeated this was no light task: many Richter products were embargoed in a number of European countries. In response he reached out beyond the seas. In the next ten years fifty Richter-concessions or daughter-companies opened on five continents, including some in India, Mexico, the Philippines and even China, where the firm maintained a permanent warehouse so as to be able to deliver more quickly than its English competitors. A decade later the RG monogram was a trade-mark familiar all over the world. And the wealth grew and grew: from 1923 until 1938, the last year of peace, the value of the stock of the limited company rose by three and a half times and its income by sixteen times.

Not much of this showed in the owner's life-style. Millionaire though he was, Richter arrived at Kőbánya at a quarter to seven every morning, dressed in his brown loden coat and bowler hat, and personally inspected the premises from boiler-house to laboratory. As he was first to arrive he was at the gate to greet staff that were late for work. For him, the factory was his only passion: he never went into the company of his peers, not even to the theatre. His family lived comfortably in their flat on the Belgrade embankment, but by no means in the luxury that by then they could have permitted themselves. Now, however, even politics recognised the manufacturer's achievements: in January 1929 Horthy appointed Richter a government senior adviser, and from then on he had the style 'The Honourable'. According to the commission this distinction was not conferred on him as a pharmacist, but *on account of his activity in the sphere of economic life*, and not surprisingly. The way that the Richter factory had boosted exports and brought hard currency into Hungary had had a perceptible effect on Hungary's balance of payments. Richter felt that the recognition of his achievement meant at the same time acceptance of his (Jewish) origins, and so was proud of it.

In the 1930s Richter had to struggle against new obstacles. Although the factory had won a series of the greatest international acknowledgements, although its functioning was indispensable to the Hungarian economy, the fact that the owner was a Jew proved more and more of a disadvantage. First he invited 'the right people' to join the board, among them a minister, a lord lieutenant and a lieutenant field marshal, in the hope that they would smooth the way for the business. This meant help only for a while, until the Jewish laws were enacted. Although in March 1939 Richter himself converted to the Protestant faith he obtained no relief from the laws restricting him economically. He resigned as chairman of the company *on the grounds of ruined health*, merely remaining a member of the board, and had to dismiss several key men. Even though he petitioned the Prime Minister to be allowed to remain as managing director for the sake of the smooth operation of the factory, in 1941 he was forced to leave that post too. His colleagues worked out a way to survive: they planned to set up a daughter-firm in Portugal, at the head of which Richter could continue to supervise the group of companies. Richter considered this, but in the end rejected the idea because he would not have been able effectively to direct day-to-day functioning from a distance. He could have done as other Jewish big businessmen did and move a large part of the company's stock abroad, but he would not do that. He buried himself in work, and not without result. In 1941 the capital of the company had to be increased, new buildings were built on Gyömrői út so that demands could be satisfied, and he was even able to afford to set up a retirement pension fund. Thirty new products were licensed in the war years, and the productivity of Richter and Co. was increased by two and a half times, bringing in enormous revenue to the state.

The state rewarded success in its own way: in 1942 Richter's employment was terminated and he was banned from the factory.

By that time his daughter-in-law, who qualified as Aryan, was at the head of management, and a majority of members of the board were Christians. They wrote to the government requesting that Richter be allowed to take part in the work of the company at least as an unpaid adviser. As there was urgent need of revenue the Treasury did indeed give permission, but another state organ reported three directors for making it possible for Richter *to work at the enterprise with a higher sphere of executive responsibility.* The dispute went on for almost two years, during which time the management of the factory met in the evenings in Richter's study at home, because no one but he had a complete grasp of the firm's multinational empire. The world outside Hungary too regarded him as *de facto* head of the business: when in 1943 Richter and Co. offered the Red Cross assistance with medicines the Apostolic Nuncio called on Gedeon Richter in ostentatious fashion and thanked him personally on behalf of the pope. By then, of course, that was irrelevant.

THE JEWISH LAWS. Hungary was the first country in the twentieth century to enact laws restricting the rights of the Jewish population. By means of the *numerus clausus* law of 1920 the state sought to ensure employment for the Magyar intelligentsia who had flocked to the country for refuge after Trianon; it was stipulated that members of the various ethnic groups might only be admitted to the universities in proportion to their numbers. Although the word 'Jewish' did not occur in the text, the law operated against the Jews, who unquestionably formed a large proportion of the intellectual professions. The laws persecuting the Jewish population, modelled on the German 'Nuremberg' laws, were introduced from the end of the 1930s. The first Jewish law of 1938 limited to twenty per cent the proportion of persons of the Jewish faith in intellectual and economic positions of employment; a year later the concept of Jewishness was defined on a racial basis, and the number that might be employed in intellectual occupations was reduced to six per cent. From then on Jews might not hold managerial positions in industrial and commercial concerns. The third Jewish law of 1941 prohibited 'mixed marriage', together with sexual intercourse between Jews and non-Jews. After the German invasion on 19 March 1944 about a hundred new regulations were brought in: Jewish-owned motor vehicles and telephones were confiscated, Jews were prohibited from cinemas, theatres and baths, their rations were reduced, and their ability to travel was restricted. The compulsory wearing of the yellow star was introduced, followed by the establishment of ghettoes. From May 1944 the Jews, deprived of the remains of their belongings, began to be deported by the Hungarian authorities to German concentration camps.

Many have posed the question: did Richter grasp his personal situation? Was he capable of appreciating that he was in mortal peril? In all probability, yes. He arranged for the Red Cross safe conduct to be given to a young man, and at the last minute before the German invasion succeeded in evacuating his son via Romania and Istanbul. He was also there when the management received the official letter from the government committee telling them to *dismiss László Richter, who has left the country.* Although his enthusiasm for work and his energy were no less, memories say that Gedeon Richter became more withdrawn and grimmer. He came into the factory until the last moment, yellow star on his coat, right until in the autumn of 1944 an army commandant took over the direction of the factory, which was categorised as of military importance. Even then he was anxious about what would become of it, and what would happen if the military managers were unable to pay the staff. We cannot say whether he learnt how, when the Arrow Cross ordered the factory to be dismantled and evacuated to the west, the employees opposed and sabotaged the preposterous instruction.

By that time the Richters were in hiding with relatives, and then, with the help of a safe conduct from Raoul Wallenberg, they moved into a tiny room in a Swedish embassy safe house. On 30 December 1944 the Hungarian Nazis, the Arrow Cross, came for them there. They lined up the occupants on the pretext of checking their identity, and took them to the party headquarters at 60 Andrássy út. There they relieved them of their papers and valuables and at dawn next day lined them up in columns, separating the men and women. Richter went over to his wife, embraced her, and went into the men's line. He was stripped to his underwear, like the rest, and taken to the Danube embankment. Not far from his old home he was shot into the river.

The column of women – perhaps because of an air raid – was eventually released, and Mrs Richter escaped. She hid in the country for a while, then went to Italy, where, rejecting all contact with the outside world, she ended her life in a sanatorium in Lugano. Two days after her husband's death, on 2 January 1945, the Russians took the Richter factory and removed the movable equipment. László Richter went to America, then to Switzerland, and from there tried to support the former daughter-companies. He had little success. The Belgian offshoot of the Hungarian firm, for example, declared itself independent, and has grown into one of the world's biggest pharmaceutical companies, Janssen. Without its founder, the erstwhile largest Hungarian-owned multinational firm fell apart. Even today, however, the RG monogram proclaims the talent and willpower of the sometime orphan boy.

... and all this great result has been achieved in the most total peace. In twenty-five years never a dissonant voice, never anything in bad taste. (...) Never has the working of a company borne the characteristic features of the person that led it as does this, the one at the head of which stands Gedeon Richter, every inch a gentleman, a man of iron resolve and outstanding talent.

Pharmaceutical Informer, 1929

The teen-age champion. Today the Petschauer Sabre Open is one of the premier fencing competitions in America.

Attila Petschauer

In 1931 Miklós Horthy, the Regent himself, received the finalist in the Hungarian fencing championship in private audience. Not the gold medallist, but the runner-up, Attila Petschauer. There had been articles in the papers for days past to the effect that the twenty-seven year-old fencer, who had, with his amazing persistence and sportsmanship, had helped the Hungarian fencing team to gold in the Amsterdam Olympics, was now the victim of deceit. The public were unanimous in seeing the jury of army officers as biased – they had awarded victory to a fellow officer rather than to a civilian. A huge row was in the offing: if it were shown that an officer had become champion through the dishonesty of others the good name of the leaders of the whole army, indeed, of the whole country would have been besmirched. For the sake of hushing up the protest the Regent received Petschauer, presented him with a signed photograph, and consoled him that he should not be upset, he would have plenty more opportunities of winning. He was right: Petschauer soon helped the Hungarian Olympian team to another victory. Before that, however, influential sporting leaders had sent him a message: they counted on him in the team, but would not like it if a Jew became individual champion in the sport of Hungarian gentlemen. Later, unexceptionable Hungarian gentlemen murdered him. Attila Petschauer was born in 1904, and began fencing while still in primary school. 'Pecsus', as his friends called him, was not really interested in anything else. He had the perfect build for fencing. According to a friend's description, *his arms are very muscular, very strong, his thighs unusually long, that was the secret of his long reach. His whole body was athletic, flexible.* He was seventeen when the celebrated Italian fencing-master Italo Santelli too watched him in a demonstration match between secondary-school teams. He called him 'the new d'Artagnan' and invited him to study with him free of charge: *If you learn fencing with me, become great champion.* He entered for the senior championship as a teenager. The public quickly fell for him because he was felt to be a brilliant fencer on the piste, and off the piste to have a real sense of fun. His humorous battle-cry of 'Hollala, oplá, alaláá' which resounded when he scored a hit became his trademark.

After leaving high school he spent five terms in law school, and then dropped out to concentrate on the sport. He was an instinctive fencer, and as a fellow fencer said: *He almost laughed as he fenced, the sword sang in his hand.* His strength lay in playful, spectacular fencing, sudden rushes, and he was known as a master of the *flèche.* From this came his weakness too, lack of tactical sense, of judgement in pacing himself – many blamed this for his failure to win individual Olympic gold despite his world-wide reputation, nor was he ever European or world champion. But he was heard of more and more outside Hungary. Many saw in fencing successes the living-down of lost military glory, and so it comes as no surprise that among others the elderly writer Jenő Rákosi saw in him a real national hero. *Attila Petschauer has brought home the triumphant Hungarian tricolour from the Vienna fencing competition. Hail to Attila's sword! (…) An athletic figure, in the flower of his youth, with the national weapon of the Hungarians, the sword, in his hand, he has gained honour for himself and the nation, and for the name Hungarian.* Others, however, were less pleased that a sportsman of Jewish birth should fight for the glory of the Magyar. There were those that tried to have him banned from fencing. Petschauer loved playing cards, and so one journalist tried to make out that he was a gambler by profession, that is, a professional sportsman. If he had succeeded in proving that Petschauer would have been banned from fencing, a sport for amateurs only.

At this time fencing in Hungary was characterised by the clash between army officers and civilian fencers. The best fencers came from the National Officers' Club Fencing Club, but sportsmen from the civilian clubs too were obtaining better and better results. The tension between the two camps was palpable not only in competitions but also in the composition of teams. Early in the century the Hungarian fencing team had twice won in the Olympics, and then in their first encounter after the First World War lost to the Italians. The return match was of immense political importance, and the leaders of the fencing association – mostly officers – would have liked it if the team to fight for the glory of Hungary were not enfeebled by the inclusion of civilian, most of all Jewish, elements. Although Petschauer had qualified for the Olympics they were unwilling to select him for the team. According to certain sources, what saved him was that a fellow competitor, Captain Ödön Tersztyánszky, one of the Olympic pool of fencers, made it known to the leaders of the fencing association that in that case he would not go either. Whatever the truth of the matter, the combination of sportsmen from different social groups gave rise to the world's most successful fencing team.

In Amsterdam it was clear from the outset that the competition would again be decided between the Italians and the Hungarians. As the youngest member of the team Petschauer achieved a superhuman task in the eliminations. Those of his team-mates that were also in the individual competition tried to reserve their strength and many lost points, but Pecsus was almost unstoppable: he won all his nineteen bouts against five other countries. In the final against the Italians too his was the final bout. Merely to defeat Renato Anselmi would not have been enough, as because of the points difference Petschauer had to win by a margin of at least three points, otherwise the gold would go to the Italians – and that he did, winning by 5–2. After the decisive bout his teammates rushed onto the piste to carry him shoulder-high, but at the last moment realised that the winner had collapsed in exhaustion: celebration had to wait for a little first aid! Next day, banner headlines announced the great success: *Petschauer wins team event! But for Petschauer Italy would have won gold!* The young fencer, who had scarcely been allowed to represent his country, was reported as *trumpeting enthusiastically an oath that he would always be ready to do what he had done in Amsterdam.*

Two days later he had to fight again, this time for victory in the individual competition – and furthermore, not against just anyone but against his team-mate Ödön Tersztyánszky, with whom he was precisely level on points. As a fencer, the army officer was in every respect the antithesis of the virtuoso, constantly moving Petschauer. In the fencing hall he was nicknamed Spot-on Ödön, and his style was marked by restrained elegance and tactical patience. In their persons military and civilian Hungary clashed symbolically, or at least so the final was seen by public opinion. Tersztyánszky had been reserving his strength, had won only once in the team event while his opponent had won twenty times. Petschauer was worn out as he stood on the piste, and was beaten 5–2. *I was tired, the previous bouts had taken it out of me. But I don't mind. I'm pleased that Tersztyánszky was the winner, and I'll be ready for the next Olympics,* he declared. Tersztyánszky may have felt that he owed the gold medal to the fact that his opponent had not spared himself but had sacrificed himself so that the Hungarian team should win. Not long after the Olympics he was killed in a motor accident at the age of thirty-nine.

After returning home Petschauer was swamped by popularity: in modern terms, we may regard him as the first 'celeb' in Hungarian sport. Stories were told of his humour and bravado. For example: at a reception after a competition in Madrid he was very tired of the way that the Spanish hosts turned up their noses and introduced themselves by ostentatiously extended titles of nobility half a sentence in length, while the Hungarians' names were short. While shaking hands with the next gentleman he smiled broadly and said: *Attila Petschauer but wipe your arse with your tail and stick it up your bum!* Immediately came the reply: *Up yours as well, my boy, I'm the Hungarian ambassador.* He became a favourite in the Bohemian art world of Budapest, and was often invited to the tables of actors and writers in the New York coffee house. He was a famously good mimic, and could imitate any language. At one memorable New Year's Eve party he performed the hit number *Sonny Boy* in gobbledygook to the raucous laughter of those present. In other words: he very much enjoyed popularity, and was pleased if people whispered to one another behind his back in the street: *There's Petschauer.*

There were, however, those who could not forgive him for publicly representing the sport of the Hungarian upper classes. According to an article in *Nemzeti Sport* (National Sport) his conduct was not worthy of fencing, which was considered a symbol of the nation: *When he's had a drink or two he acts the fool, and brings discredit upon fencers by his jokes.* Because of attacks like this he even thought of giving up fencing. *Many look on my successes with disfavour!* he stated. *But I have always fought for my Hungarianness and my country (…) In addition to that mission the sport brings me pleasure and entertainment, but I do not want entertainment that brings me nothing but irritation all the time! (…) I have done my duty, I shall give up fencing.* In the end, however, he did not give up, and helped the team to numerous international successes. The leaders of the sport made no great secret of the expectation that he should contribute to success as a team member, but not be an individual winner. To this end they were able to take steps: electrical scoring did not yet exist, and the word of the jury decided on hits. Petschauer was often disappointed over the award of points, but commented on his defeats with outwardly cheerful self-deprecation. Thus after he had been robbed of the 1931 Hungarian championship it was the press and not he himself that revealed the swindle. The Minister of Defence, Gyula Gömbös, was present at the final and his adjutant was a member of the jury. The military members of the panel and the president blatantly favoured the officers. In the final Petschauer was leading 4:1 when the president of the jury awarded five hits to his opponent – a Guards officer – in quick succession. Two members of the panel left the hall in protest at the biased judgement, and one of them actually declared to the journalists that the verdict had been false. Next day the only thing in the papers was the tale of deception. Fearing scandal, first the Minister called Petschauer in to help silence the complainants, and then the Regent himself apologised to the fencer in his own way. Petschauer never said a word about the unfair verdict, but prepared for the 1932 Los Angeles Olympics with the rest of the squad. Once again he played an active part in the team victory, but in the individual competition he lost to two fellow Hungarians and was only placed fifth.

On return from the Olympics – with two Olympic team golds and two European team championships behind him – Petschauer announced that he was retiring from competition: *Up to now I've lived for my sword, now I'd like to make a living by my sword*. He decided to go back to America and go into films. For a short while he was a fencing instructor for costume films in Hollywood, and is said to have even taken part in films, and had dreams of becoming a producer – but he did not stay there long. He could not live without the popularity that he had enjoyed in Budapest. Back at home he became a reporter on a low-class paper, writing on sport and the theatre. He thirsted for recognition, and was as proud of his articles as he had been of his sporting successes. In the evening he continued his Bohemian lifestyle, going to nightclubs sometimes with popular film actors, sometimes with the son of the Regent, and enjoying the company of elegant danseuses. Before the Berlin Olympics a member of the team invited him back – in a newspaper article – to the piste, but he declined. He parodied

Hitler in coffee houses, using a little black brush for a moustache, and took part as a reporter in the Olympics designed to glorify the Nazis. His former sporting successes had made him so well known that Hermann Göring, charged with the solution of the Jewish question, recognised him in the stadium and introduced him to his entourage: *He was the greatest fencer in the world, perhaps the greatest of all time,* and then greeted Petschauer using his walking stick to imitate fencing – presumably having no idea that Petschauer was Jewish.

In Hungary, the anti-Semitism that had risen to state level did not affect Petschauer in principle. Horthy had given him personal distinction, and that meant that he was exempt from the effect of the Jewish laws. Nevertheless, in 1940 he wrote in his diary: *I have never been asked why I constantly act the clown. Now time has gone by, rust is eating at the iron in me, and so I can confess: the wickedness of men fills me with profound sadness, and I try by clowning to dispel my black thoughts.* The black thoughts were not without foundation: in 1942 he too received a summons to forced labour. In a light suit and raincoat he reported at the recruitment centre. From this point it is not easy to know exactly what happened. According to some sources, he had – out of pride rather than forgetfulness – left his certificate of exemption at home; according to others, the commandant (later to be executed as a war criminal) simply tore it up. In any case, after a couple of weeks' training he and 260 companions were loaded into trucks and taken to the Eastern front. His relatives and friends tried to intervene on his behalf, or at least to send after him warm clothing and boots, but it was too late. Their notoriously sadistic captain did all in his power to make the lives of the forced workers unbearable. At times they had to sleep under trucks in the winter frosts, at times he threw away their food because they had not been working hard enough. On one occasion he had Petschauer tied up and beat him personally. One German officer observed these acts of cruelty, and told the Hungarian captain to let his men get on with their work.

FORCED LABOUR. The special military establishment was originally an unarmed service of those liable for conscription but found unfit; later it meant the unpaid work for military purposes of Jews and members of other social groups considered by the regime to be unreliable (e.g. non-Magyars, communists). After the introduction of the Jewish laws Jews could not become officers or even arms-bearing other ranks, but from an official viewpoint they too had to play their part in the war effort. Forced labourers built gun emplacements and tank traps for units fighting on the front, cleared mines, and in the rear cleared rubble and carried out repair work. At first they wore uniform, but later had to wear their own civilian clothes; their rations were scanty. Forced labourers sent to the Russian front were also at risk of freezing to death as winter drew on, in addition to humiliating, often brutal treatment at the hands of the Hungarians in charge of them. A number of Hungarian intellectuals and writers met death as forced labourers. After the start of the deportations to Auschwitz, paradoxically, forced labour meant a chance of survival to those conscripted.

On 20 January 1943, in a labour camp on the Davidovka in the Ukraine Petschauer met Lt. Col. Kálmán Cseh, who, like him, had taken part in the Amsterdam Olympics but as a military horseman. He had no love for his successful fellow Olympian, and decided that it was time *to make the Jew sweat*. The wrestler Károly Kárpáti, also a forced labourer, tells the story. *The guards shouted: You there, Olympic fencing medal-winner ... Let's see you climb a tree! It was the middle of winter, terribly cold, but they ordered him to strip off and climb a certain tree. They ordered him to crow like a cock while they splashed him with water. In the bitter cold the water froze onto him and in no time he was dead.* Documents that have come to light in the meantime, however, show that the powerfully built sportsman survived even that. When Red Army soldiers liberated the camp he was admitted to their hospital with serious injuries and the marks of further dreadful tortures on his body, and there he eventually died of his wounds. Of the 261 members of Labour

Company 101/4 there were a total of nine survivors. Of the successful Olympic fencing team, Endre Kabos also lost his life as a forced labourer, while János Garay died in Mauthausen concentration camp.

Many years after his death the world has begun to remember Attila Petschauer. István Szabó based the character of Ádám Sors on him in his film *A napfény íze* (Sunshine), played by Ralph Fiennes, and since 1994 the Attila Petschauer Memorial Trophy has been competed for in USA and is considered one of that country's most prestigious fencing events.

Hungary is leading 8:7! The championship depends on a single bout! We feverishly calculate the numbers of hits. 57:56 to us. We're leading by one hit. But if Petschauer loses 5:3? Then it'll be 60:61 in favour of the Italians (...) So Petschauer has to win! We go up to him, beg him, be careful! He mustn't lose! Give it all he's got. And Petschauer, always the good-humoured, light-hearted joker, who has so often entertained the audience on the piste, realises that the outcome of the Olympic championship depends on him. A great surge of national sentiment comes over him, he raises his sword to defend Hungarian glory. He takes up the challenge in grim earnest and fights (...) For victory! (...) A bad decision gives Anselmi a hit, 3:2. Petschauer attacks sharply, 4:2. Excitement is at fever pitch! One hit between him and the championship! Petschauer presses his opponent hard. Forces him to the end of the piste. The swords clash together. They glitter. A terrible head-blow and as one man they call Touché! *Petschauer 5, Anselmi 3. We rush over to Petschauer, and as we reach him to hug him, kiss him, he passes out from excitement. We hold him in our arms. When he comes to, he weeps. Everybody is celebrating, happily, wearily, exhaustedly (...) but intoxicated with triumph.*

Nemzeti Sport
(National Sport),
10 August 1928

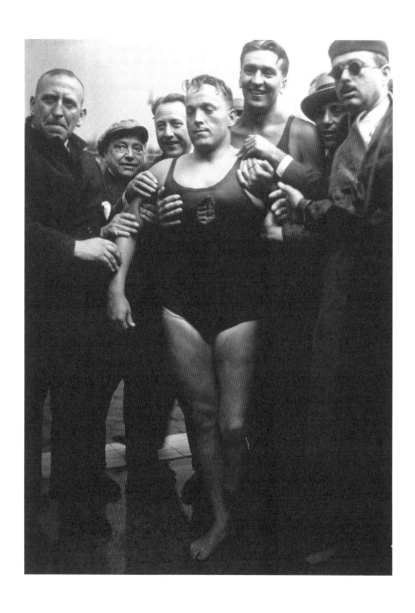

The world's first Paralympian won against able-bodied competitors.

Olivér Halassy

A Hungarian water-polo team first competed for Olympic gold in 1932, in Los Angeles. In the match against the United States a twenty-three year-old player from Újpest scored five goals, and Hungary won its first Olympic title 7:0. When the Hungarian team lined up on the pool-side after the match for the official pictures to be taken the American photographers were astounded to see that the leading goal-scorer had no left leg below the knee. In his short career Oliver Halassy won two Olympic and three European gold medals for water-polo, together with three European and numerous Hungarian swimming championships. The Paralympic games did not yet exist, yet he was the world's first handicapped Olympian. Later he was shot dead in the street over a car: in America a film would have been made about him by this time.

He was born on 31 July 1909 in Újpest, a large town adjacent to Budapest. Like many local boys he began playing football in the town boys' team, and was considered to have serious prospects. At the age of eight he tried to jump onto a moving tram, slipped off the step, and had to have his lower left leg amputated. A year after the operation he was taking part in sport again – still with the Újpest team, but this time training for swimming and water-polo. His first swimming competition ended in a dead heat, when he reached the finish at the same time as the Hungarian champion István Páhok. A year later, to everyone's surprise, he won the river-swimming championship hands down. The competitors swam down a section of the Danube in Budapest, and Halassy covered the nine-kilometre course in an hour and four minutes. The previous champion, Páhok, had a substantial lead at the halfway stage, but was beaten in a tremendous sprint finish. After that everyone began to take the one-legged sportsman seriously. The long-distance races became duels between the two of them, which Halassy won with increasing frequency. After a while Páhok said of his Újpest fellow-sportsman: *Just my luck that this Halassy's lost his leg, otherwise he'd have played football and run after the girls all the time, and I'd have been the great long-distance swimmer in Hungary. But as it is, I'm always coming second.* At the time Páhok could not even have guessed that long-distance swimming would not be the only branch of the sport in which his handicapped rival would triumph. Halassy soon won championships at 1,500 and 800 metres. Then he tried at 400 metres, but only took sixth place. Another swimmer asked him: *Oli, how can you do such a thing, you're a champion and you've come in sixth?* Halassy replied: *I've got no competition at long distance, so I'm looking for some at short distance.* He was right, and the following year he was short-distance champion too.

Meanwhile he went and played water-polo as well, but mainly for the fun of playing in a team. Béla Komjádi, the trainer who picked the national squad, noticed his conspicuous ability and encouraged him to start playing polo seriously and improve his technique. In 1927, however, the Swimming Association banned swimmers from water-polo before the European championships. Halassy was so annoyed at having to make the choice that he announced that he would give up swimming if he could not play polo. In the end Komjádi arranged, for his sake, that the remaining ÚTE championship matches would only take place after the European swimming championships. He had a liking for the young hot-head, who at the time was mainly interested in pretty girls – as well as sport. He picked him for the squad that was preparing for the 1928 Amsterdam Olympics. *Better for him to play water-polo than keep chasing the girls,* said old Komi, when he was asked whether Halassy wasn't too young at nineteen.

But Halassy wasn't the only young one, so were all the team. A newspaper article said of the trainer of the squad that he was satisfied with only three players, and considered the rest, including Halassy, as not yet ready. In Amsterdam, however, the team was among the leading group and was in with a chance for the gold. When the score was 4:4 in the semi-final against the French Halassy, the centre, scored the decisive gold – and they were in the final. Overconfidence came over the team, including Halassy. In the final against the Germans the score was 2:2 when he failed to pass to the team member on his right, and the match was lost. Halassy accepted responsibility: *I was selfish, it didn't work*, he stated. Komjádi's punishment too was severe: he dropped his protégé from the squad for a whole year.

Young Halassy was bitter about the decision and the defeat, and wanted to prove. Immediately after the Olympics he took part in an international river swim in Budapest in front of a huge crowd. The weather was unexpectedly cold, and the autumn rain had cooled the water so much that a third of the competitors were forced to give up, including István Páhok, the great rival. Halassy completed the course and won in an excellent time. The cheering crowd immediately forgave him the lapse in Amsterdam. For twelve successive years Halassy won the river championship, and, when he entered, the Balaton championship too; he also dominated Hungarian middle- and long-distance swimming. He accumulated a total of twenty-three championship gold medals and broke twelve national records. That, however, was not his greatest strength. The Újpest team, with him a member, won the national water-polo championship ten times in ten years, along with thirty-six other titles. When Komjádi called him back to the squad he praised not only his physical condition but considered him *the world's greatest field-player and the most perfect defender.* Halassy learnt quickly, and not only his throwing technique. At the time the un-der-water close-quarter combat that has come in today was not usual in Hungary. The team was accustomed to a clean game and complained to their opponents of rough behaviour in an interna-tional match. *Water-polo isn't table-tennis,* came the reply. After that the Hungarians too changed their style and took under-water hit-ting into their armoury. Halassy was especially adept and – with the slogan *if it's not table-tennis, it isn't table-tennis* – used his ampu-tated left leg to good effect on the opposition.

In the early 1930s he was considered an international star, was the king-pin of the victorious Hungarian teams in the Los Ange-les and Berlin Olympics, and helped them to gold medals in three continental competitions. His greatest success, however, came in the 1931 European championships in Paris. Hungary was playing Belgium, and Halassy gave his all throughout the match. He had learnt from the disaster in Amsterdam, had become a real team player so that the Hungarians should defend their title. The oth-ers were celebrating the victory, when Halassy said that he had to go, he had a little matter to attend to elsewhere. The final of the 1,500 metres race was starting, in which the Frenchman Jean Taris and the Italian Paolo Costolli were the favourites, and every-one reckoned that the race would be between those two. In the end, nothing went by the book. Not only because during the race there was a hailstorm over the pool and the judges could scarcely see what was going on, but because the Hungarian handicapped swimmer pulled off a miracle. Halassy drew ahead of his rivals in every length, but because of his missing leg turned badly and lost what he had gained. Finally, however, he had put them behind him and was contesting first place with another Italian, Giuseppe Perentin. He led him by a metre to take the gold and, complete-ly exhausted, was pulled out of the water by another swimmer. Even on crutches he could no longer walk and had to be carried to the changing-room. There sweet tea was poured into him un-til he recovered. He said thank you, stood up, and returned to the pool, where the match for the water-polo bronze medal was taking place. The match had to be interrupted while the spectators had eyes only for the young Hungarian swimmer. The whole auditorium rang with *Halassy! Halassy!* and in the end the jury and the referee too were applauding him.

Next day the French papers celebrated him on the front page, and in the pictures his amputated leg was clearly visible. Two days later, as the team were on their way home, the French sporting fans recognised him in the Gare de Marseille and gave him such an ovation that even the train-driver and fireman left their places. There were celebrations for him back in Hungary too, of course, perhaps even more often than was necessary. His fellow sportsmen were alarmed to see him taking advantage of his popularity in night-clubs like Arizona and Moulin Rouge until dawn two or three times a week. Béla Komjádi commented to one of his players: *You'll see, another year and it'll be the end of Halassy as a swimmer. His dissolute friends are all round him in Újpest, they drag him from nightclub to night-club. Maybe it won't matter, because this way we shall get his undivided attention as a good polo player.* Apart from Komjádi, however, everyone was sure that Halassy would win gold as a swimmer in the 1932 Los Angeles Olympics as well in between polo matches. His native Újpest even had a triumphal arch designed for the returning champion to pass under. After a long sea voyage the Olympic team travelled from New York to the west coast by train. The only opportunity for training was for them to take part in local competitions in towns on the way. Halassy lined up in the 1,500 metres in Cleveland and was beaten decisively by two Americans. After the defeat he took a decision worthy of a sportsman. On the way to Los Angeles he told Komjádi that he was going to take part in the Olympics only as a polo player, because he wanted to do his best in that. In the competitions he did indeed do that, and the team had largely him to thank for winning its first Olympic gold. After the final Komjádi said: *The way that one-legged man played was amazing!*

Next year his friend and mentor old Komi died. The loss hurt Halassy, but he remained a regular member of the water-polo squad. In 1934, after a number of trifling affairs, he married his childhood girlfriend, the daughter of a prosperous butcher in Újpest. They had three daughters, and in addition to sport Halassy took a job so as to be able to keep his family respectably. First he worked in a factory, then became a supervisor in the town accounts department. He went on swimming for another three years and played water-polo for another five. Before the 1938 European Championships in London he said to another member of the team that the game was becoming a strain, because everyone thought it natural that they were bound to win. There too they were victorious, but Halassy felt that the team was not what it had been. At the age of thirty he decided to retire.

He still played in the ÚTE, but in 1940 was taken ill in the pool. It was discovered that his heart could no longer stand the strain. He went into the heart hospital and for days lay between life and death. He never went into the pool again, but after leaving hospital returned to Újpest as director of the swimming section of ÚTE. In addition he went into business: he rented a cinema, dealt in building materials and wood, and in partnership with his father-in-law ran a small taxi firm. Because of his Olympic championship and "good background" he was above all suspicion in the eyes of the authorities. His friends included a number of far-right profiteers, with whom he went round the bars every night. Therefore no one had any suspicion of him when in 1944 he hid Jewish sportsmen in his cellar at home. A letter to the first Hungarian Olympic champion from Alfréd Hajós, of Jewish origin, is extant: *We hereby express our gratitude for your efforts in the matter of the special treatment of Olympic champions of Jewish origin. (…) I beg you to be so good as to keep us and our affairs in your further goodwill.* Halassy satisfied the request: he went on saving those that he could, and gave one persecuted person his father's military veteran's ring so that he could avoid identity checks and be able to leave the country in safety.

THE SOVIET OCCUPATION. After liberating Hungary from Nazi domination the Red Army did not leave the country for forty-seven years. (Despite this, even in the 1980s official propaganda still spoke of *Soviet forces temporarily stationed in Hungary*.) Although to many their arrival meant release from the ghetto and the Arrow-Cross prisons, in 1944-45 a large part of the population saw the Soviet soldiers as new invaders. The equipment of such factories and workshops as remained was removed by them as booty, and even the wrist-watches and personal effects of people walking in the streets were not safe. It is estimated that two hundred thousand Hungarian women were victims of rape. Civilians were rounded up in the public street or from places of refuge for *'malen'ki robot'* – little jobs – and bundled off to the USSR to forced labour. Something like a hundred and thirty thousand Hungarian civilians were taken like this; some were away for years, while a third of them actually died in the labour camps. Initially the Soviets exercised their authority under the auspices of the Allied Control Commission, which represented the anti-Nazi international coalition, and through that interfered with Hungarian domestic politics, the rules of the electoral system, and detained Hungarian citizens without reference to the Hungarian authorities.

After the war Halassy was one of those that took part in the reorganisation of competitive swimming. On 10 September 1946 he was going home to Újpest from the Swimming Association in a car belonging to his own taxi firm. In Angyalföld a Soviet military patrol waved the taxi down and ordered Halassy and the driver out. Weapons were trained on them and the vehicle demanded. We do not know precisely what happened, but the two probably resisted. The fact is that the taxi was taken away, and a few days later was found – minus its wheels – in a street a long way away. The driver and Olivér Halassy were shot dead on the spot. He was thirty-seven years of age, and his youngest daughter had only just been born. Although the incident was witnessed it was covered up at official levels; the press reported a bestial robbery and murder

The victorious Hungarian water-polo squad in the 1932 Olympics.

but said not a word about Soviet soldiers, and Halassy's relatives were threatened to silence them about what had really happened. Nevertheless, everyone knew. Thousands mourned Halassy, the most successful handicapped sportsman of all time, and Alfréd Hajós delivered the eulogy at his funeral.

Olivér Halassy wins the river championship

The competition for the Hungarian Swimming Association's Championship of the River, marking the end of the summer and of the swimming season, took place on Tuesday afternoon. The contestants started at 2.30 and the ship that accompanied them was full before then. This year the course was 9 Km in length, downstream from the tip of Szentendre Island to the MAC clubhouse. Halassy and Páhok, the two favourites, were soon in the lead and for 5 Km swam neck and neck. Then little Páhok dropped back and Halassy, constantly increasing his lead, won in fine style. The only European swimmers that could beat Halassy over this distance at present are Arne Borg and Bergess, but there are one or two competitors in America and Australia who also would be better. The little swimmer from Újpest is at present 17, that is, he is at the age when prospects for improvement are at the peak. We hope that Halassy will improve his 1,500 metre record by another minute by next year, and that if he continues to develop as we anticipate he will be the first long-distance swimmer (naturally, only in a few years' time) to swim the English Channel in under 12 hours.

Individual championship: 1. Olivér Halassy (ÚTE) 1 hour 4 min 9 sec. 2. István Páhok (MTK) 1 hour 5 min 29 sec. 3. István Szabó (MTK) 1 hour 8 min 55 sec.

Nemzeti Sport,
11 September. 1926

"How much more could I have done?"
Sztehlo rescued 1,600 children in 1944–45.

Gábor Sztehlo

In November 1944 the Lutheran pastor Gábor Sztehlo was informed that a deserted little girl was seeking refuge in the flat of an elderly married couple in Pest. He asked no questions, got into the car and drove to the address that he had been given. The couple knew nothing about the girl, only that she was Jewish and that her parents had disappeared, but they could not undertake to hide her. The portly, broadly-smiling Sztehlo took the child over and promised to put her somewhere safe. He was about to leave when the door of the flat burst open and a woman ran up to him. She asked him to take the neighbour's child as well, as the parents were supposed to go into the ghetto, but had chosen to run away instead. Right away he took the two children by the hand and set off for his car. Outside street children were standing round it with its Red Cross markings. One little boy told him that he had no one, had been left alone. Sztehlo knew that near the ghetto an Arrow-Cross raid could be expected at any moment. He made the three children lie on the floor in the car, covered them with a rug, raced past the armed men and took them to a villa in Buda. Sztehlo saved a total of 1,600 Jewish children and several hundred adults in this sort of way, and later the children of other persecuted persons, left-wing sympathisers, aristocrats and wealthy capitalists too.

In the years of communism he created the world's very first children's home to be run on modern educational principles, an island of democracy in the dictatorship. When that was taken from him he undertook the care of handicapped children. It goes without saying that his humanity and his faith naturally made him a hero. Perhaps it was only to be expected that he had to die in another country, far from Hungary.

Sztehlo was born in Budapest into a well-to-do bourgeois family. A number of his ancestors had been Lutheran clergy, but his lawyer father destined him for a career in the law. As a young man not only did he go against his father in this matter: although his parents magyarised the family name to the more euphonious Szenczy he reverted to Sztehlo out of respect for his ancestors. After leaving school he informed his father that he meant to become a theologian. The curriculum vitae that he attached to his university application is extant: *If God will help me, I consider it my principal goal to lead the Hungarian people, the simple common people, to the good life.* While still a theology student he made a year-long study trip to Finland, where he became familiar with the people's high-school movement that helped the uplifting of young people of peasant origin. Some years later he proved that he was capable of putting its concept into practice. He went as pastor to the small town of Nagytarcsa, and there in five months he set up the first residential people's high school in Hungary. The fundamental principle of the training that he devised was that talented young peasants must not be parted from their environment but be made into conscious, educated farmers that thought responsibly.

During his years in Nagytarcsa he met Ilona Lehel, the sister of a fellow pastor. Orphaned at an early age, she had been brought up in an institution, and Sztehlo's positive attitude to life, his wish to help others, pleased her. In 1936 they married and soon had two children. Ilona was cheerful, an approachable clergy wife of a modern turn of mind, the perfect partner for her husband. The school and building up the congregation might well have satisfied their every wish had history not intervened. According to his memoirs, Sztehlo had not previously been interested in politics at all: he describes himself as *an immature and naive soul, who could not see beyond the life and interests of the Church.* It was as a hospital pastor that he first encountered embittered people who had attempted suicide. *Here I could see where the Jewish laws were leading, and what measures persecution involved (…) That was very difficult service. But I needed that "growing up", and engaged in a life and death struggle. (…) The wounds that I received at this time were blessed ones.*

After the German invasion his bishop, Sándor Raffay, charged him with a new task. The Calvinist and Lutheran Churches jointly were running the Good Shepherd Association, the purpose of which was to help Jews who had adopted the Christian faith. The bishop knew Sztehlo as an outstanding organiser and delegated him to the Association with the vague instruction *something ought to be done for the Christian children of Jewish descent, some refuge created for them.* Sztehlo, then thirty-five, at once set about organising the rescue operation. From the outset he did not concern himself with two points: conformity with the racial laws currently in force, and whether those that he saved were to be exclusively Protestants. *The only question for us was: did somebody need help, or not? Were they persecuted? Deserted? If so, we took them in*, he declared.

In a matter of weeks he had created thirty-two children's homes in villas which had been abandoned or were offered by their owners, and for this he obtained the material support of the International and the Swiss Red Cross. It is typical of his initial naivety that he thought that no one could want to harm innocent children. On behalf of those in his care he asked the Minister for the Interior, László Endre, a notorious figure in the persecution of the Jews, to allot premises to the fugitive children. In reply he was threatened with internment if he obstructed the enforcement of the Jewish laws. At that he realised that saving people would have to be carried out completely illegally, concealed from the authorities. *For me that year was like a dream that I lived through weeping and laughing, starving and well fed, in difficulties and happy, confidently and desperately, freezing and warm, never mind how, but I got through. It was as if I performed everyday tasks, did what had to be done, subconsciously.* Other than himself very few knew what sort of actions the dreadful everydays demanded.

THE ATTEMPT TO LEAVE THE WAR AND THE FALL OF HORTHY. In August 1944 the Romanians, allied to Germany, dropped out of the war, allied themselves to the Soviets and moved against Hungary. Miklós Horthy, who had been seeking the opportunity to make a separate peace, abandoned his plan for a cease-fire with the British or Americans and began secret talks with Moscow. He put a stop to the deportation of the Jews and dismissed the pro-German Prime Minister. With a view to revenge the Germans kidnapped Horthy's son "as a warning". On 15 October 1944 the Regent issued a proclamation concerning leaving the war and forming an alliance with the USSR, by which time Soviet forces were already on Hungarian soil. Because of poor preparation the attempt failed that very day, the Germans deposed Horthy and placed power in the hands of the Hungarian Nazis, the Hungarist Party, commonly known as the Arrow-Cross because of their symbol, a cross barbed. Their leader, Ferenc Szálasi, assumed the direction of the country as 'leader of the nation'.

After the Arrow-Cross assumed power Sztehlo had to act more quickly. His friends urged him to greater caution, but he knew that with every day lost more lives were at risk. He obtained more and more houses and flats, even for money after a while. He asked the Church for deaconesses to supervise the children, and they looked after them together with Jewish adults who were in hiding. On the door of every house and flat he put the seemingly official notice: *This home enjoys the extraterritorial rights of the International Red Cross and it is the duty of all persons in authority to defend it.* Naturally, no such legal right existed, but for a while the notice deterred various raids – until, that is, László

Endre notified Szálasi (who had appointed him a government agent): *Tell that Lutheran priest that I know all about him. He is to stop saving Jews, or I'll break my horse-whip on him.* After that there was need for further precautionary measures. Sztehlo and his colleagues rewrote school certificates, certificates of baptism and obtained other false documents for the children. He took care that his protégés were given pseudonyms that were not conspicuously Hungarian but rather Slavonic in nature, and they – deaconesses otherwise sworn to tell the truth – instructed the children carefully in the false data. The obtaining of food meant constantly growing problems, and Sztehlo made deliveries from the Red Cross warehouse in the Buda castle district, weaving in and out among the bomb-craters.

THE SZÁLASI-REGIME AND THE ARROW-CROSS. Ferenc Szálasi, a former army officer, founded the "Hungarist" movement, with its declared national-socialist principles, in 1934, and chose as its symbol the cross barbed. He considered the Horthy regime too liberal and attacked it in articles and leaflets. The parties which he formed under various names were banned, and he himself imprisoned, several times. Even so, in the 1939 elections his party emerged as the strongest opposition group in Parliament. The Germans did not trust Szálasi, and so after invading Hungary did not at first work with him, but only helped him to power after Horthy's attempt to leave the war in October. Szálasi and the Arrow-Cross brought in an undisguised dictatorship, declared total war on the side of the Germans, and proclaimed the complete purging of the country of Jews. The Arrow-Cross special units often carried out executions without trial, invoking the military situation. Under their four-month reign approximately 70,000 Budapest Jews perished, several thousand of whom were simply shot into the Danube. When the Red Army reached the outskirts of Budapest at the end of 1944 Szálasi transferred his headquarters to Sopron, in the far west of the country, and then fled to Germany. He was executed as a war criminal in 1946.

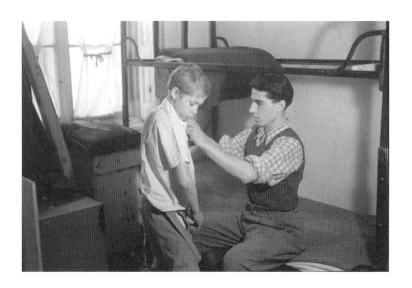

In Gaudipolis children also learned to help.

Sztehlo was careful, but would take a chance too. During one air-raid he asked for some German soldiers for help in evacuating one of the homes, and they carried the Jewish children on their shoulders or led them by the hand to a safe cellar. One of them was a teenager of seventeen who later became the world-famous chemist György Oláh. Sztehlo found time for keeping spirits up as well as saving lives. He did not allow children that had been through so much to turn in on themselves and fall into depression. He told the little ones stories and played with them, and gave the bigger ones jobs to do in looking after them. *He knew how to talk to us so as to give us confidence and dispel that hopelessness as we were down in the cellar for days on end. The mood was good. We had a lot of laughs,* recalls one of his charges. In the difficult weeks of the siege, when there were neither electricity nor clean water available to them, he told them that when they got out of the cellar they would create a community which children would direct, *where hatred was unknown and joy and peace would reign.* Thus the idea of the later children's state was born in the cellar. In the course of a year some 1,600 children and 400 adults found refuge in Sztehlo's homes. At the end of the war he was able proudly to declare: *None of our charges was lost, none was kidnapped, none succumbed to hunger, sickness or cold.*

He soon had to learn, however, that even after the disappearance of the Germans and their Hungarian allies a show of courage was called for. A tall, fair-haired teenager had asked for refuge in the air-raid shelter, and when Russian soldiers suddenly appeared they meant to execute him. Sztehlo jumped in front of the boy as he stood there surrounded by weapons, spread his arms wide and shouted *Nye soldat, not soldier!* The Russians looked on astounded for a moment, then moved on. From then on, the Jewish children were joined by the children of Hungarian civil servants that had fled from Transylvania, or of communists far away in hiding. There was even one little boy who turned up on a scooter, carrying a gun, and could speak Russian. Sztehlo decided that he could not abandon the saving of children. He said to a friend that *if anyone was attacked or persecuted he would stand up for them. Whether they were Jews, aristocrats or Horthyist officers, he would always stand up for the persecuted.* Parents that survived the Holocaust soon reclaimed their children, but no one came for the orphans. More came in the shape of war-orphans, who were roaming the streets often in gangs and living by theft. If the police caught the odd one now and then the state orphanages did not take them in, and they could find refuge only with Sztehlo. *Children of ten to fourteen had to be specially taught how to play, because all that they could remember was playing soldiers, they didn't know what to do with peace-time toys,* Sztehlo reminisced, and decided to create a home for them. First they occupied a villa that was standing empty, left by its owner, an aristocrat, and then the family of the Jewish industrialist Manfred Weiss offered them the Buda rest-house belonging to their factory, where two blocks of flats were placed at their disposal. Food was provided for them by the Swiss and the Danish Red Cross, and by a communist official whose child Sztehlo had saved during the war.

On the thirty-acre site Sztehlo created a self-supporting children's republic. The "state" of the 800 refugee children was officially called the Pax Children's Home, but its citizens referred to it as Gaudiopolis, City of Joy. The republic had its own constitution, a parliament consisting of children enacting laws, and indeed, there was even a currency known as the "Gapo dollar". Attendance at school was compulsory, but working was voluntary. For work there were payment and praise, and so everyone gladly took a share in the control of the city-state. The children also put on shows, published a newspaper, and started a library and a choir. Sztehlo held regular religious services, but attendance was not compulsory; there was complete freedom of religious observance in the children's state. This eventually led to a partial split with the Churches: the bishops of both Calvinist and Lutheran Churches would support the institution only if it took in children of those denominations. Sztehlo, however, would not relinquish his principles, and so after a while the children's home was supported financially only by the Red Cross and a Freemason organisation. As the Hungarian state was swept towards the new dictatorship it looked amiss on the experiment in the democratic upbringing of children. According to one former resident: *The home became a crucible of the classes of Hungarian society, where at first the orphaned Jewish child and the son of the policeman had looked askance at one another. In a little while, nevertheless, no sense remained of those extreme contrasts, or of the class warfare that raged outside.*

For five years Gaudiopolis was able to demonstrate that liberty, equality and fraternity were more than empty words, then the authorities had had enough of the children's republic, and at the beginning of 1950 they nationalised the home. They offered Sztehlo the post of director of the new state institution, but naturally he would have had to comply with the educational principles laid down by Communist Party headquarters. He was unwilling personally to destroy what he had created, therefore he declined the offer and painfully took his leave of the children. He continued to work as an assistant pastor in a Budapest congregation, but there too got into trouble with the authorities of state and Church for supporting with food and medicines class-enemy families that had been relocated.

Finally he found the sphere in which he could be of most help to the fallen: in 1951, under the auspices of the Church he established a home for seriously handicapped children. Here too his ideas about the purpose of the institution differed radically from what was usual at the time: essentially, he put into effect what we now call integrated upbringing. He put children with grave disabilities and those with less serious difficulties into the same room, so that the healthier could experience the pleasure of doing something intelligent and helping, while the less fit learnt to whom they could turn for help. He also organised work therapy and had teachers of the handicapped trained. In the course of ten years he created sixteen Lutheran homes nationwide for the handicapped, children and adults alike, more than those supported by the other historic Churches put together. When during the revolution of 1956 the frontiers were open for a brief time his wife decided that they should emigrate for the sake of the children. Sztehlo, however, was unwilling to give up running the homes for the handicapped. *Here they all love me. This love cannot be spurned*, he told her, and decided that he would let the family go to relatives in Switzerland but he would stay in Hungary. It was five years before he could obtain a passport and visit those that he loved. During the visit he suffered a heart attack – the result of overwork. The doctors advised him to stay there, because in Hungary his life would be at risk because of his condition. His passport soon expired, so that even as a visitor he could not return to Hungary.

He served as pastor in a number of small villages near Bern. The faithful soon came to love him, but for a long time none of them knew anything about his past. Until 1971, that is, when those that he had saved proposed him for the Nobel Peace Prize. Although the German politician Willy Brandt was awarded the prize that

"He relieved the hopelessness of the months we spent stuck down in the cellar, and we had a lot of fun."

year the world outside Hungary took note of the life-saving clergyman. He had a hand in one Hungarian Nobel Prize, none the less: György Oláh, whom he had hidden, was awarded the Nobel Prize for Chemistry in his new country, the USA, under the name of George Andrew Olah. In 1973, aged sixty-three, Sztehlo was awarded the highest Israeli distinction, being elected among the Righteous of the World. His medical condition prevented his attending the award ceremony as he could no longer travel, but he was preparing, if he received Swiss nationality, to visit his native Hungary. In 1974, two months before he anticipated taking the oath as a citizen, he received a letter from his former protégés. Some hours later the postman came across him in the churchyard:

he had died, sitting upright on a bench, with the letter in his hand; it was the forty-second anniversary of his ordination. *The whole of Hungary should feel a pang of conscience over him*, wrote one of his former pupils. To ease that conscience a couple of years ago a street in Budapest was named for him, a memorial tablet placed in Bécsi kapu tér, and a statue erected in his memory.

How much more I could have done, had I not been so unprepared, ignorant, lacking in ideas in March 1944. But until then my eyes had looked at only a little circle, had not seen beyond the life and interests of the Church. (…) How blind and self-confident was the Church! Not only ours, all the Churches. It should have taken up its task differently, and not forfeited the trust of Christianity. All that burdens my conscience too. I learnt all sorts of things. I believe and hope. First of all, that Christianity is the world not of dogma but of love. (…) Of living, lively, active love. Whom did we fail? The individual? The priest? The servant of the Church? The Church itself? Society? Every class? The little man who thinks "I just don't matter"? Or the responsible agent who covers up with "I couldn't have done anything else"? Whom did we Christians fail? (…) You will say: there's been enough repentance, enough mea culpa! Really. Here that's not the point, it's a question of learning. Of admission of sin, without which repentance can't be sincere. Of learning to look and see so that we come to recognise sin.

Gábor Sztehlo,
In the Hand of God, 1994
(edited from his diary by Éva Bozóky)

Margit Slachta as head of the Sisters of Social Service.

Margit Slachta

On 3 August 1941 a party of five left Budapest for the eastern frontier: a count, a countess, two Catholic priests and a nun. They travelled first by train, then by car, towards Kőrösmező, beyond which lay the Ukrainian theatre of operations. They were not on an official journey. To anyone that met them they might have seemed old-style tourists who wanted to look round Kárpátalja, then annexed to Hungary from Czechoslovakia (and now in Ukraine). They were, however, carrying out the most courageous action of their time. Other than them no one had appeared that would speak up loud enough to be heard when the Hungarian state deported several thousand Jewish citizens to certain death within the framework of an "alien control procedure". The delegation prepared an outspoken account of their experiences on the journey, which ended with the words: *We know that at this moment we represent an unpopular affair. But we consider it our duty to raise our voices where to keep silent would be to sin against our consciences.* The spiritual leader of the group, the fifty-seven year-old Margit Slachta, head of the Sisters of Social Service, said in a letter to the wife of the Regent Miklós Horthy that what they had experienced in the concentration camp at Kőrösmező was a disgrace to the Christian religion and besmirched the honour of Hungary. By her steadfast persistence she soon brought about the end of the deportations, and thus saved the lives of thousands. Describing herself as a Christian feminist, Slachta battled to the end of her life with similar relentlessness.

She was Hungary's first female Member of Parliament, and spoke out as courageously for the rights of women as she did against Nazism and Communism. Her male fellow politicians on both sides of the House alike often ridiculed her speeches in Parliament. Even before the war she was regarded as an old-fashioned eccentric, and after the war she featured in the comic papers as a reactionary, ultra-conservative nun. She never relinquished her principles, considered by the majority inopportune, so that in the end she was driven from Hungary.

THE MASSACRE AT KAMENEC-PODOLSKI. Between 1939 and 1941 more than 10,000 Jews fled to Hungary from Nazi-occupied Austria, Czechoslovakia and Poland. The Hungarian authorities wished to free themselves of the Jewish refugees who did not possess Hungarian citizenship, and in the summer of 1941 a decision was taken to expel them. Within the framework of an alien control action some 20,000 were deported, including some who, although they were Hungarian citizens, had failed to identify themselves as such. The deported Jews were held in an internment camp established at Kőrösmező on the eastern frontier of Hungary, and from there – despite the denials of the German army – were transported by train and lorry over the Carpathians to German-held territory of the USSR. The Germans could not feed the horde as they wandered, hungry and thirsty, and tried to drive them back into Hungary. Since the Hungarian authorities resisted that, the Germans arranged for the refugees to be liquidated. Some 11,000 were killed at Kamenec-Podolski, and the remainder taken to concentration camps. After that the Hungarian government stopped the deportations. That was the first mass killing in the history of the Holocaust in which the number of victims exceeded 10,000.

She was born in 1884 in a noble family of Polish origin in Kassa (today Košice in Slovakia), where her father was managing director of the municipal savings bank. Religion did not have a particularly important role in her parents' life, and their six daughters were brought up in bourgeois comfort. Margit, a pretty, slender teenager, came by herself to a deep religious feeling and desire to do good in the community. In a sudden decision she enrolled in the teacher-training school of an order of nuns, where she qualified as a teacher of French and German. She had just begun her teaching career when the savings bank became bankrupt, and the well-to-do bourgeois family was suddenly beggared. Her father decided to start a new life in America, and a few months later they were on board an emigrant ship, awaiting a turn for the better in their fortunes. But not the entire family: the young teacher had said no to emigration and stayed in Hungary. Even at that early date she did not see teaching as her main goal in life, but rather the improvement of the situation of women living in poverty. On her study trips in Europe she had encountered the first feminist movements, but their brazenness had alarmed her, and at the same time she did not find the traditional charitable institutions of the Churches sufficiently effective. It was at this time that she met the Catholic Social Mission Society, founded by Edit Farkas, which was primarily active in the sphere of working-class women: it gave assistance, found work, provided free training and legal advice. The Mission Society was a modern social institution and an order of nuns all in one: its members were allowed to play a part in the community, but they took an oath of poverty and chastity like that of nuns.

In 1908 Margit was one of the first to put on the blue skirt and veil of the Society, but she appeared among the working women more often in a fashionable ordinary modern dress and broad-brimmed hat. From then on the duality of public life in the world and the private life of a religious was with her all her days. She gave up teaching so that she could devote all her energy to the defence of women and to social work. She soon realised that without equality in law women's situation could not be effectively improved, and so she called more and more determinedly for the introduction of universal female suffrage. Together with the Social Democrat and the scarcely visible feminist movements, the Catholic Margit became the spokeswoman for suffrage reform. She chose the sub-title "The paper of Christian feminism" for the newspaper *Christian Woman*, which she founded, and wrote a series of articles on the broadening of women's rights. She represented both the principle of the conservative, religious family and the idea of equality in law, which was reckoned radical. In social work too she followed new lines. She rejected the paternalistic charitable action of the Church and brought to Hungary the implement of professional social policies. *We must not only think of the relief of misery and suffering (…) but try to put a stop to the causes of poverty and wretchedness,* she declared. She drew up scientifically based studies of the living conditions of women living in poverty, and made recommendations for long-term government programmes.

Margit was a convinced conservative who proclaimed progressive left-wing ideas. It is not surprising if neither the authorities nor the left-wing movements knew what to make of her activity. She did not even join any of the major tendencies, but in 1918 joined the little Christian Socialist Party, then formed a women's branch of it under the name of Christian Women's Camp. It aroused no little surprise when she, being of the royalist party, was among the first to welcome the electoral reforms of Mihály Károlyi of the republican party, but it merely followed from her earlier principles. She was active in politics during the Republic of Councils too: with a view to reducing hunger she addressed a petition to the government for the cultivation of fields that were lying fallow, and indeed also organised a collective farm on a Catholic basis. After the revolutions had failed the right-wing government charged her with the distribution to the poor of grants of aid that had been collected. She immediately showed that she was not merely a person of principle but also a wonderful organiser: she put an end to the queues that had snaked outside the relief points, introduced a system of record cards instead, and her colleagues delivered the grants to those in need at their homes. In those days her name became familiar nation-wide, and she frequently addressed political meetings. At that time the right-wing ideologue, bishop Ottokár Prohászka, wrote of her in his diary these lines, both laudatory and critical: *Sister Margit was here and spoke very well. I like that delicate, gentle, genial young woman, she is a really fine spirit; it's just that she's very radical, and easily acquires the life-style and habits of the lower classes, e.g. she is extremely undemanding, is satisfied with everything, even sleeps on the floor, etc.*

In January 1920 Margit's long-standing political demand was met: that was when the first Hungarian Parliamentary elections were held in which women too took part. During the campaign she tried to persuade her fellow women to take advantage of their hard-won rights, to vote, indeed, to stand as candidates. In the election, however, not a single party put up a female candidate as they had no confidence in women's ability to compete against men and win. That meant a great disappointment to Margit, and so when a by-election had to be held in a Budapest constituency she decided to stand herself. The Superior of the order too thought that her candidacy, like other things, was merely a symbolic contribution to her political activity. The surprise was all the greater when in the election Margit polled more votes than her three male opponents put together. In Parliament even her party would have liked to see her as a sort of cosmetic, token woman, while the rival parties were frankly contemptuous of her. When in her maiden speech she addressed the problem of reducing infantile mortality several male members simply laughed at her.

Despite rejection she turned out to be one of the hardest-working MPs. In two years she spoke twenty-eight times, often calling for expressly social-democrat reforms. This puzzled the left-wing movements outside Parliament. Whether she spoke on the defence of the rights in the workplace of women that were bringing up children, or whether on compulsory holidays for factory workers, the national daily *Népszava* did not fail to remind its readers that the nun had picked up her programme from "socialist women". For that very reason the left-wing press took pleasure in attacking her when she voted with the majority in Parliament for a law that made it possible for those that "profiteered to excess", that is, usurers that preyed on the poorest, to be sentenced to flogging. Although it worried her later that she had supported the introduction of corporal punishment the left continued for years to associate her name – unfairly – with the "cane law". However, she found no more supporters on the right: the conservative Hungarian Women's National Association, founded by the writer Cécile Tormay, was so far from agreeing with the extension of female suffrage that it even put up posters discrediting her. Tormay's real problem was presumably that Margit had remained a staunch member of the royalist party even after Miklós Horthy had been elected Regent. This also brought her into conflict with the Superior of the order, Edit Farkas, a close friend of the Horthy family; before the next elections she refused Margit permission to stand again.

Even outside Parliament, Margit was reluctant to give up her political activity. The leaders of the Mission Society, however, would have liked to make it an order of nuns more and more traditional and insulated from society. The internal dispute came to a head: in 1923 Margit and a few companions were expelled from the order. In response she formed her own order, the Sisters of Social Service – known also from their veils as the "grey sisters" – of which she was elected Superior. She directed the Sisters for the next forty years; in a couple of years the order became international, with members in Transylvania, Czechoslovakia, Switzerland, France, Canada and the USA, where they engaged in social work, protection of mothers and children, and adult education, and took part in the work of women's rights movements. Margit herself spent much time abroad, from where she always returned with new ideas. One of these was the setting up in Budapest of Everyone's Christmas Tree, and her name is also linked to the initiation of higher level training of social workers. She struggled for women's right to education, and so was the first to speak out against the *numerus clausus* provisions that limited women's access to university education. She did not, however, only stand up for women when she felt that fundamental rights were restricted. When the first Jewish law was debated she published a statement on behalf of her party to the effect that an organisation established on a Christian basis *could not accept the Jewish law.* She spoke more than once in public about the conflict between racism and the New Testament, and in her paper *Lélek Szava* (The Word of the Spirit) she joined battle with Nazi and Arrow-Cross ideology.

Se did not merely protest verbally but also took action. In the winter of 1941 she moved so effectively against the "alien control" action at Kőrösmező that the Regent put a stop to the deportations. A year later she was in Slovakia where she witnessed inhumane anti-Semitic behaviour at first hand and organised another protest movement. First she requested the assistance of the leaders of the Hungarian state and Churches: *While the large body of Jews are deprived of their rights, left exposed to everything and struggle in despair, Christians crowd the churches but offer no defence to the hapless and defenceless, eagerly sucking up the poison of hatred. (…) It is likewise a torment to my conscience that I share in the crime when I do not make every attempt to help in stopping this depravity* – she wrote in her letter. When she saw that her words fell on deaf ears in Hungary she went to Rome to call personally on the pope for action. She was successful. Thanks to her determination, on the pope's orders a pastoral letter of protest was read out in all Catholic churches in Slovakia, which contributed greatly to the stopping of the deportations. Back in Hungary, she addressed Christian women in the winter of 1943 on the subject of forced labourers: *Let your heart go out to the man in the labour-camp, whom the spirit of the age cuts off from community with his fellow men. Dare in these deadly*

serious times to drive from your heart indifference, lack of love, hatred. László Endre, one of the leading figures in the persecution of the Jews,
condemned this incitement against the laws in a furious statement,
and from then on Margit was regarded by the Hungarian extreme
right-wing as a declared enemy. After the Arrow-Cross took power, however, it did not concern her that she would be directly threatened. She hid fugitives in the order's house in Budapest and obtained
forged documents for others. She never asked the members of the
order to join in the life-saving activity: nevertheless, many of them
did join her in risking their lives. Of them, Sister Sára Salkaházi and
the teacher of religion Vilma Barnovits were shot into the Danube
by the Arrow-Cross, along with the people that they were saving.

THE OCCUPATION BY THE GERMANS AND THE DEPORTA-
TIONS. After the heavy military defeat suffered on the Don Bend
(the Second Army was annihilated by the Red Army, with the loss
of at least 60,000 men and most of its equipment) the Hungarian government entered into secret talks with Britain about leaving the war
and the conditions for a preliminary cease-fire. The German command learnt of the talks, and in consequence Hitler decided on the
military occupation of Hungary. The Germans entered Hungary on
19 March 1944 with hardly a shot being fired. Horthy was cornered
and appointed Döme Sztójay as Prime Minister, so legitimising loss
of independence. The Hungarian economy was put to the service of
German war interests. The Gestapo immediately set about arresting anti-German intellectuals and politicians, while the Soviets began to bombard Hungary, which had until then been spared. In the
course of a few weeks the Hungarian authorities stripped the Jewish
population of what remained of its property, and those living in the
provinces were confined to ghettoes. Beginning in May – under the
supervision of Adolf Eichmann – 450,000 provincial Jews were deported to Auschwitz and other concentration camps. There was not
time for the Jewish population of Budapest to be similarly treated
merely because the Germans were unable to accept the transports so
quickly had the Hungarians sent them.

After the war Margit continued where she had left off. She testified in court for an Arrow-Cross man who had been condemned to death; he had once noticed during a raid on the house of the order that there were Jews hiding there, but had not taken them away. That was enough for the left-wing press to accuse her of saving Arrow-Cross men. She planned to re-establish the Christian Women's Camp and stand in the 1945 elections. The new Christian party, the Christian Democratic People's Party, did not consider that appropriate, and so in the end she re-entered Parliament on the list of the liberal Social Democratic party, as a non-party candidate. In the Parliament, which consisted of men, she was received in just the same way a quarter of a century before: her speeches were interrupted by cat-calls, her proposals ridiculed. Her policies were truly not timely: while the parties were arguing over the republican form of state, she argued for the restoration of the monarchy. The communists and their allies spoke of her as an outdated figure of the clerical reaction, but the Christian politicians also found her too headstrong and did not support her. Only one independent MP had a good word for her principled quality: *There's only one man in the national assembly!* In 1947 she re-organised her party and once more won a seat, as did three other women. In the Parliament which was moving to the left, however, she was marginalised. First she was excluded from Parliament for sixty days for making a statement critical of the USSR, and then finally silenced. When Parliament voted to nationalise the church schools despite her objection, before the singing of the National Anthem at the end of the session Margit quoted from the Book of Psalms: *They that led us away captive required of us a song (...) let my tongue cleave to the roof of my mouth*, and then remained conspicuously seated. The disciplinary committee found that form of protest a good pretext for suspending her for a year.

Margit was aware that not only her political career but her very life was in danger. Fearing arrest, she hid in a convent for some months, and then one summer night in 1949 she crossed the

"Take a forced labourer to your heart!"

Austrian frontier together with her sister. Not long afterwards she emigrated to the USA, where she lived to the age of ninety. For a while she took part in the work of the political émigrés, then completely lost connection with the world around her. She never returned to Hungary, and passed away in the house of the Sisters of Social Service in Buffalo. To this day she lies buried far from her homeland.

I travelled with a small group to Kőrösmező, and on to Havasalja and a num-
ber of other places from where nowadays internments, concentrations and ex-
pulsions take place. (…) We saw people with their certificates of national-
ity in their hands, disabled veterans who had lost arms, shuffling old people,
children with measles, who, after two days' travel, were waiting for hours in
the rain for further transport in open wagons. We saw the gallows erected at
the station, and the crow perching on it, to mock those hapless people. (…)
For me it was only half of the matter, that everyone is the child of God, and
so no one should be treated unjustly and cruelly. The other half is the percep-
tion of what is going to become of us if the country slips from the principles of
law and slides deeper and deeper into demoralisation, into silent anarchy. And
that which is today silent, in what an explosion is it going to burst out later,
especially in time of dearth, if there are no Jews left, on whom it is the custom
for the law to use fists and violence.

Margit Slachta,
letter to Miklós Horthy
13 August 1941

Ocskay in 1944 as commandant of 101/359 Labour Battalion.

László Ocskay

In December 1944 armed Arrow-Cross men burst into the building of the Jewish grammar school in Budapest. Officially, a forced labour company was stationed on the school premises, sorting and repairing military and workers' clothing, but it seemed to the Arrow-Cross that for the work in question there were too many Jewish men and women crowded into the building. In the course of the raid they lined up two thousand people in a marching column in the yard. *Nobody bring anything with them, we're on our way to the Danube!* they howled. While preparations for the evacuation were taking place one forced labourer managed to telephone the company commander, who was in bed at home with scarlet fever. *Can you hold them up for twenty minutes?* he asked. There was not much prospect of that. The first of the column were just leaving when the gate was flung open and a detachment of SS-men on motorcycles drove in. As they stood in the yard, the people destined for death were sure that this sealed their fate. To their amazement, out of the car that was leading the motorcycles came the person sheltering them, the fifty-one year-old László Ocskay. He ordered the Arrow-Cross men to clear off that instant, because the building, as military premises, and those working there were under the jurisdiction of IX Mountain Corps of the SS.

Ocskay, the Hungarian Schindler, pulled off a dozen such tricks for the sake of the "clothing collection company" under his command. If need be he bribed people, if need be he made use of his military connections. Some sources say that he saved 1,700 people, some say 3,500. He died in America, a forgotten, sick man, working as a night-watchman.

He was born in 1893 in a noble family that went back to the Middle Ages. After leaving the Piarist Grammar School he went on to study agriculture, but did not complete the course: he was scarcely twenty when he started a family, marrying the daughter of a landowning family. He was among the first to volunteer when the First World War broke out, and that same year, by then a hussar officer, was one of the first to be seriously wounded on the field of battle. In military hospital he barely escaped an amputation: his left knee remained permanently rigid, and he had to wear an orthopaedic boot for the rest of his life. He would not agree to being discharged on medical grounds and insisted on being able to remain a reserve officer. After he had recovered he farmed his family's estates in north Hungary – as long as history allowed him to. After the Peace of Trianon, that is, the family estate was assigned to Czechoslovakia, and as Ocskay was not prepared to give up his Hungarian citizenship the Czechoslovak authorities sequestrated the estate along with the ancestral mansion. They moved to his mother's native Nagykikinda – assigned to Yugoslavia – and in 1933 moved back to Budapest where the cultivated gentleman of the old school, who spoke several languages, quickly found himself a post.

He joined the Hungarian-American Vacuum Oil Company as a financial adviser. At that time the oil industry was very much on the increase in Hungary and foreign companies with concessions paid their employees well. The Ocskays lived in upper-middle-class style in their central Budapest flat, keeping a maid and a German lady companion. The head of the family had the entrée to the Hungarian landowning élite and the officer corps, and because of his ancestry the salons of the aristocracy too were open to him. Despite his crippled leg he was full of life, something of a bohemian in society, often to be seen in night-clubs. He took no part in politics, but his anti-Nazi views were no secret. When the Jewish laws were brought in Vacuum Oil repatriated its two American managers of Jewish origin, replacing them with Christian Hungarians. In this way the company did its utmost to look after its employees, keeping them on in protected positions. In this Ocskay, himself of impeccable pedigree, played a part. This was perhaps when a Jewish organisation, the National Council of Jewish Offices and Ex-servicemen, noticed him; it collected warm winter clothing for forced labourers. This was necessary because from 1943 on forced labourers were sent to the front not in uniform but in civilian clothes. The less well-off could not take appropriate things with them and many froze to death. Losing unpaid workers did not please the military commanders either, and so it was decided that for the sake of more effective organisation the collection of clothing should take place in a military framework. A friend of Ocskay's, a world war veteran of Jewish origin, invited him to accept the position of commandant of a labour company that collected clothing. He knew that the honest, anti-Nazi army officer would do more for the persecuted than collect warm clothing.

Ocskay soon made up his mind. He left his job in the oil business and in 1943 returned to active service with the rank of reserve captain. By the spring of the following year he had created a warehouse providing clothing for forced labourers and was organising systems of collection, mending and delivery. All that, however, he regarded as a secondary task. His real aim was the saving of the forced labourers in Royal Hungarian Auxiliary Pioneer Company 101/359.87. His plan was to enlist as many as possible in his company and then try to protect them from persecution. The company was good cover for this: clothing collectors could move freely around the city, and women were needed for the needlework.

The captain mobilised all his contacts – social, business and military – to that end. He was closely acquainted with the senior officer responsible for the labour units, and always learnt from him in good time about plans affecting his company. As, after a while, he was concealing not only forced labourers but also members of their families he needed a huge amount of food. He also made contact with the International Red Cross, citing the distribution of clothing, and obtained rations from them. Vans "on military duty" belonging to his former workplace delivered clothes and food, and ordinary police had no powers to stop them. He could obtain cash – needed *inter alia* for bribing supervisors and others in positions of authority – from the Vacuum Oil holiday fund and a Catholic aid organisation.

After Szálasi came to power the Arrow-Cross tried almost at once to liquidate the whole company. The gateman, who was in league with them, cut the phone lines at night, switched off the electricity, and let the party thugs – armed with hand-grenades – through the gate. They identified everyone, looked for deserters from the army, and threatened to set the building on fire. Some of the forced labourers alerted Ocskay from a telephone box in the street. He was there at once, and by taking decisive action – gun in hand – made the Arrow-Cross leave the building. A few days later he resorted to another trick at the risk of his life: he put Hungarian military uniforms that were waiting to be repaired on young Jewish men, who went round the families of the forced labourers and brought those that they could to the secure company HQ. Nor did he permit his protégés to be taken away one by one. On one occasion two forced labourers received summonses to report to a company stationed in the provinces. The military commander told them that he hoped that they had said good-bye to their wives as next day they were off to the front. Early next day came a document signed by the Minister for Defence: the two men were engaged on work where they were irreplaceable and were to be sent back to Budapest at once. Ocskay could mobilise his contacts to exceptional effect. When, at the end of October, the Hungarian military command 'lent' the forced labour companies to the Germans every company in Budapest was marched to the west of the country to forced labour – with the sole exception of Company 101/359.87

In November there were so many in the company that they needed somewhere bigger. Ocskay obtained the use of the Jewish grammar school building in Abonyi utca in Zugló, the villa region of Pest. It had been closed by the Arrow-Cross not long before, and there the company settled in. As well as the spacious classrooms a kitchen with a water supply was at their disposal, and they were able to cook three times a day right until the siege. In the new place they were also able to perfect their cover: they began to make underwear and clothes and opened a cobbler's shop, where members of forced labourers' families worked as experts – with false papers. If any inspectors came they saw forty sewing machines rattling away, and it cannot have occurred to them that the seamstresses were working on the same garments for days on end. Even so, they often came close to being discovered. On one occasion Ocskay had to send a suspicious employee to the front with rapidly produced call-up papers, and on another a keen customs official who impeded his vans had to be bribed to keep his mouth shut. A few courageous forced workers even formed a so-called transportation section, which carried out dangerous missions in the city: sometimes they rescued women from the centre where they were awaiting deportation, sometimes they brought Jewish orphans to the school. Ocskay registered new arrivals personally: by that time there were among them several well-known actors, journalists and sportsmen.

From Arrow-Cross HQ a few hundred yards from the grammar school the strange company was regarded with ever greater suspicion. On one occasion they swooped on forced labourers working outside the building clearing rubble, carried them off and deported them. Another time a small boy was caught when he ran into the street after a ball, and he was only returned for payment. After these incidents Ocskay took the most reckless step in the life-saving action. Through intermediaries he contacted two German officers, Major Werner Otto Florian and an SS Sergeant-major by the name of Weber, who at the time were blaming the Nazi leadership for having dragged the German people into a losing war. He discussed with them the idea that the company should – only as cover – also repair German uniforms. The result was that the Hungarian guard was relieved and a unit of the Waffen SS consisting of Hungarian Swabians took its place. They were all much happier to guard the school than to serve on the front line. From then on the German guards prevented the Arrow-Cross from entering the building on several occasions. According to one survivor: *If there were Arrow-Cross skulking around in the neighbourhood Ocskay would appear with a German major, they would stroll around in the yard and the major would fire a few shots from his revolver into the air. Then the Arrow-Cross always backed away.* One witness also described the surreal scene when on Christmas Eve Ocskay entered the school, flanked by German officers: *In paradoxical fashion the Germans drank a toast to us, saying 'Let's drink to your liberation and the victory of the German people'.*

The hardest time for the concealed community was the weeks of the siege. By that time forced labourers were receiving only military rations and their families and other fugitives could not obtain food. Eight people died either of hunger or lack of medication. Furthermore, there was hardly room for them all in the cellar, and nowhere for them to sleep. According to extant documents, at the end of 1944 Ocskay also made contact with Raoul Wallenberg. By that time there was little that the Swedish diplomat could do for the persecuted, and he himself was looking for shelter. Ocskay took Wallenberg into his own home, and it was from there that he set out on his fateful journey to report to the Red Army. In those days personal tragedy struck Ocskay too. While he was doing his utmost for the people in his charge no one knew that at home his wife too was gravely ill and needed care. She died on 13 January 1945.

DIPLOMATIC LIFE-SAVERS. Diplomatic pressure, especially the activity of the Vatican ambassador Angelo Rotta, had played a great part in stopping the deportations in the provinces. Horthy wanted to improve his country's international reputation, and so accepted the request of the embassies of the neutral countries (Sweden, Switzerland, Spain, Portugal, Turkey and San Salvador) to be permitted to issue safe conducts (*Schutzbrief*) to "protected Jews" that were in any way connected to them. After the Arrow-Cross came to power Szálasi too – in the hope that his regime would be recognised abroad – at first accepted the functioning of the diplomatic "protected houses" that offered refuge to Jews. Later the Arrow-Cross regularly broke into the protected houses and often deported, or shot into the Danube, those sheltering there. The largest number were saved by the Swedish mission, and in this the embassy secretary Raoul Wallenberg played a large part, issuing several thousand protective documents, setting up thirty protected houses, and often risking his life to rescue people from the ghetto. Karl Lutz, the deputy consul at the Swiss embassy, played a similar role, as did Ángel Sans Briz, the Spanish *chargé d'affaires*; after his departure the Italian Giorgio Perlasca took his place "as an impostor", and saved lives by making himself out to be a Spanish diplomat.

After the Soviet invasion Ocskay dressed as a civilian to avoid becoming a prisoner of war. Not long afterwards there came the time for him to take his leave of those that he had saved. The survivors held a service of thanksgiving for him in a synagogue. One that took part recalls: *At the end of the ceremony we lined up on both sides of the pews, and Ocskay went all along and shook everyone by the hand.* A few months later someone that he had rescued wrote an article about him in a minor paper, but he never received official thanks from anyone. He tried to put his firm on its feet, but shortly afterwards he too had to flee. He was a Horthyist officer and a servant of American capitalism all in one, and later was also accused of having supplied the Germans with oil during the war. According to some sources he was taken in for questioning on a number of occasions, and actually imprisoned for a short time. It is almost certain that he too would have been one of the accused in the so-called "oil cases" if he had not – at the last minute – left the country together with his children in 1948. (The former management of Vacuum Oil, who had all taken part in supporting the life-saving action, were not long later prosecuted on trumped-up charges and sentenced to long periods of imprisonment.)

He settled in Austria with his son's family and an American company gave Ocskay a post in Graz. In a few years' time his son found a job in the USA, and the recently retired Ocskay followed him there. He lived in Kingston, in modest circumstances compared with his earlier life, and supplemented his pension by working as a night-watchman. He never spoke to anyone about his heroic achievements in Budapest. In the 1950s those that he had rescued made numerous attempts to find him, but without success. In the end a friend of his, whom he had gone to see in the cold of winter wearing just a jacket, decided to let the Holocaust organisations know of Ocskay's plight. A foundation identified him and began to reveal his life-saving activity. They even gave a dinner in his honour in New York, but had no time to do more. At the age of seventy-three Ocskay fell in the street, fracturing his femur. He was taken to hospital and his friends organised a collection for the cost of treatment – but the amount raised was only used for his funeral expenses. The Hungarian Schindler passed away on 27 March 1966 in Kingston, where he lies to this day.

The first articles about what he had done appeared only after his death, and since then witnesses have come forward one after another. He was not at first awarded the Yad Vashem award because the documentation of the clothing-collection company had been destroyed in bombing, so that no proof could be found that he had risked his life for the sake of those protected in the company. Then, following an appeal from a survivor living in America, written recollections of members of the Ocskay Battalion began to be compiled, and on the basis of their evidence he was awarded the distinction of Righteous Gentile in 2002. At the end of his life, all that he said to a friend of his about his heroism was: *I did no more than any decent, God-fearing man would have done.*

One foggy night in early autumn, after midnight, men with guns and grenades stormed the building of the community and the company's HQ. They demanded that the deserters hiding there be handed over together with the food. Then they threatened that if there was any opposition they would fire the building and burn us all inside. (...) There was a single name on the lips of those besieged in the building: Ocskay. He had to be informed somehow, as without him everything and everybody was lost. A few slipped out along Dohány utca, hidden by the thick fog, rang Ocskay at his home and told him the situation. He instructed them to resist until he got there. (...) An hour later – it had seemed like a year – Ocskay appeared from the direction of Wesselényi utca: despite his lameness he seemed to be running. He was in uniform, a sub-machine gun slung round his neck. He introduced himself loudly, and made it known that the premises were his responsibility and those there were under his command, and that no one was to be taken away and nothing removed without his permission. Ocskay's one-man relieving force triumphed, the attackers withdrew (...) empty-handed, grumbling and threatening. Dawn was breaking as the company fell in, weary and shattered by the excitement and the fear of death.

Recollections of Dr. László Sándor,
Equality
New York, 5 January 1966

He addressed the persecuted as "gentlemen" and "comrades in misfortune".
Reviczky in 1946.

Imre Reviczky

For days the new conscripts had been waiting for their fate in the barracks at Nagybánya (today Baia Mare, Romania). There were some for whom there were no beds and who had to spend the night in the open. The commander of Forced Labour Battalion X had sent out 1,500 call-up papers in Northern Transylvania, which again belonged to Hungary, and the men assembled were waiting in trepidation for what came next. Major Teleki had prepared an important speech, and was enjoying his role as he was outspokenly anti-semitic. He kept a horse-whip in the leg of his boot and used it too if he wanted to make his authority felt. He went up onto the platform and began to speak. He smiled broadly as he announced that next day the conscripts would be taken by train to the front, where sooner or later they would all perish. He was not allowed to finish his speech. A lorry turned into the barack yard and from it emerged a bald officer with the insignia of a lieutenant-colonel on his shoulders. He went up to the major, showed him a document, informed him that he was taking over command with immediate effect, and himself stepped onto the platform. The crowd ranged in the yard watched the scene in silence. "I am Lt.-Col. Imre Reviczky", he introduced himself, and began to speak. Now it aroused surprise that he addressed all present – soldiers and forced labourers alike – as 'Gentlemen' and 'Comrades in misfortune'. He told them that there was need of several thousand more pairs of hands in the war, and that he considered manual labour "under the circumstances" to be of equal value with the bearing of arms. He ordered that all should regard it as such, he continued loudly, because forced labourers deserved the same respect as the soldiers doing the fighting.

Some of the officers blanched as they looked at the new commander, who announced that he would personally enquire into any abuses and complaints. That was an unambiguous message to forced labourers who feared the revenge of those in charge of them. He added that if he saw any officer with a horse-whip he would transfer him at once to an active unit. Aged forty-seven, Imre Reviczky commanded the Forced Labour Battalion for eighteen months, during which time he saw to the safety of some forty thousand Jewish, Romanian, Ruthenian and Serbian forced labourers, of whom at least ten thousand had him to thank for their lives. When, after the war, they thanked him, all that he said was: *I haven't done anything that deserves gratitude and celebration. I don't deserve anything for trying to be a human being!* A human being he remained even when deprived of his position and pension he scraped a living delivering coal.

He came of a noble family that went back to the Middle Ages. The Revickys had Hungarian, Slovak and Polish ancestors, and most of their land was in Upper Hungary, nowadays Slovakia. They were not outstandingly wealthy, and the men of the family mostly had to find employment; they included county administrators, diplomats and army officers. Imre Reviczky was born in 1896 and grew up on the family estate at Bánóc (today Bánovce nad Ondavou, south-eastern Slovakia), where his father farmed. As well as Hungarian he learned the language of the local peasantry from his Slovak nurse. After leaving school he followed his two brothers into officer cadet school.

He received his commission as an infantry officer in 1916, and was sent to the Transylvanian theatre. Two years later he was in

Kassa (today Kŏsice in Slovakia) when news came of the collapse and he learnt that the Czechs had occupied his native village.

After losing the war Hungary was only allowed to retain reduced armed forces, and most of the professional soldiers had to be dismissed. Some of the redundant officers – among them Reviczky – were offered positions as physical training instructors by the state. He took that task seriously as well and his pupils soon obtained excellent results in national sporting competitions. It was in 1931 that he could resume his military career, as international restrictions on the army were lifted. He became commander of a garrison in southern Hungary. Before the introduction of the Jewish laws the proportion of officers of Jewish origin was quite high, about twenty per cent, but at that time they were starting to be dismissed. Reviczky, however, cultivated good relationships with the Jewish officers under him, and relieved them of duties on Saturdays. Nor did he like the way that officers from upper-class families spoke condescendingly to the other ranks of humble origin. He was friendly and polite towards everyone, and for that reason the lower ranks had an exceptional respect for him. His son too took him as a role-model, and in 1938 he too enrolled at the military high school.

THE VIENNA AWARDS. When Nazi Germany began the revision of the peace treaty of Versailles that had ended the First World War the Hungarian political leadership too saw that the time was ripe to regain the parts of historical Hungary that had been detached. At the international conference convened in Vienna the Italians and Germans decided to re-draw the map of Central-Eastern Europe. In 1938 Hungary regained the southern part of Slovakia, where there was a Hungarian population, and the Kárpátalja on the eastern frontier, at the foot of the Carpathians, where the population was Ukrainian. The second Vienna Award took place in 1940, after the outbreak of the Second World War, and concerned Transylvania: northern Transylvania, with a population of 1.3 million Hungarians and a million Romanians, went to Hungary, while the south, with 400,000 Hungarians, remained in Romania. By this means Hitler wished to acquire two allies who, in exchange for the satisfaction of their territorial demands, would compete for the Germans' trust. As a third step, after the German attack on Yugoslavia Hungary occupied the regions of that country where there was a Hungarian population. At first the revision met with undiluted pleasure in both the Hungarian territories returned and in the mother country, and it only later became clear that the price of the territorial expansion was entry into the war with the USSR on the German side. In the Treaty of Paris that ended the war the Vienna Awards were not recognised, and Hungary lost again the territories that had been gained by the revision.

Reviczky was delighted at the first Vienna Award, under which part of Upper Hungary returned to Hungary. His native Bánóc remained Slovak; nevertheless he requested a posting closer to the places of his youth, and was promoted major and sent as commander of a unit near to the Soviet frontier. His enthusiasm evaporated, however, when in 1941 Hungary, in alliance with Germany, declared war on the USSR in exchange for the frontier alterations. He thought from the outset that the war was madness, and tried in his own way to reduce the losses of personnel. The first time that he clashed overtly with the regime was when his subordinates informed him that a goods train was stuck in the station, and from locked wagons in it people were signalling for help. Reviczky immediately had the train opened and it turned out that it contained Jewish families being deported; they had been unable to prove their Hungarian citizenship in a night-time raid and so, under an "alien control" action, the authorities were deporting them to Ukraine, where war was raging. Reviczky turned the train round, thus saving those expecting deportation from certain death.

That same year he was promoted lieutenant-colonel and appointed to the command of the 22nd infantry regiment at Léva (today Levoče, Slovakia), and then ordered to the front. Although he

As a young officer. He was a soldier for 34 years.

was opposed to the war he held his ground courageously against attacks. His son Ádám was fighting not far away as a lieutenant. Six weeks later Reviczky was declared incompetent and relieved of his command. The fact was that he had been reluctant to implement the so-called "partisan order", that is, to take reprisals on the Ukrainian civilian population for attacks by partisans. He was sent home, an enquiry was instituted against him, but in the end he was exonerated. Nevertheless, his service record was endorsed 'leftwing', which effectively precluded further promotion. He was given the kind of posting that no officer wanted. In May 1943 he was appointed commander of Forced Labour Battalion X, which

Forced labourers – Jews, non-Magyars and other "unreliable elements" – clearing rubble.

meant control of fifty labour service companies and supervision of a few fighting units all over Northern Transylvania. Although he had 40,000 men under him everyone regarded this appointment as a punishment. One of his son's fellow officers commented on the news: *I'm sorry for your father! Being in command of Jews in this day and age? He's done for! If he's hard on the Jews, for that reason. They've got the ear of Horthy and his wife, and he'll get it in the neck! And if he goes the other way, we'll go for him!* Reviczky chose the second alternative.

HUNGARIAN DEFEAT ON THE EASTERN FRONT. Hungary entered the war in June 1941, a few days after the German attack on the Soviet Union. At first only minor units were sent to the front, and Hungarian soldiers mainly served in the occupied areas of what is now Western Ukraine, for the most part operating against partisans. Their turn for involvement in significant fighting came only from early 1943, after the counter-attack by the Red Army. On the Don Bend the 250,000-strong Second Hungarian Army and forced labourers suffered the severest losses in Hungarian history. In temperatures of minus 30° more than half were killed, wounded or captured – and most of those captured died in Soviet captivity. Armed soldiers and unarmed Jewish forced labourers alike were among those killed and captured.

As he took over command in the Transylvanian mining town of Nagybánya (today Baia Mare, Romania) he put a stop to cruelty and the humiliation of forced labourers. Among those under his command were not only Jews but also 'nationalities' regarded as unreliable – Romanians, Ukrainians and Serbs. All of them performed hard and dangerous work: they built roads and railways in territory that was regularly bombed, in addition to felling trees, working in mines and military establishments and clearing rubble. From the first moment Reviczky regarded them as if they were armed soldiers. He ensured that they received clothing and equipment, and the same rations as the soldiers. But he did more too. Among other things he did not permit men with families to be sent to the front, and did all that he could to withhold as many as possible from the futile war. He called for public works at Nagybánya for all sorts of reasons in order to be able to keep men in the rear. When he heard from a local monk that another Roman Catholic church would be useful in the town he immediately undertook to have it built by the forced labourers. By that alone he saved fifty from serving at the front.

On one occasion, however, he went even further. An embittered young man escaped home to his lover from forced labour, was arrested on the train, and the court martial meant to make an example of him. When the Nagybánya HQ was officially informed of this Reviczky sent a strongly worded telegram requesting that the escapee be returned under heavy military escort to his unit. Meanwhile the boy's father tried to intercede with the colonel, who said only "Go home and don't worry about a thing, Mr. Salamon! Your son's in the safest place in the battalion guardhouse." He began every day by reviewing complaints, and tried to help anyone that he could. When it became known that one of his men had been giving privileges in exchange for money and valuables he immediately ordered an investigation. It turned out that the officer had been treating the conscripts sadistically, but that his harshness had in fact raised the 'rate of exchange'. Reviczky immediately sent the corrupt captain to the front. News of the incident soon went round, and not only among the forced labourers. There was one officer who called the commander – behind his back – a hireling of the Jews, and was watching for him to do something for which he could report him. Reviczky was aware of this, and was scrupulously careful not to accept gifts or favours from anyone. When members of forced labourers' families waited for him at his quarters with parcels of gifts he sent them home, and told them: "I've got a son fighting at the front as well. If you want to help me, pray for him!"

He disposed of his quarters in Nagybánya not as officers usually did. On his arrival Béla Steinfeld, a well-known art-collector, offered him his house, which under the Jewish laws he had to share with the soldiers. Reviczky admired the villa – and then moved into the ruinous bailiff's cottage down the garden. There he lived, at 1 Petőfi utca, for eighteen months together with his wife, who was fully supportive of her husband's standing up for the persecuted. When their landlord had to put on the yellow star Mrs Reviczky made a point of inviting him round for coffee. The colonel's immediate colleague, his most important assistant, was a Jewish forced labourer – Sica, the quick-witted Nagybánya taxi-driver, who had joined up with his Ford car. As after a while Reviczky no longer trusted his junior officers Sica arranged his most important personal and official affairs. After the German invasion the requests of those that queued up at his door changed: previously families had asked for husbands and children to be allowed home; from then on they asked for them to be taken in.

On a single night in May 1944, in Nagybánya as elsewhere, the gendarmes rounded people up and took them to a ghetto. Some were not allowed even ten minutes to get their belongings together. When the paper *Új magyarság* triumphantly reported that *Clearing the Jews from Northern Transylvania has been a great step in the defence of the life of the Hungarian nation!* Reviczky issued several thousand call up papers on his own initiative to unknown people so as to save them from deportation. *My father's activity changed fundamentally,* Ádám Reviczky recalled later, *he sent SAS-invitations to thousands. In some cases those affected did not themselves immediately understand his intention, because they did not want to believe the fate that awaited them!* Reviczky refused one after another to carry out the inhuman orders, and therefore often clashed with the newly appointed anti-Semitic mayor of the town and the German HQ. Despite the gendarmerie's prohibition he made his men night after night write the call up papers which in several towns in Northern Transylvania were delivered straight to the ghettoes. On one occasion he gave a travel permit to a forced labourer to visit his family in the ghetto of a distant town. The man in question was asked for his papers, and because of the travel permit a military legal investigation was instigated against Reviczky, and he was ordered to report to Budapest. His enemies were rubbing their hands with glee: *That old Jew won't be coming back, and you're going to die here!* – shouted the commander deputising for Reviczky, as he declared the forced labourers unfit one after another so that he could have them taken back to the ghetto. Reviczky cleared himself, however, and returned a fortnight later.

In August Romania went over the Allies and Soviet and Romanian forces moved against Northern Transylvania. In Nagybánya the Romanian inhabitants were locked in an internment camp, while the youth were enlisted in *levente* companies. Reviczky knew that by this the situation of Hungarians cut off on the far side of the front could only be worsened. He protested to headquarters in Budapest about the order, and personally removed several from the camp. He sent the Romanian forced labourers to places near the front so that they might escape and join their own people, and he forbade the pursuit of any escaping. When he received orders to send Romanian cadets aged between fifteen and eighteen by train to Western Hungary he had the available railway trucks loaded with firewood and sent them, then reported that unfortunately he had insufficient transport at his disposal. He did the same with the Transylvanian Jewish forced labourers and the other ranks. He organised companies by places of origin, local units, and carefully sent them in the direction of their homes, which the majority reached.

In September instructions came from Budapest for him to evacuate the town and move westwards with what remained of the battalion. He delayed carrying out the order on various pretexts, and some of his officers accused him of sabotage. The front was approaching Nagybánya when the Arrow-Cross took power in Budapest and Horthy abdicated. Those in the barracks followed events over the radio, broadcast through loudspeakers. When the first Arrow-Cross onslaught had quietened down Reviczky made a short speech to the forced workers: *Gentlemen, as of now you do as you please, you are free men, because I took my oath to the Regent*. That very day the German HQ ordered him to hand over control of the labour companies. He refused. He sent most of the forced labourers to a distant hilltop "to extract timber". All of them escaped. The battalion moved off towards Budapest, and Reviczky's wife too went with them in a car. The colonel stayed behind: he wanted to attend to a few things.

It had come to his knowledge that the retreating Germans were planning to blow up the bridges over the River Zazar after them, together with the mines and chemical plant. Indeed, a specialist German commando had by then placed the charges on the bridge in the centre of town. Reviczky and a handful of men that remained removed the fuses, and the Germans did not want to become involved in a fire-fight with them as the Russians were by then on the edge of the town. Nagybánya was spared from pointless destruction. The people that he had saved tried to persuade Reviczky to remain in the town, but he did not want the Arrow-Cross to avenge themselves on his son, and so left at the last minute in pursuit of the retreating force. A few days later he caught up with the column and assumed command. He deliberately avoided contact with HQ, and slowly, with several intervening days of rest, they reached Western Hungary. He was still officially commander in the region of Karácsony, but was almost forced to go into hiding when he appeared at his son's wedding. A few hours later he had to go on. He learnt that he had been relieved of the command of the battalion, but he still issued back-dated open orders and travel permits so as to be able to save as many as possible.

He was given command of a hastily assembled infantry regiment not far from the Austrian frontier. There in March 1945 the Arrow-Cross arrested him. He was imprisoned and his wife was not allowed to visit him. A military judge told her simply that the charge against him was treachery in time of war, sabotaging the evacuation of Nagybánya, and withholding *levente* units that had been ordered to the front. The trial did not last long, and Reviczky was sentenced to death. He had the confusion caused by the approaching Soviet forces to thank for his life. He managed to jump onto a lorry, hid under a tarpaulin and escaped from the prison. He reached Budapest after an eventful journey and offered his services to the Ministry of Defence of the Provisional National Government. After the end of the war he was promoted to full colonel and appointed commander of a provincial depot. He also went back to Transylvania, where he was fêted as a hero. The recognition he deserved did not last long.

First he was taken off the active list without any explanation, and then in 1950 discharged from the army entirely: the People's Army had no place for a 'Horthyist' officer. Two years later he was informed in a curt letter that his pension would no longer be paid, and from then on he had to support himself as an unskilled worker. At first he worked as a laboratory assistant, then as an employee of the Fuel-trading Enterprise, where he earned only 800 forints a month. The former colonel delivered coal to local people from the cellar in Budapest. Even that he endured with head held high. Coal-dust stained his skin, but he was always elegant and very polite to all. In the summer of 1956 a Hungarian-language newspaper in Romania carried an article about the wretched existence as a Budapest coalman of the life-saver who had been hailed as a hero. As a result a subscription on his behalf was started in Transylvania. Eventually there came the first newspaper article in Hungary too, which began with the words: *I am ashamed to describe ...* It seems that at last someone in authority had felt shame, because although no one apologised to Reviczky his officer's pension began to be paid again a few weeks later. He was not able to enjoy it for long: he died of a heart attack in early 1957 at the age of sixty-one.

It was only after his death that he was given the recognition that he deserved. The Yad Vashem Institute awarded him the title of Righteous Gentile, and streets are named for him in Budapest and three towns in Israel. The Chancellor of Austria wrote the foreword to the German edition of the biography written by his son, and the Hebrew translation is compulsory reading in the Hebrew University in Jerusalem. *My father was not a giant, the others shrank to dwarves in their human condition*, wrote Ádám.

How cruelly hard it must have been for Imre Reviczky. He could see the filthy flood all around him. He could see that this was no life for human beings. He had to change it, he alone. Perhaps there were others like him elsewhere, but not in his vicinity. It is much easier to assist with the help of society. (...) We shared our misfortune with one another, and so it must have been easier to bear than it was for him to do good by himself. He had one thing in his favour: he knew what he meant to do. That gave him courage. He had no fear, and very likely his wife's unconditional agreement must also have given him support. Such a stance, however, adopted in solitude is not hard to sustain for a month or three months, but dreadfully hard to maintain for years. (...) To oppose and not go under (...) and to be victorious. He was a supernatural being, scarcely imaginable.

Memoirs of András Szilágyi,
sometime forced labourer
1981

Géza Soos as head of Soli Deo Gloria in the 1930s.

Géza Soos

At dawn on 9 December 1944 a strange group was crouching
in the bushes beside a military airfield in Western Hungary:
five men and a woman with a child in her arms. At a given signal
they stole out to the Heinkel III transport aircraft that was waiting, fuelled up, for the Minister for War Production of the Szálasi government. They climbed in and started the engine. Clearance
for take-off was requested and received. Weather conditions were
exceptionally bad, there was a thick fog, and so when the aircraft
deviated from its goal and turned south-westward German fighter
aircrafts did not give chase. In Adriatic airspace, however, which
was controlled by the Allies, the aircraft with its German markings was almost shot down. By lowering the undercarriage the
aircraft-thieves indicated that they wished to land, which they did
a few kilometres from the small Italian town of San Severo. The
plane was surrounded by American soldiers, and there emerged
from it three Hungarian Air Force officers, a Dutch prisoner of
war who had escaped from the Germans, the pilot's wife and
child, and a thirty-two year-old civilian, the leader of the party. He produced from under his shirt a canvas bag containing two
documents. The one contained a coded message to be transmitted
on Soviet radio before the liberation of Budapest so that the Hungarian resistance could prepare for the armed struggle. The other
document was what later became known as the Auschwitz Proto-

col (The Vrba–Wetzler Report), and was the first to give details of the workings of the Nazi death-camp.

Géza Soos, official of the Hungarian Foreign Ministry and leader of the Soli Deo Gloria movement, was one of the bravest in the anti-fascist resistance, and was at that time wanted by both the Gestapo and the Arrow-Cross authorities.

He was born in Budapest in 1912, son of a respected judge of the Supreme Court. As a boy his profound and sincere religiosity was notable even in the church-going Calvinist family, and by the age of ten he was reading the Bible every day. As a teenager he took part in the camps of the Soli Deo Gloria Association – founded by Calvinist theology students – and this left its mark on his later life. From then on he regarded active religiousness as his aim, performed social work in the notorious slum quarters of Budapest, organised food distribution and student canteens, cared for needy families. As a law student he became principal secretary and deputy president of Soli Deo Gloria, and on graduation its president. As a polyglot and trained lawyer he found a post in the Ministry of Justice, where the anglophile Prime Minister Pál Teleki took note of him; at the age of twenty-four he became his secretary.

In 1938 he took part in a conference at Évian as a member of the Soli Deo Gloria delegation. The persecution of the Jews in Germany, and the possibility of rescuing them, were the main topics of the consultation on refugee problems convened by President Roosevelt of America. Before Soos left Hungary he had been summoned for questioning by Miklós Horthy himself. *He asked me to behave very circumspectly, and at the same time to take a thorough look at what was being rumoured about the persecution of the Jews.* That Soos did; he informed himself fully, and it became clear to him that it was not a matter of rumours, the lives of the Jews of Germany were in danger, and presumably the same was in store for those living in the countries in the German sphere of interest. He wrote a report on the threatening situation: this was read in Hungary and then pigeonholed. Young Soos, however, decided to devote his life to the cause of refugees and the persecuted.

He soon had the opportunity to demonstrate that he took his decision very seriously: he took part in the saving of the Poles that fled in large numbers into Hungary after the invasion of Poland. The Soli Deo Gloria centre in Budapest and its holiday house on the Balaton quickly became the prime places of refuge for young Poles that had fled their homeland. He was firmly convinced that he was firmly convinced all democratic power had to be mustered against German danger.

Together with Domokos Szent-Iványi, his colleague in the Ministry, he founded the anti-German Hungarian Independence Movement, and in parallel with that tried to build up a network of cells. He stated the primary objective thus: *The most imperative task of the moment is (…) to resist German expansion by every possible means. We cannot just sit by and watch anti-Semitic propaganda put out on Nazi money, when the Nazi German embrace is so deadly.* As a diplomat he could still travel freely in the 1940's, and he sought connections with the British and American embassies in Finland, while in Switzerland he made contact with both the Protestant movement and the Zionist organisations. This all proceeded very slowly, of course, in the greatest secrecy – much more slowly than the extreme right-wing gained ground. At the same time tangible results were achieved. He succeeded in persuading the director of the Good Shepherd Commission, set up for the protection of Jews who had converted to Protestantism, to join him, and thus to put the actual life-saving activity on a more or less legal footing. At the very end of 1943 Szent-Iványi organised an official government unit called the Special Office, and the anti-German Miklós Horthy junior, son of the Regent, was appointed as its head. In this way the office, which enjoyed political protection, acquired numerous items of important government information which could not otherwise have been shared with the members of the illegal opposition movement. (This official unit later became known as the 'Back-Out Office', because it was there that Hungary's exit from the war – soon to be frustrated – was planned.)

On 19 March 1944, after the German invasion, Soos and Szent-Iványi meant to build up Hungarian resistance on the broadest possible basis. They made contact with the missions to the Jews of the Christian Churches, and with various Jewish organisations including even the Zionists. Even an attempt on the life of the pro-German Prime Minister, Döme Sztójay, was contemplated, but was later abandoned on account of the risks involved. One member of the group recalled: *It was our rule – all the more effective for being unwritten (…) that what we did not know could not be extracted from us even by the greatest torture. From that it followed that gossip was forbidden, that we did not wish to know what did not concern us, and that we did not ask one another questions out of idle curiosity.* Soos was aware that the Gestapo would have him watched because of his overt involvement in saving the Poles, and so after the invasion he slept in a different place every night. He could only see his family in secret, and did not tell even his wife what he was doing.

As a result of this strict security even now it is not known how Soos came by the so-called Auschwitz Protocol. It had been compiled by two young Slovak prisoners who had managed to escape from a building under construction in the death-camp, and gave a detailed account of the course of the deportations and the existence of the gas-chambers. The document may have come into Soos's hands directly from them or through the Slovak anti-fascist resistance, and he realised at once that its contents could have an effect on the course of the war. Previously there had been no reliable information about what happened to the German, Polish or Slovak Jews that were herded into the camp, or of what fate awaited the Jews of Hungary, and so the Hungarian political élite had soothed their consciences with the belief that the Jews were 'only' being taken to a labour camp. Soos had the German document translated into Hungarian and had six copies of it made.

Three of these went to the heads of the three Hungarian Christian Churches, one to the head of the Zionists in Hungary and one to the Regent's daughter-in-law, the widow of István Horthy; one copy and the German original Soos retained himself. Mrs Horthy received the document on 3 July and that day the Regent read it too. It is one of the saddest facts in Hungarian history that for various reasons not one of the addressees brought the contents of the document to light.

It was at this time that Raoul Wallenberg arrived in Budapest as secretary of the Swedish embassy, and looked for allies in his life-saving action. He knew on whom he could depend among the Hungarian government officials. *I was one of the first that he called on after arriving in Budapest, and I spent a long evening with him and his friend*, Soos recalled later. Wallenberg gave him and the Good Shepherd Commission 1,500 blank Swedish protective letters, and Soos and his colleagues organised a 'news service' among the 2,600 Jewish houses in Budapest. According to the plan, as preparations for deportations became known two or three young non-Jewish persons were to appear at once in the houses marked with a star of David and go out with the Jews that lived there into a near-by square or park, where they would sit or lie on the ground and await the armed police. Thus it would have been possible to take away the persecuted only by force, one at a time, and so prevent "the murderers killing them in secret and undisturbed". In the end this action did not take place, and as the summer went on the deportation of the Jews of Budapest was stopped.

After the Arrow-Cross took power the links between the resistance and officialdom mostly ceased, and they themselves became the persecuted. By this time Soos risked his life in every action that he took. At the end of November 1944, for instance, he received information that the Germans were transporting captured aircrew and Polish Jews that had been arrested along the Újpest quay. He sent word to Wallenberg, and together they freed the prisoners in a daring move. They simulated an accident on the embankment: a young woman's face was smeared with blackcurrant jam and she was made to lie on the road. When the German lorry carrying the prisoners stopped, with the help of their six companions they disarmed the soldiers and tied them up in a riverside warehouse. In this way they not only saved the lives of five British and American Air Force officers and nine Polish Jews, but also later secured the release of a further forty Jewish prisoners 'in exchange' for the four Germans.

By this time it was obvious that Soviet forces would sooner or later reach Budapest, and that the Arrow-Cross would maintain the terror to the last minute. Some of the leaders of the anti-German movement, including Domokos Szent-Iványi, travelled to Moscow in October to discuss a possible cease-fire. As all communication with them was lost, their companions looked for another connection with the Allies. There was a secret meeting in a house in Óbuda, to which the anglophile former Prime Minister István Bethlen and Raoul Wallenberg were also invited. This was where the plan was devised for Soos, whom the Gestapo were now hunting high and low, to fly to Italy, which had been liberated by the Americans. Later he summed up his aims: a) to renew the connection with the Allies (…); b) to inform them that the Movement had organised itself by uniting as far as possible all the democratic powers and was requesting orders and weaponry from the Red Army; c) to ask what arranged signal the underground forces in Budapest should expect if the Soviet command considered mobilisation of the internal forces necessary when beginning the attack. Furthermore, they intended to hand over the Auschwitz Protocol to the Allies; it had produced almost no reaction in Hungary. Before leaving on this perilous journey Soos went under cover of darkness to take his leave of his wife. *I was ill, he was grave and taciturn*, she recalled later. *There was a great spiritual battle going on inside him – you could see it on him. He didn't answer my questions about where he was going and why, or when he would be back. From that day there wasn't a single letter or message from him for six months.*

THE END OF THE WORLD WAR. By the end of 1944 the Red
Army had liberated Eastern Hungary, and the anti-German political movements had established the Provisional National Assembly in Debrecen, while at Sopron, in the west of the country, the
Parliament convened by Szálasi was still sitting. The siege of Budapest lasted almost three months, from December to February, and
in ferocity of fighting and numbers of dead could only be compared
with the battle for Stalingrad. The Red Army drove the Germans
back house by house, while because of the constant bombardment
a million civilians took to the cellars, where many starved to death.
The retreating German forces blew up the Danube bridges, and the
city was in ruins by the time that the last German soldier left at the
end of February. Fighting continued in the west of the country for
another two months, and in its final hours the Szálasi régime began
conscripting boys between the ages of fourteen and eighteen. Many
of the enfeebled Hungarian Jews that had been driven to forced labour but were incapable of marching were shot on the side of the
road; among them were several significant figures of Hungarian literature. By the end of April the Red Army had driven the Germans
out of Hungary, and did not leave the country for forty-seven years.

After the adventurous escape the mission was, for the most part,
a failure. In Italy Soos and his companions were interrogated for
weeks by low-ranking extremely distrustful British and American officers. By the time that the significance of the message that
they had brought was appreciated it was too late, the siege of Budapest had begun, and the Red Army had liberated Auschwitz. The
American Secret Service held them as prisoners of war for a while
'in friendly detention', but even after that they were not given permission to return home. In the end it was late 1945 before Soos managed to meet his family in Switzerland. They could have started a
new life there, but he wanted to have a personal hand in rebuilding
Hungary. He went back to Budapest without his wife and found
employment in the Foreign Ministry. He was, however, soon called
on by representatives of the Communist Party, who first asked him

to join the party, and when he refused tried to persuade him to sign a declaration of collaboration. As he was not prepared to do that he was automatically branded an enemy. His passport was withdrawn and his arrest was initiated. A former comrade in the resistance put him in touch with a state security officer who arranged for him to flee the country again. He was never again able to return home. In 1947 it was resolved in Parliament, on the proposal of the Minister for the Interior, that his Hungarian citizenship be revoked.

Soos began his life all over again. At the age of thirty-six he enrolled in the Protestant theology department in Geneva and two years later was ordained. When he had officially become a servant of God he asked to be sent to serve in refugee camps in Germany. He arrived as a refugee himself, but soon he was organising the social and spiritual care of 14,000 migrants from Hungary and other East-Central European countries. One of his reports illustrates the superhuman work that he did: in a few weeks he travelled 6,000 kilometres by car and train and found individuals in such need that in addition to emergency parcels he also gave them his own money, and indeed his spare clothes. He lived with his wife and children in a cramped little flat, but there were always whole families living with them until they found permanent accommodation. Donations even enabled him to establish a correspondence school in Munich, sending schoolbooks to emigrant families all over the world.

In 1951, at the invitation of an American Protestant high school, he and his family settled in the USA. While teaching at the school he went round the major Hungarian communities in the country. He was almost constantly travelling, and when it was pointed out to him that he was overburdening himself he replied: *We have a fearsome responsibility. If we have today once more to look in the eye a single friend of ours who is languishing in prison, how can we bear it?* At his home in Montreal, North Carolina, the door was always open to Hungarian refugees. In September 1953 he entertained the former colonel Ferenc Koszorús, sometime member of the Hungarian resistance movement. They set off together for Pittsburgh in Soos's car. The weather was bad, the car skidded and hit a concrete post. As his passenger was badly injured Soos ran to the nearest house to call an ambulance. He helped to put the unconscious Koszorús into the ambulance and got in beside him. On reaching the hospital the apparently uninjured Soos was found dead beside his unconscious friend. He was forty-one-years of age. It has never been made clear whether he died of a serious internal injury or – as his family and friends thought – the Hungarian or Soviet Secret Service had executed him. Even today we have less than complete knowledge of what he did for his country, for Hungarians suffering persecution and for the large numbers of refugees abroad. What we do know, however, would amply justify memorial tablets, statues, and streets named after him. Not one of which exists.

God called me at a very early age. At the age of ten I was already reading the scriptures and praying daily. I knew that God was the Lord of my life, and that I had to obey Him (…) When war broke out I joined the resistance movement so as to go to the defence of the persecuted and preserve the honour of my country against Nazi aggression. I carried out a number of dangerous missions. God always kept me out of the Gestapo prison. On my final mission in Italy I organised the first Hungarian Calvinist assembly in Rome. In 1946 in Budapest the communists once again tried to get rid of me, as I refused to join the Communist Party or to sign a declaration of obedience. I had to flee to Switzerland again, where my family were living at the time. I soon realised that all roads were closed: no decent man could collaborate with the Communists. (…) I grasped with joy this opportunity to have the chance to dedicate my life entirely to the service of my Redeemer. (…) In my work as a pastor it is my view that (…) pastors, presbyters and believers must work together. They must feed the flock together, taking especially into their care the weak and sick, and looking for the lost.

Géza Soos,
My Creed
Új Magyar Út, 1954

Ilona Elek, the most successful woman fencer ever.

Ilona Elek

On 5 August 1936 Adolf Hitler looked in fury at the result of the women's épée in the Berlin Olympics. Two days after a black athlete had won the gold in the 100 metres sprint, the Nazi propaganda weapon had backfired once more. The twenty-four-years-old Austrian Ellen Preis, the previous Olympic champion, stood – slightly disappointed – on the lowest level of the winners' rostrum. In second place the German Helene Mayer, aged twenty-six, with horror on her face made a Nazi salute towards the seat of honour. The world's press had, until the last moment, thought that the tall sportswoman would take the gold for Nazi Germany. No one had anticipated that Ilona Elek, aged twenty-nine, would deservedly be standing on top of the rostrum as the first female Hungarian Olympic champion. All three had been lucky to take part in the Olympics, as they were Jewish. Threefold attempts had been made to prevent Ilona Elek, the most successful ever fencer in Hungary, from fencing: firstly, she was a woman, secondly she had been born Jewish, and thirdly her sport was a middle-class reserve.

Ilona Elek – Csibi to everybody – was still at grammar school when she read that the actress Gizella Tary had won an international fencing competition. The idea of women fencing was so unlikely, seemed so ridiculous, that the leading Italian fencer Nedo

Nadi declared "Let's give women flowers, not épées". After Tary's successes, however, an inventive fencing-master decided to open Hungary's first fencing club for women. The quick-thinking Csibi – her hair cut boyishly short – persuaded her sister Margit to see how they would look in fencing kit. At the club everyone was accepted who paid the subscription and bought the equipment. The Elek girls joined the club with money obtained from their parents for music lessons. They tried to keep their new hobby secret, because such unladylike occupations were strictly forbidden at school. When a group photograph was taken of the team they stood in the back row and pulled their necks in so as not to be recognised. Even so they failed: after their first win the newspaper gave an account of the girl fencers, and so they were hauled over the coals at school.

After leaving school, even so, they almost stopped fencing. Csibi was accepted to study piano at the Music Academy, and the director called in her father and told him that fencing would make her wrists stiff, so she had to give it up. She was on the point of saying goodbye to the piste when the leader of the fencing association saw her in a match and realised how talented she was. *I don't know what sort of a pianist she'll be, but I'm sure there'll be a hundred like her. But I do know that a fencer like Csibi is scarcely born every hundred years!* He persuaded her to continue her career as a fencer with the trainer of his choice, the Italian fencing-master Italo Santelli. From then on she competed seriously, and in 1928 was picked as reserve for the squad for the Amsterdam Olympics. In the end she was not taken and followed the Olympics on the radio with her sister. That was when she first heard of Helene Mayer, the German gold medallist, who was referred to in the sporting papers as "the first woman to completely master the technique of fencing". Mayer featured more and more in the papers and popularised women's fencing worldwide. But only outside Hungary – there it was still considered extravagant foolishness for a woman to pick up a sword.

Nevertheless, from then on Ilona Elek prepared as hard as she could to go to the next Olympics. The Italian maestro Santelli noticed that she made a lot of mistakes in practice, but never in competition. "Csibi is a prima donna, she has to have an audience", he said. And he was quite right, Csibi liked winning and being admired by the audience and the press. Hungarian officialdom, however, did nothing for her sporting career. When the Hungarian Fencing Association was selecting its squad for the 1929 European Championships in Naples it was decided to leave the women at home to save money. In the end, Csibi's father, not the Association, paid for her to go, and she finished on the fifth place. Shortly after that, nevertheless, her sporting career almost came to an end. When the jury was unfair to her sister Margit in a competition she called the leader of the jury aside and – according to his recollection – *informed him unambiguously of her opinion of the judging.* The all-male jury decided to make an example of the impudent female sportswoman: she was banned from competition for two years. That meant that the Hungarian women fencers also went to the Los Angeles Olympics without her.

During the years of her ban Ilona kept on training. She practised early in the morning and in the evening, as she and her sister were working as representatives of a tourism business to finance their expensive hobby. In 1933, when the European Championships were held in Budapest, she was able to compete again. She could no longer call on the Fencing Association for travel expenses as this time they were not even prepared to pick a women's team. Their excuse was that the women would *jeopardise the good name of Hungarian men's fencing.* In the end, through the intervention of Italo Santelli, they were given permission – and won the championship. Ilona also competed in the individual event, and the international press spoke of her as the least nervous fencer in the world. *The real difficulties came only after this,* she reminisced later: *the men had simply smiled at female competitors until then,* but from then on regarded them as rivals in the struggle for the sparse state funding. In the fencing halls whispering started: the women had really only won by good luck, they would not be able to repeat that result in the future. They were

Ilona Elek on the podium as Olympic champion. In front of her is the Austrian Ellen Preis and behind her the German Helene Mayer. (Berlin, 1936)

able to travel to the 1934 Championships in Warsaw only thanks to money wheedled out of sponsors. They wiped the floor with everybody, and Ilona fought her sister for the gold medal in the final. Csibi went home champion, and from then on brought back international trophies one after another, but the world of men's fencing still denied the women recognition. One champion fencer summed it up in *Magyar Sport* (Hungarian Sport) with the words: *Sports of contest are altogether unsuitable for women. This also applies to close-quarter combat sports like fencing, which is none too suitable for female characteristics.*

Furthermore, at this time it was not Csibi's only misfortune to have been born female. Not long before the Berlin Olympics she was excluded from the Army Officers' Fencing Club (which brought together the best competitors) because of her Jewish origins. She transferred her allegiance to the upper-middle-class sport association, but soon had to leave that too. Finally the Detectives Athletic Club accepted her – that was open to 'civil sportsmen' including even Jews, and she prepared for world-class competition in a club much worse equipped than that of her rivals. At the time she was not the only one in Europe to be in such a situation. In 1933 Helene Mayer, who had been German champion six times, was unable to provide the Nazi authorities with documentation on her father's Aryan antecedents, and so her sporting funds were withdrawn and she was excluded from her club. She emigrated to America and would in all probability have taken part in the Berlin Olympics under the American flag had the government of her native country not blackmailed her. She was informed that the safety of the members of her family that remained in Germany would be guaranteed if she put on the swastika and won a gold medal for the third Reich. Ellen Preis, the champion in the Los Angeles Olympics, also had to contend with the racial laws. She had been born in Berlin and held dual German–Austrian nationality. Her German club had kicked her out because of her Jewish descent, and she competed in Austrian colours while she could.

Ilona had to take part in six selection competitions in Hungary to ensure her place in the Olympic squad. She met the requirements, but her sister was not permitted to travel: she was said to be too young, and room was needed for men. As two Olympic Games were not held during the war Margit lost three opportunities for world competition in the course of her life. In Berlin the male épée fencers and the épée team were eliminated out in the preliminary rounds, and as there was no women's team competition only Ilona represented Hungary in the finals. Despite her international successes, the press considered that she had a chance of the bronze medal, and that the gold would be between the two previous Olympic champions, Helene Mayer and Ellen Preis. And not only the foreign press: the fencer Attila Petschauer, who was only at the Olympics as a journalist, reported from Berlin to *Az Est* (The Evening) that *victory could not be taken from Helene Mayer.* Margit remarked ironically: *It's just as well that Csibi hasn't read the article.* In fact, Ilona moved steadily towards victory, losing only three of twenty-one bouts, and so quickly and easily did she defeat first Preis and then Mayer (the latter a straight 5:0) that the audience did not even have time to get over it. The German competitor was not able to present Hitler with the promised gold medal, and the Nazi salute visible in the pictures taken on the podium was born of fear of reprisals. In any case, along with the African-American athlete Jesse Owen, with his four golds, the Hungarian Jew Csibi Elek succeeded in humiliating the Führer and those that proclaimed the supremacy of the German race.

After Berlin, the first Hungarian female Olympic champion received the recognition that she deserved. Nevertheless – perhaps weary of the many years of struggle – Ilona announced her retirement. She returned to the piano and continued her studies at the Music Academy. Helene Mayer too gave up competition after her defeat, but before the 1937 World Championship in Paris the German fencing association tried to persuade her back by blackmail. After that the Hungarian association too began to beg Csibi to return to the piste. She did not want to lose the chance of a re-match with Mayer, so she agreed. By that time, and thanks to her, women's fencing was taken so seriously that in Paris the more important encounters were fought in the presence of the President of the Republic. Led by Ilona, the Hungarian women's team won 9:7. In the individual competition, however, Mayer had her revenge – though by a single hit. After that Csibi decided that retirement could be postponed a little, because she wanted to face her most important rival once more. She was not to know that thanks to politics it would be 1951 before she could compete in a world championship again.

After her victory Helene Mayer did not return to Germany but continued to compete as an American citizen. Ellen Preis too was forced to emigrate after Austria joined the Third Reich. Of the three of them – the three Helens – only Csibi remained in her native country, and won Hungarian and international titles until she too was banned from the piste. On 9 May 1944 *Nemzeti Sport* (National Sport) announced in a brief article that (…) *at sporting venues under the control of the state, therefore, Jews that are obliged to wear the distinguishing mark laid down, so-called yellow-starred persons – may not attend sporting competitions or other events*. Csibi realised from that, that she might never again compete for the glory of her country. She survived the rule of the Arrow-Cross in Budapest by hiding. After the war she immediately resumed fencing. She trained in a war-damaged building that had neither heating, lighting nor glass in the windows, and soon won the first post-war championship of Hungary. She also did a lot as an organiser to put Hungarian fencing back on its feet. When Gyula Sédey, former head of the fencing association, was sentenced to death by the court because, under the Arrow-Cross, he had assumed the title of Chief of Police in Budapest, Csibi organised a petition for mercy in which it was shown that Sédey had committed no crime and had personally intervened everywhere for the condemned. In the end he was pardoned.

Politics, however, did not allow her to compete for long. If she had previously been banned as a Jew, she was now prevented from fencing because, according to official communist evaluation, it was *the upper-class sport of trouble-makers, gentry and the select, remote from the people*. It was seriously enacted that fencing, as a sport alien to socialism, was simply banned in Hungary as it was throughout the Soviet bloc. The Hungarian team was not even allowed to compete in the 1947 World Championships in Lisbon. The authorities changed their minds only because of the large number of gold medals that could be expected, and so permitted Hungarian fencers to take part in the 1948 Olympics in London. Ilona – now forty-one – easily defended her title. After an interval of twelve years she was the sole competitor to retain a title from the Berlin Games. Now she was regarded as one of the most successful fencers of all time. In 1951 – when, incidentally, she became world champion again – she was awarded the highest international recognition, the Feyerick Prize.[8] The citation said: *She deserves the prize. Not only for her achievements that have amazed the whole world (three individual World and two Olympic championships) but also for her spirit that has striven for pure sport, (…) the spirit with which she has struggled for the sake of fencing, even under the most difficult circumstances, for her country and the Interna-*

tional Fencing Federation, and for the great family of fencers. She was not allowed to travel to receive the supreme award, which no active sportsman had previously been awarded. Indeed, in the summer of 1952, before the Helsinki Olympics, her name together with her sister's featured in the secret police report containing the names of sportsmen *to whose travelling abroad there is an objection on national security grounds.* Eventually, after a lengthy argument the political commission decided that sportsmen of dubious reputation might travel, but eight policemen would go with them. At the Helsinki Olympics only a subsequently questioned jury decision robbed Ilona of her third gold medal. She was shown on the scoreboard as level on points with the Italian Irene Camber, and so a deciding bout had to be fought. The Hungarians registered a complaint against the referee in the match – on the basis of his previous decisions – but the organisers rejected it. The complaint was not unfounded, as the referee awarded a hit to Camber, and so Ilona only received the silver medal. (It was later revealed by film footage that the questionable hit had been foul.) In Helsinki Csibi even had the chance to meet Mayer, who had moved back to Germany and had by then given up the sport; she died a year later of breast cancer. *Helene Mayer, dear blonde Hee! Everybody else may forget you, but your comrades in arms never will!* reminisced her former greatest opponent.

All her life she was disappointed with judging, especially after that, and she did not receive praise for her silver medal but was criticised for missing the gold. It is not surprising that she was one of the most consistent international supporters of the introduction of the mechanical registering of hits. *Let the bout be decided on the piste! That's the idea of mechanisation!* she wrote. *The machine can't be intimidated or influenced. Even the best theatrical performance can't affect its decision.* She could have retired again, but she decided to take revenge for the unfair decision at Helsinki. At the age of almost fifty she began to prepare for the Melbourne Olympics. As world champion she had not been required to take part in qualifying events, but the fencing federation finally abolished this rule. Not long before the

Olympics she was informed that she would not be allowed to travel. Disappointed but with head held high she gave up active sport. It is typical of her nobility of spirit that during the 1956 revolution she gave refuge in her flat to the communist sport administrator who had had the final word in preventing her going to the Olympics. Nor did she feel dissatisfied that at Melbourne there were no Hungarians in the women's épée final: she accepted the position of team captain and for many years assisted the branch of sport that she had made great. She and her sister wrote the history of her sporting career, and then at the end of her life she returned to music, which she had given up for fencing. The first female Hungarian Olympic champion, who had brought glory to her country despite two political régimes, died in Budapest on 24 July 1988.

(…) We have been really unlucky competitors. A lot of people will smile at that, and quite a few have asked, not entirely without malice, how it would have been if we had actually been lucky? Still (…) We were unlucky, because between the often mentioned two Olympic gold medals one of the bloodiest periods in the history of the world occurred. Though the results – two Olympic championships, three individual and eight team world championships, and very many domestic and international victories – contradict that statement. That is merely appearance, because when the Second World War broke out we were really at the start of our careers, our successes. We reached the real peak of our form in the years during and just after the war, that is, in those times when sporting links had been broken off. After the war, however, we fencers could not take part in either world championships or international competition for a long time. But – as we have already said – that was when our strength and skill were at their height. What would we have achieved then?! But it's all in the past (…)

Ilona and Margit Elek,
That's how we fenced
1968

László Kozma, convict and computer pioneer.

László Kozma

On the afternoon of 25 November 1949 László Kozma, 47, university lecturer and technical director of Standard Electric Co., had just got ready to go to the theatre. He was leaving his office to meet his wife when in front of him stopped a man in the uniform of the dread State Security Authority, and called him into the adjacent room. *I'm Captain Sárközi. Please be seated, comrade director! Here is some blank paper. Be so good as to describe in detail the sabotage that has taken place in the factory since the liberation. Now, it would be a shame to waste time, as you mentioned on the phone this afternoon that you had tickets for the theatre this evening.* The engineer, who had recently received the state's highest distinction for his inventions, was astonished at the question, and said that he was unaware of any sabotage in the factory. From then on he remained day and night for a year in the suit that he had put on for the theatre: he was arrested without any charge, and as he was not prepared to play the role of false witness was sentenced to a lengthy term of imprisonment. After the Nazi concentration camp he had not gone to America but returned to Hungary, to build for his country the first automatic calculator and at the same time to modernise Hungarian long-distance communications. Therefore he did so: he worked on it while he was in prison and waiting decades for rehabilitation. If he had headed for the West after the war we would today consider him one of the greatest figures of computer technology.

History strained at his career in every way, but because of his incredible staying power and talent it could not break it. He set out to be an engineer from childhood. He left school in the very year when the *numerus clausus* rule restricting the admission of Jews to universities was announced, and so because of his Jewish origins he could not be accepted at the Technical University. For lack of anything better he started work as an electrician at Egyesült Izzó (United Bulbs), an electronics firm making telephone exchanges. His bosses soon noticed that the hard-working electrician was interested enough in the drawings of telephone circuits that he had started to learn English so as to be able to read technical descriptions in the original. First he was made a laboratory assistant, then a few engineering scholarships were set up for him so that he could nevertheless obtain his degree – outside Hungary, in Czechoslovakia. He studied at one of the best technical universities of the time, that at Brno. From there his way lay straight to the international firm that was developing telephone exchanges, the American Bell Telephone factory in Antwerp. As an engineer at the start of his career he did routine jobs to begin with, but there too his talents were quickly noticed. Year after year bigger and bigger developments were entrusted to him, and he was scarcely thirty when he had played a key role in the building up of the automatic telephone network in several European countries, including Switzerland, Belgium, Holland and Italy. He registered more than twenty-five patents, more than the other engineers in the factory put together. He was considered one of the most successful specialists in his profession, and his private life too was shaping up nicely: he married and soon had two children.

At the end of the 1930s design of electronic calculators was beginning in three places in the world: the University of Harvard, the American centre of Bell Telephone and its Antwerp factory. By then the American government knew for a fact that in a future war a decisive role would be played by means of rapid calculation that would enable the precise aiming of projectiles to be worked out. When Kozma was entrusted in Antwerp with the development of an 'automatic calculator' he had no idea at all that his work could be of military significance. *As far as I was concerned, the work was just something of interest. I was simply pleased at being entrusted with a completely new kind of task, but what it all added up to I had no idea at all at the time.* The first Kozma calculator was built by 1938 out of telephone exchange components, two years earlier than its American counterpart. It was capable of compiling and sorting data in seconds, and in it there appeared several of the basic ideas of later computers. The improved variant of the first prototype could perform division, and could control multiple work-stations simultaneously. Developments proceeded at the same time in America and in Antwerp in such a way that neither knew of the other's results. The next step was to have been the uniting of the two proto-computers, but meanwhile war broke out. The German army invaded Belgium, but the Americans immediately loaded Kozma's machine onto a ship. Exactly what happened after that is a secret, because the calculator never reached America. The official explanation is that the ship was sunk by a submarine, and according to others the Americans were entitled to suppress the militarily important invention in this way.

In any case, during the German occupation Kozma continued his work in secret, but after a while the director of the factory felt that the illegal laboratory was dangerous and closed it. Under German orders the firm soon had to shed its Jewish engineers, and deportations began in Belgium as elsewhere. Kozma and his family were forced to go into hiding. Although he could have escaped through France to America, he decided that he would rather return to Hungary and produce the computer there. Once again he found employment as a mere electrician at Egyesült Izzó. *Between November 1942 and November 1944,* he recalled, *we lived, but it was hard. Sometimes I worked at Izzó, and at other times I did forced labour in a company doing rubble-clearance and rescue work. My life was often in danger. (…) In November 1944 I was deported, first to Fertőrákos, then to Mauthausen and Gunskirchen.* Even in concentration camp, he worked. At night, by the light of floodlights that shone into the barracks, he designed a new sort of telephone exchange in a notebook which he concealed from the guards. Later he reminisced that this work gave meaning to his life and kept him from giving up the struggle.

He returned home in the summer of 1945 after being seriously ill. He found only his two children: his wife had disappeared. He therefore decided not to go back to Belgium, but to try to look after the two of them in Hungary. Although he had never been active in politics he joined the Communist Party because they seemed the most prepared to take steps for the rebuilding of the country. He became a research leader at Standard Eletric Co., which was owned by Bell Telephone, and felt that he was at last going to be able to realise his plans. He dreamt of a flourishing Hungarian telephone business, and a young team of engineers that he had trained himself. He directed the post-war modernisation of the Hungarian telephone system on the basis of the plans that he had devised in Mauthausen, and for that received the state's highest award, the Kossuth Prize. He was appointed to a teaching post at the Technical University, where he was one of the founders of the electrical engineering department. His wife, who had vanished, was found to have died, and a few years later he remarried. It seemed that ahead of him there lay at last a peaceful scientific career and quiet life. There was only one reason for his life to take another turn: his place of work. There were scarcely a dozen factories in the world making telephone exchanges, but in the socialist camp Standard was the only one. The authorities wanted to acquire the business come what may, but it could not be a simple matter of nationalisation because the factory belonged to the investors in a militarily allied country, and international treaties governed its workings.

The American owner was prepared to let the factory go to the Hungarian state for a fair price, but negotiations dragged on, and the Hungarian purchaser also wanted to acquire the patents. It seemed much simpler to find a pretext for taking the factory off the Americans. In 1948 the technical director of the factory went abroad for a year, and Kozma, at the worst moment, undertook to replace him for a year. Not long after that the first show trials began, but no one at Standard was under suspicion. When the managing director of the factory, Imre Geiger, complained of being followed in the street Kozma told him that as long as they did their jobs they could come to no harm. His colleague's easy-going attitude did not reassure Geiger. A few days later he and his family tried to leave the country, but were caught at the frontier and arrested. Not longer after that the Secret Police captain that was investigating the factory called Kozma into his office and informed him that he was not under suspicion of sabotage, but that as technical director he must have noticed suspicious activities. As Kozma could not give an account of such the Secret Police took him to 60 Andrássy út and kept him there for months, without officially arresting him, as a 'witness'.

THE COMMUNIST STATE SECURITY SERVICE. When the dictatorship of the party-state came into being it was of key importance that the Communist Party had assumed control over internal affairs as early as 1945. The most important organisation for political reprisals were the Államvédelmi Osztály (State Security Department, aka ÁVO) and the Államvédelmi Hatóság (State Security Authority, aka ÁVH), of which Mátyás Rákosi, Secretary General of the Party, was the actual director through his appointees. The headquarters of the ÁVH were the former Arrow-Cross Party centre at 60 Andrássy út in Budapest. Thus they also had access to the data on former Arrow-Cross members. Although several of the senior officers of the ÁVH were of Jewish origin the opportunity to join the communists was offered to several thousand Arrow-Cross activists, and many of them became members of the new instrument of repression. Political reprisals had begun in the period of coalition, but after the formal communist takeover in 1949 the

ÁVH cellars were full of innocent captives. In the first half of the 1950s the ÁVH became a fearsome, nation-wide terror organisation that watched the people by means of a network of informers tens of thousands strong and was liable to carry off simply anybody and intern them without trial. Although the ÁVH was formally disbanded in 1953 – after its leaders had been condemned as Zionist plotters in a Soviet-style show trial – for many years the majority of Hungarians still referred to those that worked in the State Security organs as 'ávós'.

They tried by means of threats, blackmail and sleep-deprivation to persuade him to make a confession incriminating Geiger and Robert Vogeler, the representative of the American owners. When that did not succeed they invoked his duty as a communist. *You've been awarded a Kossuth Prize, you enjoy an increased salary, you've got a highly responsible position, and all thanks to the party. Are you refusing to help now, when you ought to?* asked an ÁVO colonel. *I knew that there was no point in heroics. Especially that you can only be heroic if you're biologically strong, and living properly, in tidy circumstances. If anybody tries to offer opposition they lock them in the cellar and they're broken in a couple of weeks,* he wrote later in his memoirs. He soon realised that they had no evidence at all or, indeed, any idea of sabotage, and they were expecting him to invent something. He told a tale of a couple of industrial accidents and manufacturing problems, from which the ÁVO fabricated a show trial. He was confident that if his confession were made public the workers in the factory and those who understood technical matters would know that the charge of sabotage was false. When they had got from him what they wanted they left him to himself in the cellar. He spread his coat over him against the winter cold, and his feet that had been frozen during the war were bad again because of the cold. He later said that conditions at 60 Andrássy út had been worse than at Mauthausen.

SHOW TRIALS. Show trials organised on Soviet lines played an important part in the consolidation of the communist dictatorship. From as early as 1945 actions against war criminals were rich in elements that took no account of the norms of the rule of law, but in them the majority of the accused had actually committed crimes. Later the communist supervisors of the police and the legal profession had a predilection for ridding themselves of their political rivals who had governed in coalition with them, the leaders of the Independent Smallholders Party and the Social Democratic Party, through trumped-up legal proceedings. In addition to taking total political power they also acquired economic authority partly by means of show trials: they accelerated the nationalisation of private enterprise by dreaming up imaginary affairs involving sabotage and espionage. By the use of theatrically managed lawsuits they were also able to keep sympathisers with the Communist Party in a constant state of readiness for action against 'enemies of the regime', and to enforce the silence of the terrorised majority. The leaders of the party-state also dealt with their rivals within the party by means of show trials. The communist Minister for the Interior László Rajk was accused of espionage and executed in 1949, which turned many former sympathisers against the authorities.

He had to learn by heart a previously written confession, and in the end did not have to appear at the hearing. The authorities intended the Standard case to be a public attraction, and feared that he might play his part badly. At all events, not only the Hungarian press but also foreign reporters, including those from the *Times* and the *Guardian*, judged that the proceedings had been properly conducted. It did not occur to anyone that neither the accused, the witnesses nor the judge hesitated for a second to speak their lines but reacted in theatrical fashion to cues. Evidence was offered against Imre Geiger, Robert Vogeler and the rest without anyone picking up that their evidence consisted of complete technical impossibilities. Meanwhile the workers of the Standard factory, now renamed Beloiannisz after a Greek communist partisan,

*László Kozma and his colleague with the
first Hungarian punched card in 1958.*

held factory meetings to demand the weightiest penalties. It later
emerged that Geiger had been promised two years in prison if he
would play the part of saboteur and American spy. In the end he
was sentenced to death and executed. The American and English
accused got off with ten or fifteen years. A Catholic priest who
had, to his misfortune, rented his Balaton holiday house to Geiger, was likewise given ten years.

Kozma continued to be held as a witness while the trial proceeded. And as he was still there, he was given a few sheets of paper and a pencil so that he could begin to redesign the electrical
calculator that he had prepared in Belgium. As in the concentration camp, now too he found relief in work. One day the guards
confiscated the notes that he had made. After the case had been
concluded an ÁVO colonel summoned him again: *Look here, up
above they've decided that we can't release you yet. You know too much and
you'd talk. (…) We'll sentence you to two or three years, but after two*

or three months at the most we'll release you. (…) There was need of this prosecution. We've got to show the imperialists what we're made of. You were of assistance to us in it, so to speak, you've done the party service. The confession intended as evidence had been rewritten as a damning self-accusation. A hearing took place behind closed doors which the press could not report. The purpose was simply to put everyone that knew the truth about the background of the show trial out of circulation. Instead of the promised year or two Kozma was given fifteen. A penalty of that magnitude carried automatic sequestration of property, so that his wife too was immediately rendered destitute.

Kozma spent a year in solitary confinement in a provincial prison, in complete isolation. Apart from the guards he only met the domestic staff who emptied the toilet, and who turned out to be some of the condemned Arrow-Cross men. *They'll be bringing in some more Jews,* said one, *something's going to happen outside.* After a while Kozma was given some translation work to do. He had to translate technical and political texts of a confidential nature from English, and from that he could be aware that he would not be released for a long time yet. In 1952 he was transferred to a Budapest prison, where he could be made to continue his engineering work. He became a member of the group of condemned scientists permitted to research the possibilities of cybernetics, officially reckoned a pseudo-science by the Soviet authorities. He actually developed two patents on behalf of his former workplace. He considered that his old colleagues would realise that the documentation came from him and would let his wife know. Eventually he was allowed to resume work on his calculator designs, and in addition planned the SB-model country-wide telephone exchange. After a while there were almost a hundred working in the prison engineering office, and Kozma became leader of the communication technology team.

Kozma's wife first learnt officially in November 1953 that her husband was serving fifteen years for crimes against the people.

Not long afterwards they were permitted to meet once a month, but neither of them spoke of what had happened to him. A few months later Kozma was again summoned to make a confession, and was told that his sometime interrogating officer was being interrogated in the next room: *The fellow's sitting there in the next room shaking in his shoes,* said the ÁVO officer with a knowing wink. Another six months went by, and he received a brief official letter in prison: *The Council of Ministers of the Hungarian People's Republic has remitted as an act of clemency the prison sentence prescribed and the additional punishment of a ten year ban from public affairs.* The letter therefore did not say that he was innocent, only that he was pardoned. Even so, it was another six months before they ventured to release him. If, that is, it had emerged that the Standard had been taken from its owners by means of trumped-up accusations the Hungarian state would have had to pay huge indemnities.

Of the former Standard colleagues only Kozma, then fifty-two, was pardoned. He began teaching in the electrical engineering department of the Technical University. It was a long time before he could obtain a certificate of good character, and so could not occupy a senior position. According to his pupils he did not like being called 'Professor' but preferred 'engineer', because, as he put it, *The good engineer is a creative man, an independent personality, he can assess his activity precisely and work it out.* Once again he started work on designing and constructing a calculator for training purposes. The MESz-1 (Technical University Calculator -1) was not up to the technical level of the contemporary American computers, but even so it was the first Hungarian computer and remained in use for about ten years for a variety of scientific purposes.

Kozma's rehabilitation was a half-cock affair. His innocence was not made clear, but he was given back his Kossuth Prize and appointed Dean of the electrical engineering department. In 1961 he was elected a member of the Hungarian Academy of Sciences. The official party paper, *Népszabadság,* carried an article about him titled *At last the wound heals.* Of course, the wound could not heal because no one ever apologised to him for the treatment that he had received. It was only at the end of his life that he learnt that before the former Hungarian coronation regalia – smuggled to America after the war – were returned the Hungarian state tacitly paid an enormous sum in compensation to the European Standard factories. In return no one raised the matter of the show trial or the memory of those wrongfully executed or imprisoned. Kozma worked to the end of his life, took part in his old age in the development of the first Hungarian crossbar telephone exchange and the automation of the Hungarian telephone network. He died at the age of eighty-one, and a crowd of his students accompanied him on his final journey. In 1996 the American IEEE Computer Society resolved to admit the first Hungarian computer constructor to membership of the Computer Pioneer Association, which lists the creators of the modern science of Informatics.

(...) *I have never found peace of mind. In the 1920s I left Hungary because I could find no place in the Horthy regime. I went to Belgium, where I was well off until the Germans came, when I became a* sale étranger. *I came home and was considered a stinking Jew. I had to enlist for forced labour, then was deported to Mauthausen. All these people were my enemies. But now the situation was different! It was declared by the ÁVH that I would be serving the party if I took upon myself crimes that I had not committed. That I did not really understand, but perhaps we would have been the example for others to follow – beware, you have to do your work well because otherwise you'll be next. So I became – as a new variant – a traitorous villain!*

László Kozma,
The Prison Years of a Kossuth Laureate, 2001

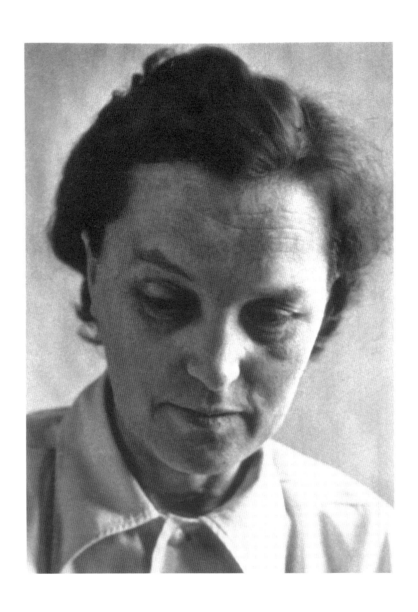

Interned in the Arctic without sentence.
Sára Karig at the age of 41 after her release in 1955.

Sára Karig

It happened to be Monday 1 September 1947, but the thirty-three-year-old English teacher did not go to work that day. She was taking part in the work of the electoral committee of a Budapest district as a Social Democratic Party delegate, handing out voting papers to voters on the electoral roll. Sára Karig was not politically active, and was doing the administrative job – hardly an interesting one – out of democratic conviction. When she looked out of the window at about 6.15 in the morning she saw an open lorry on which workmen in overalls were waiting. She remarked to herself that it was not very nice to be going on an excursion on election day. Then it came to her that the previous day a huge number of blue voting papers had been brought from the State Printer with the official explanation that anyone that was unable, for any reason, to be at their usual place of residence might use these to vote. When one of the communist members of the electoral committee had helpfully offered to take the blue papers that had been left in to the centre, she told him not to. *Comrade Karig, Siberia isn't that far!* said the man menacingly, which Sára had not known how to take, but in any case it had aroused her curiosity over the voting papers.

It was only next day, when she saw the bus-loads of workers, that she realised what was going on. *I didn't think it right either ethically*

or politically for a country to have its principles corrupted right at the start.
She phoned round the voting stations to ask that if anyone arrived
with blue voting papers she should be given their details. The first
call soon came: a factory worker had voted with a blue paper. Sára
immediately informed the other voting stations that if anyone of
that name appeared there too their voting paper should be with-
held together with their personal documents, and the person concerned handed over to the police on duty for electoral fraud. In a
few hours the number of reports and arrests rose to several hundred, and Sára informed the national leaders of the Social Democratic Party. That evening, after voting had ended, the Communist Party activist of the previous day reappeared and demanded
the blue papers that had been issued. *I'm handing them over to the law,*
replied Sára, and went home. That very day the political scandal
broke out: the other parties and the press too became aware that
the communists had polled 22% by means of fraud.

Next morning, when Sára set out for work four policemen
were waiting for her outside the house. They asked her politely
to go with them to make a statement. She was ushered into a car,
its windows curtained, and then handed over to detectives of the
Red Army. She was not allowed to let anyone know, and her documents, jewels and money were taken from her. Some months later all that she was told was that her presence would impede the
democratic development of Hungary. She was deported without
so much as being informed of a charge, and was made to work for
six and a half years in one of the harshest Soviet labour camps,
Vorkuta. She was one of the bravest Hungarian women of the
twentieth century: she put her life at risk for the sake of Polish
refugees, British prisoners of war, exiled Jews and orphaned children alike. She knew at all times that she was morally in the right
and so always had the strength to start again.

She was born in 1914 into a family of school-teachers in the
small Hungarian town of Baja. Her father was a lecturer at the
Baja teacher-training college, and also head of the local school of

music. He played the organ in the Calvinist, Lutheran, Catholic and Orthodox churches and, indeed, in the synagogue. Although he was a Lutheran elder he married a Catholic teacher, and together they decided that they would bring up their children in both faiths at once, so that when they grew up they could decide which denomination to join. The three grew up surrounded by books and musical instruments, in great freedom and moderate poverty – there was seldom money for new clothes, but always for a language teacher. When she was still quite little the younger girl displayed a keen sense of justice. On her first day at the Catholic elementary school she was fidgeting on the bench, for which the nun taking the class rapped her on the knuckles. In response Sára took the stick off her and hit her back. She was immediately expelled, and it was only in exchange for a cow that she was allowed to become a private pupil. At the age of twelve she was sent to Germany to study at the convent of the Institute of the Blessed Virgin Mary. By the time that she had finished she was fluent in English, German and French. On returning to Hungary she went as a boarder to a school in the provincial university town of Szeged; there she took her matriculation examination and enrolled in the English and German department of the university.

In the early 1930s Szeged was characterised by a particularly lively intellectual life. In the mornings Sára would go to lectures, and in the afternoon would spend time with Albert Szent-Györgyi. He was one of the most important biochemists of his time and had not long returned to Hungary from America; some years later he was awarded the Nobel Prize for Biology and Medicine for the isolation of Vitamin C. Szent-Györgyi became very fond of the open-eyed girl, took her rowing in his family boat, and from time to time gave her little secretarial tasks. She went regularly to events held by the *Szegedi Fiatalok Művészeti Kollégiuma* (Artistic College of the Youth of Szeged), and at lectures on village studies and avant-garde art became acquainted with one of the greatest Hungarian poets, Miklós Radnóti. She was interested in so many things all at once that she had no idea what career to choose. She wrote articles for a newspaper, did some translating, and meanwhile took a course in nursing, then left the Arts faculty as she wanted to enrol in the medical school. In the end she studied for two terms in the law department too, before qualifying as a chartered accountant. In love too she lived a comparatively indulgent life: she had numerous boy-friends but did not want to settle down with anyone. *Marriage wasn't invented for me,* she admitted.

Her mentor Albert Szent-Györgyi recommended that she should see the world while she was young, and so she found work as an *au pair* girl in England. She spent three years there, and in addition to working as a children's nurse she studied at Durham University and then obtained a certificate as a teacher of English in London. In 1937 she returned to Hungary and, to keep herself, took a post as English and German correspondent in an industrial firm, where her immediate superior was Pál Justus, a Social Democrat ideologue. Until then Sára had not involved herself in politics – more precisely, she had considered herself an 'individualist anarchist' , but Justus convinced her that in difficult times it was the duty of the intelligentsia to take part in public life. Difficult times, what is more, were approaching fast: the world war broke out, and then the first Jewish law came into force. As one who valued liberty above all else she was horrified to see her Jewish friends, as law-abiding citizens, adhering to every restrictive piece of legislation: they left their places of employment uncomplainingly, gave up their telephones and cars. Sára had different ideas. *I had one motivation, that something ought to be done, because one can't endure the feeling of defencelessness and helplessness,* she said later. Together with a number of friends she swore: if the laws are inhumane, one should not obey them.

She infringed the first regulation in 1939 for the sake of Polish refugees who had come to Hungary because of the German invasion of Poland. She rented a flat in her own name and handed it over to a Polish family. As it turned out that she only had to show proof of income and the flat would be rented to her she acquired ten in different districts. Then she became a voluntary worker with the International Red Cross, and was able to drive her own Fiat Topolino with an international driving licence. A colleague admitted to her that he was working for the firm with false papers: in fact he was a Jew from Pozsony (today Bratislava, Slovakia) with a Hungarian name, and had fled to Hungary from the persecution of Jews in Slovakia. He asked her as a colleague at the firm to help him find his relatives that had stayed in Pozsony, as from 1941 deportation of Jews to labour camps had begun in Slovakia. Sára went to Pozsony and, thanks to her determined attitude – by displaying a Red Cross certificate that entitled her to nothing – she succeeded in retrieving one of her colleague's relatives from among those awaiting deportation. She returned to Hungary with two important items of experience: firstly, that in Hungary too further persecution of the Jews would result from continued alliance with the Germans, and secondly that a bureaucrat was surprisingly easy to convince with a document that looked authentic.

It soon became apparent that Sára had an unsuspected talent: she could produce remarkably convincing forged documents. When a regulation was introduced in 1941 permitting soldiers returning on leave from the front to marry in one day by an accelerated procedure, she invented a life-saving method. She obtained and copied the papers of eight soldiers who had returned from the front and gave them to her friends. Then she officially married them in her own name – in front of eight different registrars. As no central record was kept the fraud was not discovered, and the brand-new husbands immediately acquired 'legal' registration documents. After that successful action she forged a whole range of documents – not only registry statements, but everything from tram season tickets to club membership cards, so that personal identification could be as authentic as possible. From her illegal workshop at home she provided numerous figures in the resistance, Catholic and anti-fascist, alike with blank certificates of baptism, licences and stamps.

I never joined the resistance movement. I did my own personal resisting, she recalled the time when she had risked her life on a daily basis. At the time she worked in the office of a wine-dealer, but her work was far from dull: she hid the secret armoury of the resistance movement in the cellar. In addition to the Poles, in the flats that she rented she hid English pilots who had escaped from POW camps and other refugees. In March 1944 she became a voluntary helper of the Swedish Red Cross office that rescued children. The original plan of Asta Nilsson, the leader of the organisation, was to place Jewish children – rescued from ghettoes or hiding with friends – in a Swedish Red Cross children's home. This was in fact set up, but Sára succeeded in persuading the Swedes that it would be a safer solution if the children were given forged papers and placed in existing Hungarian orphanages and Church-run old people's homes. She found places for more than a thousand children in some fifty establishments. She managed to save them all, whereas the Arrow-Cross caught the Swedish orphanages unawares. As the front approached she arranged for the placement of orphans escaping from the war zones while continuing to produce forged documents at home as well as reproducing anti-fascist leaflets. At this time she was closely connected to Raoul Wallenberg, who passed on to her children that had been rescued from ever more hazardous situations. *I wasn't afraid of death,* she explained her courage later, *but of becoming completely warped physically and spiritually.*

Soon after the war was ended she was visited by a British major who presented her with a decoration for her saving of prisoners of war, and at the same time asked whether she would like to take British citizenship. Although that was the only official gratitude expressed to her by an organ of state she declined the opportunity. She wanted to share in the creation of a free, democratic Hungary. She continued where she had left off. She became a representative of the governmental commission that was set up to assist prisoners of war, Hungarians left homeless outside Hungary, and Jews returning from concentration camps, and went to the British Council as a lecturer, organising the language training of teachers of English in secondary schools.

It was from that that she had taken time off to assist in the 1947 election as a delegate of the Social Democratic Party. When she reported the abuse of the blue voting papers as a district election agent she had not reckoned on the seriousness of the political scandal that she was going to cause. That day the police also arrested several fraudsters, but on the orders of the communist Minister for the Interior also released them. The Social Democratic Minister of Justice resigned in protest on the very day of the election, but several non-communist coalition politicians too protested at the frauds. Finally the Soviet General Sviridov, President of the Control Commission, pacified them by saying that even so a coalition government had been formed and it was not worth making a fuss. As the parties were occupied with their own internal struggles, and the communists had only achieved 22%, no one demanded that the elections be repeated. This result, however, proved amply sufficient for there to be no further need to hold a democratic election in Hungary for many years. After Sára disappeared the Social Democrats tried to discover what had happened to her. The leader of the Communist Party, Mátyás Rákosi, did indeed promise to investigate the matter. Not long afterwards he informed them that she had been questioned by the Soviets but then released – presumably she had gone to the West. Those that could read between the lines knew that Sára's fate was a warning to meddlesome partners in the coalition.

THE COMMUNIST SEIZURE OF POWER. After the Second World War the Red Army occupied and held Hungary, nevertheless for some years it appeared that a Western-style parliamentary democracy was in the making. Between 1945 and 1948 left-wing parties formed coalition governments, but the Communist Party, backed by the Red Army, gradually ousted its allies from power. In the 1945 election the communists came only third, but obtained for themselves the Interior portfolio and control of the armed organs of security. By means of what the party leader, Mátyás Rákosi, who had returned from Moscow, called only 'salami tactics' they immediately set about systematically appropriating power. While offering an amnesty to any Arrow-Cross activists that would join them, they used trumped-up accusations to force into prison or long-term emigration the leaders of the rival coalition parties. In the 1947 election they obtained by fraud a better position than their support warranted. And in 1948 they eliminated their main rival, the Social Democrats, by a fusion of parties. In 1949 they formally ended coalition government and assumed control of the country. The one-party state came into being, the totalitarian dictatorship of the Communist Party with Rákosi at the head.

After a brief interrogation in Budapest the Russians took Sára off to the Soviet occupied zone in Austria. She was not accused of anything, merely had to write out her biography again and again. At first it seemed that after a short show of power she would be allowed home. *The chief Soviet military lawyer informed me that he did not regard the charge against me as proven, and he would recommend to Moscow that I be freed.* Then, after she had spent four or five months in the collecting prison at Neunkirchen the answer came: the presence of Sára Karig *would hinder the democratic development of Hungary*, and so the relevant committee of the Soviet Ministry of the Interior had decided that she was to be interned 'indefinitely' in the USSR. In the same light autumn coat and dress that she had been wearing at the time of her kidnap from Budapest she was put on the train. The locked railway carriage loitered for two days in a station near her home, then took her further eastwards. She was put off the train at the labour camp at Lwów, where, on the strength of her experience in health-care, she worked as assistant to the camp doctor for two months before being loaded onto another train; this one did not even stop with her until reaching the Arctic, where she had to spend the next six years.

The Corrective Labour Camp at Vorkuta had been established in 1931 to work one of the biggest coalfields in the Soviet Union. In an area as big as London, 160 Km north of the Arctic circle, more than a hundred sub-camps operated; at one time a total of between a hundred and two hundred thousand common criminals and prisoners of war worked there, in inhumane conditions. Because of the daily 10–12 hours of heavy physical work in temperatures of twenty or thirty degrees below zero and the poor rations the majority of prisoners could not endure more than a few years, and 80% did not survive their sentences. When Sára arrived she was sent to a clay mine which worked in three shifts. *I looked at things with a positive will to live: that was my life if I'd got to live it out there, and if I'd got to die I wasn't going to be given another.* In the evenings she talked to the other prisoners about literature and history, or recited poetry to them, and they in return taught her Russian. She endured the hard physical work for two and a half years, and her health was ruined. Her ears were so inflamed from one infection that without proper treatment she would have died of complications. Her knowledge of Latin caught the attention of a camp doctor, who performed the necessary operation. After that she was able to stay in the hospital area as a nurse, and after recuperating she was given other work. Because it was thought that she knew no Russian she was put into a book-binding workshop, where she had to bind confidential documents into volumes. Every day she managed to put aside some of the flour used for making glue so as to make pancakes for her fellow prisoners on special occasions. In order to prevent scurvy she brewed an infusion of pine needles, thus avoiding vitamin deficiency.

In almost seven years her constitution was so weakened that there seemed little likelihood of her surviving a further year in the camp. Then in 1953, after the death of Stalin and a strike by prisoners that was ended by a volley, many of the foreign prisoners were allowed home from Vorkuta. Sára reached home in rags, four stone lighter. She was tormented by insomnia and claustrophobia. It was months before she was able to leave her home and mix with people once more. She felt that she had been forgotten while she was away. She had not been convicted of anything, but as a liberated prisoner no one would offer her employment. Eventually friends obtained her work translating from English, German and Russian. Slowly the work restored her enthusiasm for life and at the age of forty she decided to make a fresh start: *I thought that everything that was to come would be something extra. It seemed that I was starting a third life.*

After the easing of the communist dictatorship she became an editor in a publishing house. In addition to editing collections of stories and book series she translated an anthology of Australian, African, Bulgarian, Russian, Ukrainian, Finnish and Latvian writers, while works by Bulgakov and Agatha Christie also appeared in her translation. She received numerous Soviet awards for her literary work – a sort of rehabilitation – and others from Bulgaria and Finland. She was seventy-two when she met with recognition here in Hungary in the form of a prize for young writers! She never boasted about what she did during the war, and so it came as a surprise when the Israeli Yad Vashem Institute awarded her the distinction of Righteous in the World. At first she would not even go to the presentation ceremony. *I don't want an award for that,* she said. *I had friends among the refugees, and there were some who couldn't be rescued. What I did helped me to live through that period sane and with a clear conscience.* In the end, however, she travelled to Israel in 1987.

Sára Karig spoke of her life in no more than a couple of interviews. She was in no hurry to write an autobiography. She lived by journalism and translating, but at the end of her life also brought out her first book of verse: a collection of poems jotted down on scraps of paper in the camp. The woman who on paper had had eight husbands never married and had no children. But she was not lonely: she surrounded herself with friends, relatives and dogs. In one of her last interviews she said: *I now know that prison and concentration camp aren't the worst things that can happen to you. The worst thing is not being able to look into a mirror, or into yourself.* She died in 1999 at the age of 85.

> Life is a nightmare, death of no account.
> We excavate a cutting for the line
> and tortured bodies toiling on the mound
> can never tell when they've achieved the norm.
>
> The crack of ice, the ring of pick are heard.
> The trusties stand on watch, but there's no need
> for them to shout 'Keep at it' – if you dared
> to take a break you'd soon be cold indeed.
>
> The razor wind of Arctic winter night
> slashes alike at prisoner and guard,
> and arching overhead the Northern Lights
> mark the extent of Stalin's mindless wrath.

Sára Karig,
written in Vorkuta
c. 1950

Simon Papp shortly before his arrest.

"I thought that I would stand spiritual bankruptcy better"

Simon Papp

Even after retiring the sixty-seven-year-old oil engineer worked every day. He had for decades been considered the best in his profession, and had opened up the most important oil- and gas-fields in Hungary, Romania, Serbia, Croatia, Turkey, Albania, Canada, Australia and New Guinea. When in 1953 a sectioned map with research data was placed on his table he said unerringly where it was worth drilling. After work, however, he could not go home, and his guards took him back to his cell. Simon Papp, the creator of oil drilling in Hungary, was serving a life sentence in Vác prison. The death sentence handed down in his show trial for sabotage had been commuted simply because without him the Hungarian oil industry would have been crippled. In return for his work he was allowed, as a favour, to exchange monthly letters with his wife, who had been relocated to the provinces. For a long time he did not understand why the letters came unsigned and typewritten. After seven years he was pardoned, and it was only then that he discovered that the ÁVH had been corresponding with him in his deceased wife's name in case he stopped working in his grief. Even after that he had to go on working, as his retirement pension had been withdrawn. He had been a professional of impeccable honesty, and the Arrow-Cross and the communists alike accused him of sabotage when every oil-well dried up even though it was thanks to him that Hungary had become a producer of oil and gas.

Simon Papp was born in 1886. His mother came from an Austrian mining family, his father was a headmaster in the ethnically Romanian Kapnikbánya (today Cavnic, Romania), and so he was brought up in a very cultured environment. He matriculated at the grammar school in the well-known mining town of Nagybánya (today Baia mare, Romania), where he fell in love with geology, in which he took a degree at the university of Kolozsvár (today Cluj, Romania). His talent was noticed at once and he was offered an assistant lectureship, and in that capacity he took part in the 1910 discovery of the Kissármás (Sărmăşel) gas-field in Transylvania, where the then most important gas well in Europe was found. He was conscripted in the First World War, but the government soon realised that he was of much greater use as a geologist, because oil was indispensable to the war effort. During the war Papp was, despite his youth, of crucial importance in the development of the gas- and oil-fields in the Austro-Hungarian Monarchy – in what are now Romania, Slovakia and Croatia. The Republic of Councils likewise required his work as a 'mining-adviser senior geologist', as did the government of the restored monarchy. He was capable of saying, from the shape of the hills in a region, where he would carry out worthwhile drilling for oil. It was not surprising that one of the biggest oil companies in the world, the British Anglo-Persian Oil Company, also noticed his talent and offered him a contract.

Papp spent twelve years opening up oil-fields in various parts of the world, in effect travelling constantly. His expertise was required not only in Albania, Yugoslavia, Germany and Turkey, but also in USA, Canada and Australia, not to mention such exotic places as New Guinea, Tasmania and Fiji. In the latter places he carried out anthropological research as well as looking for hydrocarbons, and he built up a significant collection of the implements, weapons and jewellery of the indigenous peoples. He sent home a bottle of crude oil from every oil-field that he discovered, together with several rare minerals. His wife Irma accompanied him on his longer journeys, and they spent only short periods in Hungary. Papp was certain that here in Hungary too the earth still concealed significant deposits of oil: *While I was making a living abroad I came home a number of times, and always tried to persuade the appropriate Hungarian authorities that (...) the possibility existed that even in 'mutilated Hungary'[9] we could find hydrocarbons. In this, however, my efforts were in vain.*

In 1932 he became tired of globe-trotting. After returning to Hungary, instead of the appropriate government committees he succeeded in persuading the management of Standard Oil, the world's biggest oil company, that it was worth devoting money to oil exploration in Hungary. As a world-famous expert his opinion was trusted and through a daughter company a concession was bought from the Hungarian government to prospect for and extract mineral oil in the Dunántúl[10]. Papp was engaged as head geologist. The decision was a good one: in 1937 he discovered significant quantities of gas and good quality oil in Zala county, western Hungary. The first well was soon in production, to be followed by several more. The firm established Magyar-Amerikai Olajipari Rt (MAORT, Hungarian-American Oil Ltd.), which in a few years became one of the most important industrial concerns in Hungary, and its output covered 100% of the country's increasing demand for oil. It is to the credit of Papp's many-sided engineering ability that his name is associated with the construction of the pipeline connecting the Zala oil-fields to Budapest – at the time Europe's longest oil pipeline. It is no wonder that in 1941 the Hungarian government too engaged him to direct prospecting for gas in Northern Transylvania, then re-attached to Hungary, and the gas-fields that he discovered have since then been considered among the most important finds in the world.

The Second World War put an end to a successful period in Papp's life and in the history of the Hungarian oil industry. At the end of 1941 Hungary broke off diplomatic relations with the United States and the American management of MAORT were expelled. The firm was not nationalised, but the government, thirsty for oil because of the war, 'made use' of it, entrusting Papp with its management in an agreement with the Americans. He did not suppose that thanks to his new position a political power struggle would shape his future life and in the end ruin it. From the outset the government, under German pressure, urged increased productivity to the detriment of prospecting. Papp tried to make them understand that the yield of the wells would decrease after a time, and that if new ones were not found it would be impossible to make good the short-fall. His warning fell on deaf ears, the opening up of new oil-fields was stopped, and production from the existing ones was increased. The peak of production was reached in 1943, and from then on the quantity of oil produced began to decrease steadily. The political response was not slow in coming. Shortly after the Arrow-Cross came to power the new secretary of state for industry summoned Papp and informed him that the Arrow-Cross Party was charging him with sabotage for not trying to produce more oil. He was also accused of still employing Jewish persons in key positions in the firm. Perhaps he was in no greater trouble simply because the Germans would dearly have liked to get their hands on the business. Papp chose delaying tactics, quoting more and more technical problems, thus succeeding in preventing the most important installations being dismantled and carried off to Germany.

Scarcely had the Germans and their Hungarian henchmen left than he had to protect the company from new dangers. After the front had passed through, MAORT came under Soviet military control, and the invading Russian soldiers even ravaged Papp's private home. They thought that the hundreds of bottles of oil from all parts of the world were alcohol, and when it turned out that they were nothing drinkable poured them all out. Naturally the Soviets too instructed the firm to increase production, then when they saw that in the person of the managing director they were confronted with a real expert they called on Papp to transfer to the then forming Hungarian–Soviet oil enterprise. *After I refused to do that on the grounds that I had no reason to leave MAORT they warned me that I was going to regret that very much.* After the war was over MAORT was not threatened by nationalisation as it was owned by the citizens of an allied power. The American managers actually returned and Papp remained managing director. Behind the scenes, however, the growing new power too had its eyes on the huge property. As early as the summer of 1945 Mátyás Rákosi had said to those close to him that it would solve the party's financial problems if MAORT were to come under the control of reliable communist cadres. At the time he had still to be satisfied with attaching a party agent to the firm, who reported 'illegal fascist organisation'. Papp was called in for questioning because according to the accusation he had been in the service of the Germans during the war. He soon cleared himself of that charge and was otherwise under no suspicion at all – not even when the Hungarian government appointed an agent to the firm who forced the increase of productivity and impeded the continuation of prospecting. All that Papp could do was to repeat his warning that the enforced increase of productivity could lead to a catastrophic situation. He was proud that in 1946 he was elected to the Hungarian Academy of Sciences in recognition of his geological work. He was planning to retire and devote himself exclusively to science.

In the following year the American owners invited Papp, now 61, to a farewell visit to New York, and his retirement was officially announced. He was loaded with rewards and recognitions, and a colleague advised him not to return to communist Hungary. He replied that he had no reason to fear going home. He retired, but still went into his workplace as an advisor, and was looking forward to an active old age. On 12 August 1948 he returned home from a trip in the country with his wife to be told by the housekeeper that on the previous day the political police had called on him. He went immediately to the MAORT centre in the Gresham Palace and informed the American president Paul

Ruedermann that he had a feeling that he was about to be arrested that very day. He asked Ruedermann to escort him and his wife to the American embassy. That Mr Ruedermann was unwilling to do because he did not consider it necessary. *He said that I was taking too black a view of the situation, and it was unthinkable that I, who had done so much for the discovery and opening up of oil and gas in Hungary, should be arrested,* he later wrote in his memoirs. Papp went home, and half an hour later two ÁVO officers came to his home for him. All that they said to his wife was that they were taking him away for a few hours, to make a statement. It was seven years before he was allowed back.

The planners of the show trial that soon took place themselves knew precisely that Papp and the management of MAORT were innocent, but there was no other means of acquiring the firm as it was American property. The government wanted to make it clear to the international community that it had been unable to meet its obligations under war reparations to provide oil because of sabotage. In addition, the court case provided political theatre to replace the shortage of bread, and the tale of saboteurs in the pay of the Americans offered good basic material for this. Furthermore, the nationalised firm could be packed with party cadres, who used it as a pay-office. These three reasons were quite sufficiently pressing for the life of the world's best oil engineer to be ruined without a second thought. Papp's interrogation began that same evening. His interrogating officer informed him openly that he regarded him as a marvellous catch because he was a university teacher, and academic and a managing director, and this provided a marvellous occasion for the organisation of a sabotage case of high propaganda value. In the days that followed the entire management of the firm were arrested, including the representatives of the American owners. All of them were subjected to selected physical and psychological torture. Paul Ruedermann, who refused to make a self-incriminating confession, was kept for a long time without food or drink. Finally even he broke. He put it on record that he had been sent from America to Hungary with orders to reduce oil production. The ÁVO-men made Papp translate his confession, from which he realised that sooner or later his interrogators would achieve their aims in his case too: *There was nothing else for it, if I didn't want to be physically wrecked. And so I thought that I could endure mental ruin better, especially in this case when I would receive protection from neither the Americans nor the Hungarians.* In his torment he then confessed to a total of twenty-seven items, saying everything that was asked of him. He 'confessed' that before 1945 he had helped the Nazis by increasing oil production, but after the liberation had reduced it so as to damage the people's economy. In making these confessions he became so embittered that he attempted suicide with potassium cyanide hidden in his suit, but his guards spotted it and his stomach was washed out.

In the autumn of 1948 there appeared a thoroughly edited, grey-bound publication entitled *Report of the Hungarian Ministry for the Interior on the MAORT Sabotage Case.* This piece of propaganda contained the personally signed confessions of the accused, together with the false data and witness statements. The authorities essentially needed only this publication, the trial was necessary for the closure of the case and the silencing of those concerned. Even before the verdict was pronounced the political committee of the party-state had decided on taking MAORT into state ownership. The American citizens who had been tortured were escorted to the Austrian frontier and expelled from Hungary in exchange for a ransom of 80,000 dollars each. They then publicly withdrew their confessions in Vienna. Papp offered scarcely any defence in the case, which was heard before a large audience. On the day before the hearing he had been visited in his cell by ÁVO officers and threatened that if he dared deny the earlier confessions *he would come to a very sticky end.* The radio broadcast the most exciting parts of the hearing live. Thus the indictment by the public prosecutor Márton Bodonyi was heard, according to which *Simon*

DRÁMAI SZEMBESÍTÉS
Papp Simont, a MAORT szabotáló vezérigazgatóját
Kertai György geológus-tanárral szembesítik

IV. ÉVF. 49. SZÁM   1948 DECEMBER 4   ÁRA: 2 FORINT

*1948 headline: "Saboteur in the pay of America". The communist
authorities orchestrated every moment of Simon Papp's trial.*

Papp was prepared to produce oil for Hitler, the executioners of the Hungarian people, Horthy and Szálasi, but would not give it to the tractor of
the Hungarian peasant ploughing his own land, the nationalised factories,
and the Hungarian people that had been liberated from plundering and op-

pression. With that the play came to an end. The court sentenced Papp to death *for a crime intended to overthrow the democratic order of the state*. One person present who expressed audible horror at the verdict was swiftly seized by the ÁVH and spent five years as a prisoner at Recsk.[11]

NATIONALISATIONS. After 1945 collectivisation of private enterprises without compensation began almost at once in Hungary. First to come into state ownership were the mines and the bigger heavy industrial firms, followed by firms employing more than a hundred staff, including the banks. After the communist takeover in 1949, all firms employing ten or more became state property. Nationalisations were, for the most part, carried out 'Putsch' fashion, with identical actions taking place on the same day in similar privately-owned firms (e.g. chemists', restaurants, hotels, butchers' shops), when armed police would appear on the premises together with the 'worker-directors' appointed by the state and, in the name of the working people, take over the business from the former 'exploiters'. In the cases of some foreign-owned firms compensation was paid to the owners, but they were frequently taken from their owners by means of show trials. The big agricultural estates were nationalised by declaring that they would be distributed among poor peasant families. In actual fact, however, the land belonging to the latter too was nationalised when they were forced into Soviet-style collective farms. In the first half of the 1950s theatres, cinemas and sporting venues too became state property, as, with few exceptions, did schools. Apartment houses in towns were also taken from their owners, and for years their peeling render proclaimed the magnificence of the totalitarian state ownership.

A number that were in the secret knew from the outset that Papp's death sentence would not be carried out, because his expertise was indispensable to the state. So it proved: in January 1949 his punishment was commuted 'out of clemency' to life imprisonment. In addition, he was formally excluded from the Academy, and his wife relocated. MAORT production went into crisis, the minister responsible decreed an end to wasteful expenditure and allotted funds to the resumption of experimental drilling, because it was realised that without opening up new oil-fields production could not be increased. Naturally, no one told Papp about that. He was kept in solitary confinement for years, to insulate him as much as possible from news of the outside world. He was in a number of prisons over the course of his seven-year captivity, and in each of them made to work. He was pleased to have something intelligent to do, and with his help the state kept Hungarian hydro-carbon prospecting alive. He studied the results of the various surveys in his cell, and indicated the places where he recommended drilling. Thus in 1951 he discovered the Nagylengyel[12] oil-field, which was considered the most important find in Hungary for ten years. It is typical of his captors' cynicism that they even made him design the water supply for the labour camp at Recsk.

In June 1955 he was set free 'out of clemency' after numerous foreign scientists had called for his release at an international conference in Rome. It was only then that he learnt that his wife had passed away. Because of his years in prison his entitlement to a retirement pension had lapsed, and so at the age of seventy he had to start work again. He found a post as junior geologist with the National Oil and Gas Industry Trust, with great loss of professional status. In 1962 he was able to retire a second time. One of the world's great geologists, he died at the age of eighty-five after struggling for years for rehabilitation: justice was never done.

After a while ÁVO Lieutenant Ferenc Torda came to see me again and read what I had written. It failed to satisfy him. He declared that every word that I had written was a lie, and so he would teach me to write the truth about everyone. But I had written the absolute truth about everyone. He made the vile threat of making me eat the paper bit by bit. He succeeded less than fully. (...) Then I was taken into the reception cell. There my spectacles were taken away. Then I was taken down into the cellar, two storeys underground. I was pushed into a corner, where there was a plank bed and wooden pillow. No straw mattress or blanket. In the morning I was turned out into the corridor, where there were iron troughs in which one could wash. There were no soap, no towel. (...) I was kept there until 24 November.

Simon Papp,
My Life
Zalaegerszeg, 1996

"I will accept no conditions".
Áron Márton with his followers in the 1970s.

Áron Márton

The Hungarian bishop knew that he would be risking his life, and so before writing to the Prime Minister of Romania about the situation of the Magyar minority and the separation of Church and state he secretly appointed trustees to deputise for him at the head of the Catholic Church in Transylvania while he was away. Áron Márton, then aged fifty-three, received no answer to his letters, only a request personally to call on the head of government. He set out from the episcopal seat at Gyulafehérvár (today Alba Iulia, Romania) on 2 June 1949. As at other times, he took a taxi for himself and a colleague to travel to the near-by station and from there by train to Bucharest. That day the taxi company did not send the usual driver. Despite the suspicious circumstance Bishop Áron and Benjamin Ferencz, head of his office, got into the taxi. On the way to the station the car slowed down, and the new driver informed them that something had gone wrong with the engine. An all-terrain vehicle stopped next to them and the Romanians in it readily offered to take them to the station. As the bishop and his companion took their seats beside them the men produced police identity cards and announced that their passengers were under arrest. To the bishop's questions they replied that only they had the right to ask questions, and then they blindfolded the prisoners. Márton was charged with plotting and treason, and spent a total of six years in Romania's harshest prisons followed by a further ten under house arrest. At first they wanted to question him, later only to come to terms with him. The Romanian communist authorities succeeded in this no more than had the earlier Hungarian and Romanian right-wing régimes. In prison and at liberty alike, Márton remained the spiritual leader of the Magyars of Transylvania, and all his life was the spokesman for the rights of the minority and religious freedom.

He was born in 1896 into a family of farm-workers at Csíkszentdomokos (today Sândominic, Romania) in the purely Magyar Székelyföld, and even as a schoolboy made up his mind to go into the Church. While still in his final year at grammar school he lived in the seminary, and so could have avoided military service, but he joined up three days after his matriculation examination. He served through the First World War, being wounded three times, and was discharged in the rank of lieutenant. The horrors of war filled him with doubts, and it was perhaps for that reason that he did not return to the seminary. First he worked as a day-labourer, later in a forestry office. He was courting a girl named Erzsi, and his family were planning the wedding when again he decided differently about his life: he announced that he was going to become a priest after all. By then the priesthood was not the comfortable career that it had been five years earlier: it meant the representation of a diminished Church and a diminished ethnicity.

Márton was ordained in 1924, and as a young priest made long journeys on foot and alone in the Székelyföld Alps for the sake of the sick or dying. In addition to his pastoral work he was also entrusted with religious education, and it turned out that he was not only a brilliant preacher but also a sensitive teacher. At first he worked as a teacher in a grammar school and a teacher-training college, and then was summoned to the biggest town in Transylvania, the multiracial Kolozsvár (today Cluj-Napoca, Romania), as university chaplain. His voice had a novel effect compared to those of the aloof, rigid priests, and the young people were soon flocking to his sermons. He saw the key to the future of the Magyars of Transylvania in education, and so established a teachers' periodical. He could see much more clearly the danger lurking for Europe, as was borne out by his 1934 article titled *Hitler is not to be trusted*. Not long afterwards he was put in charge of the church of St Michael in the main square of Kolozsvár, and from then on crowds came to hear him preach.

Even so, many people were surprised when in 1938 the pope appointed Márton, at the age of forty-two, as his apostolic delegate to the dioceses of Transylvania and bishop of Gyulafehérvár. By the choice of Áron Márton – a man of peasant origins, who could speak the language of the common people but was also at home in journalism – he broke with the tradition that for the most part bishops of aristocratic birth should be at the head of the Catholic Church in Transylvania. The youthful primate stood at the same time for modernity and a return to the social traditions of the Church. From then on he signed himself in archaic form, Bishop Áron, and in the very first sermon after his consecration he invoked universal human values and preached against war – that at a time when the political leaders of the West were seeking compromise with Hitler.

In the summer of 1940 came the Second Vienna Award, which re-drew the frontiers of Central Europe under pressure from Nazi Germany and fascist Italy. Under the terms of that, Northern Transylvania was re-annexed to Hungary, while Southern Transylvania, together with the episcopal seat, remained in Romania. Márton decided that he would not abandon his seat but would accept the fate of his faithful people, now in the minority. He directed from beyond the frontier the dioceses that had fallen under Hungarian jurisdiction, but frequently protested to the government in Bucharest against the loss of rights suffered by the Magyar minority. However, he did not only act in the interests of the Magyars: when the Romanian authorities, currying favour with Hitler, wanted to hand over the German Catholic schools in Transylvania to a Nazi youth organisation, the Volksgruppe,

The youthful preacher's voice had a novel ring.

he prevented the order being carried out. Trouble soon flared up with the authorities on the other side of the border too. He was the first of the Hungarian Church leaders to speak out decisively against the persecution of the Jews. On 18 May 1944, scarcely three days after the establishment of the ghettoes but before the start of deportations, Márton inducted seminarists in Kolozsvár. In his sermon he overtly and roundly condemned the policy of the

Hungarian government. As a Kolozsvár student who was present recalls, his voice did not ring out harshly, but rather he spoke with 'obstinate sweetness': the essence of the spirit of the true Catholic was identity with the persecuted, irrespective of their religion. He encouraged the seminarists to disregard the immoral laws. *Imprisonment in defence of justice is not shame but glory,* were the concluding words of his sermon, which those present listened to with bowed heads. No church leader in Hungary had yet said anything of the sort. It was not until two months later that Cardinal Jusztinián Serédi of Esztergom promulgated an ambiguous letter – by which time the Jews in the provinces were already being deported.

THE CHURCHES AND THE PERSECUTION OF THE JEWS. The Christian Churches played a large part in the rise of anti-Semitism in Hungary between the world wars. Anti-Semitic articles appeared frequently in Christian newspapers, and the representatives of the Churches in the Upper House of Parliament voted in favour of the first two Jewish laws. They did not, however, consent to the third (racial) Jewish law and endeavoured to exempt Jews that had been baptised from the restrictions. Jusztinián Serédi, head of the Hungarian Catholic Church, frequently intervened on behalf of Jews that had converted, but for tactical reasons was not prepared to take open steps. In the summer of 1944 he issued a pastoral letter in which – although it also contained anti-Semitic expressions – he spoke against the deportations, but in the end it was not even read out in churches. László Ravasz, the leader of the biggest Protestant community, the Calvinist Church, acted similarly. A number of Church leaders and clergy, however, did act more decisively in the interests of the disenfranchised Jews despite the passivity of their Churches. After the Arrow-Cross came to power institutional life-saving by the Churches increased considerably. The Catholic Holy Cross Association and the Protestant Good Shepherd Commission no longer protected only the interests of Jews that had been baptised, and many that were persecuted found refuge in religious houses, Church schools and orphanages.

No text of the sermon is extant – it was delivered without notes – but a Sister of Social Service who was present made notes and sent them to Margit Slachta's convent in Budapest, where they were reproduced and circulated in secret. The caution was justified, because next day the parish priest of the church where the sermon took place was summoned to the Kolozsvár police headquarters and instructed to inform Márton that he was lucky that he was a foreign citizen, otherwise he would be prosecuted. The bishop was in no way put out, and in reply sent official letters to the Chief of Police, the *főispán*[13] of the county, the Minister for the Interior and the Prime Minister in which he called on them to prevent the heinous crimes that were in the making. In it no trace remained of softly-spoken sweetness. To the Minister for the Interior Andor Jaross, for example, he wrote: *In the measures that you are taking you fail to come up to the level not only of Christianity but of humanity. I ask you with respect, but in the full meaning of the word, immediately to retract your latest measures, or if you find that impossible to resign at once from your office.* The response was not long delayed: the leader of the Catholics in Transylvania, as a Romanian citizen, was expelled from the territory of the Kingdom of Hungary. In the months that followed Márton took part in rescue operations from outside Hungary, sending instructions from Gyulafehérvár for monasteries, nunneries and schools to give refuge to the persecuted.

Even after the exodus of Magyars Márton did not leave Transylvania, and believed seriously that the affairs of his native country could be resolved justly. During the Paris Conference after the world war he called for the right of self-determination for the Transylvanian Magyars, so that they might decide for themselves to which country they wished to belong. He was a believer in European organisation, not violent revision, and with that in view urged a more just demarcation of the frontier. He made clear his position in a letter to Petru Groza, Prime Minister of Romania, with whom he later clashed sharply over the nationalisation of Church schools.

Márton never made a secret of his opinion, but at the same time was not naive: in his circular letter he tried to prepare his clergy for the persecutions that could be anticipated. He detailed in particular what was to be done if a bishop were arrested or how marriage could be solemnised in church without a priest. He appointed secret delegates and deputies who would be able to ensure that the Church organisation was still capable of functioning. When the state, in cahoots with the Romanian Orthodox Church, essentially banned the Greek Catholic denomination (which acknowledges the authority of the Roman Catholic pope) he wrote a circular letter to the Roman Catholic bishops: *The terrible events that have befallen our Greek Catholic brethren leave no room for doubt that days of steadfastness even in the face of martyrdom will follow for us too.* He did not have to wait long. When in the summer of 1949 he was away in the Székelyföld holding confirmation services a series of scandalous articles about him appeared in the press, and on occasion the authorities even marched a military band past the church during his sermon. When it was rumoured that he was to be arrested during the Palm Sunday pilgrimage at Csíksomlyó (today Șumuleu Ciuc, Romania) his followers put him on a horse and surrounded him as a living cordon so that he could not be reached. He preached in calm tones about religious freedom and freedom of conscience to a hundred and fifty thousand people.

The authorities knew that if they were to kidnap Márton from a mass or from the bishop's palace they would risk a public disturbance. They therefore decided to arrest him by stealth as he was on the way to see the Prime Minister. After his disappearance in mid-journey no official statement concerning his whereabouts was made for two years. The pope appointed him titular archbishop, but he did not hear of it at the time: he was imprisoned in the cellar of the Ministry for the Interior in Bucharest. It was two years later, in 1951, that the accusations against him were made known: according to the lawyers Márton had intended, with the aid of priests, aristocrats, bankers, renegade communists, Hungarian nationalists and American imperialists, to overthrow the socialist régime in Romania and to annex Transylvania to Hungary. The 'evidence' was the memorandum that he had sent to the Paris peace negotiations in 1946. The bishop did not even know some of those that were accused with him, and he held views that definitely conflicted with those of others. He said as much in the hearing of the show trial, in which he denied the charge of conspiracy while acknowledging the memorandum urging the peaceful drawing up of frontiers, of the content of which he had spoken openly earlier. He asked the court to take into consideration that he was the initiator and so the responsibility too was his. *I would like there to be peace at last between the two peoples, and if that means prison I will accept it,* he said in his final address to the court. Under torture and blackmail, the other accused admitted conspiracy. One was kept alive during the hearing by injections so that he could confess, but one former communist lost his mind under interrogation, praised Stalin in court and accused the Romanian government of Nazism.

THE POST-1943 MAGYAR MINORITY IN TRANSYLVANIA. During the Second World War approximately 100,000 Magyars fled from Romanian-controlled Southern Transylvania, while the Hungarian authorities deported 125,000 Hungarian Jews from Northern Transylvania. By the time that the whole of Transylvania became part of Romania again after 1945 there were only 1.5 million Magyars in the country, but even so this was considered the largest ethnic minority in Europe. As most of the former political leaders of the Magyar community had left the country the Catholic and Protestant Churches played a greater part in the protection of the interests of the Magyar minority. The measures taken against the Churches by the communist authorities (e.g. the nationalisation of schools, the persecution of clergy) were often also actions taken against the Magyar minority. In 1952 the Székelyföld, where most of the inhabitants were Magyars, was given limited self-determination under the name of Magyar Autonomous Territory, but at the same time Magyars living outside the autonomous territory were refused the right to the use of the Hungarian language in education and public administration. A few years later the Romanian state also began to limit the sphere of rights of the autonomous territory and ran down the Magyar schools and universities. Eventually in 1967 Nicolae Ceauşescu formally ended the autonomous territory and declared that *the nationalities question has been definitively solved*. A significant part of the destruction of villages that took place in the 1980s affected settlements with Magyar majorities.

On 6 August 1951 the Bucharest military court sentenced Márton to ten years imprisonment for conspiracy and to life imprisonment with hard labour for treason. One of those sentenced with him died of starvation, others were killed by the hard labour, but Márton survived. After the daily sixteen or seventeen hours of work he held prayers for his fellow prisoners to keep their spirits up. When he was transferred to a prison near the Soviet border, where a death camp also operated, he reckoned that he was to be killed like the three Greek Catholic bishops who had been imprisoned with him. It was only many years later that he was told why his life had been spared. Petru Groza, the Prime Minister, had personally visited the prison on several occasions: on the first, he had tried to persuade Márton to break with Rome and join in the creation of a Romanian National Church; later he had asked him to plead for clemency. Márton would do neither. After the death of Stalin the wrongfully imprisoned archbishop became more and more embarrassing to the authorities, and so in 1955 the Romanian National Assembly revoked his sentence. He was kept for a month on a cure to put on weight, so that the traces of his sufferings should vanish, and then allowed home.

The government was anticipating that as he resumed direction of the diocese he would fall out with the collaborators (the so-called 'peace-priests') and the conflict would end in a rift in the Church. After returning home, however, Márton called together those in the Church that were collaborating with the communists, pointed out to them of the error of their ways, urged them to repent, and declared forgiveness for those that regretted their actions. It was thanks to his moral standing and wisdom that the Catholic Church collaborated much less with the authorities in Transylvania than it did in Hungary. After that, naturally, he was openly considered an enemy, and the Securitate (the notorious Romanian secret police) watched him constantly, even placing listening devices in his study. That was unnecessary: he spoke his mind openly, just as he did at masses. According to a Ministry of the Interior memorandum of 1957 he was *far from changing his ways,* and so his re-arrest was justified. In the end a gentler retaliation was put into effect – house arrest. For ten years Márton was not allowed to leave the area of the bishop's palace and the cathedral. He was able to receive visitors during his palace-captivity, but they were watched and often harassed. As he was himself – several of his dogs were poisoned, and on one occasion some unknown person fired at him as he walked in the palace garden. The story of his scrutiny and state harassment has to this day not been made fully known, which is not surprising: in its several decades of history the Securitate compiled the most extensive material on him – 77,000 pages in all. He himself wrote about this to the principal of the office of ecclesiastical affairs: *I have often felt the power of your authority, and if you want to make me feel it in future too I shall endure it.*

When in 1967 the Romanian Deputy Prime Minister informed him that the ban on his leaving his palace was lifted, he merely enquired: *What are the conditions? Because I shall not accept any.* As it had been realised that he could not be broken he was released without any conditions. He served his Church and the Transylvanian Magyar community for a further thirteen years. When he went to Rome for the first time he was received as a living martyr, and at the ceremonial reception in the Vatican the pope did not allow Márton to make obeisance to him but hurried forward and embraced him. Shortly after that he was diagnosed with prostate cancer. He offered his resignation four times on the grounds of health but the Holy See would not accept it. At the end of his life he had difficulty in walking and his hands trembled, but he was up at dawn every day to celebrate mass. Finally, in the spring of 1980 Pope John Paul II accepted his resignation; he lived a further six months, dying on 29 September 1980 as the bells pealed for St Michael's Day. Ten years later his diocese initiated his sanctification; as miracles have to be proven, decision on this has not yet been reached. Humanity and unquestionable honour do not count as miracles: they are much more.

Yesterday I was informed that the Jews and Christians rounded up in recent days under the heading of Jews are to be transported. One cannot hear without horror and profound shock what is said concerning the treatment and impending fate of such transports. My duties call me back to my place of work, Romania, but I consider it my duty as a human being, a Christian and a Magyar to beg the agents of the authorities concerned, with feeling and in the name of God, to prevent the inhumanity, or if they are incapable of so doing to take no part in an act the purpose of which is the destruction of thousands of people. In these fateful days every responsible person must feel that the fate of our nation and with it the fate of us all is in the hand of God, and we should therefore not call down upon ourselves the vengeance of God by the commission of, or the collaboration in, sins that the catechism lists among the heinous, and retribution on earth for which will not, as experience shows, fail to come.

Áron Márton,
letter to the Royal Hungarian Ministry,
the Office of the Főispán of Kolozs County
and the Chief of Police, Kolozsvár
22 May 1944

*György Cziffra went from utmost deprivation
to the world's greatest concert-halls.*

György Cziffra

It was still dark in the small hours in the Budapest slum when his mother woke the small boy. She dressed him in the sailor suit and patent leather shoes that she had bought with the family's last money, and they set off hungry, with no breakfast. From the outer suburbs of Pest it took them two hours on foot and by tram to reach the Castle District of Buda, where they were invited to audition with Ernő Dohnányi, director of the Music Academy. The meeting had been arranged by a door-to-door salesman who had heard the eight-year-old Gypsy boy, György Cziffra, play the piano. He was a delicate little boy, looked small for his age. He seldom even got out of bed, and this was the longest journey in his life. At the address that they had been given a concierge stopped them. It turned out at once that there was no audition, they were not expected. *The director's sick and tired of child prodigies,* said the concierge. At that moment the director's car turned into the street and stopped with a loud bang: it had had a puncture. Dohnányi got out of the car and spoke to the arrivals. The mother explained that someone had made fools of them, took her son's hand and moved away. Nevertheless, while the wheel was being changed the director invited them in for a quick audition.

The small boy sat down at the piano and began to play in the style that he had developed himself while he was ill. Half an hour later Dohnányi called someone on the telephone and said simply *This isn't a pearl, it's the Kohinoor diamond itself.* Young Cziffra had that puncture to thank for being accepted at the Music Academy at the age of eight. Later he had to start again three times. First, he all but died of starvation on the Russian front, then he was made to break stones in a labour camp so that he should never again be able to play the piano, and then as a bar pianist in smoky dives, where he became addicted to alcohol. All three times he managed to get back on his feet. He became one of the most significant pianists of his time, known world-wide – and never forgot where he came from.

THE GYPSIES IN HUNGARY. *The Roma or Gypsies – traditionally 'cigány' in Hungarian – have lived in Hungary since the Middle Ages; they migrated from the Balkans into Transylvania, and from there into the middle of the country. The Lovari-speaking Romungós arrived in great numbers in the fifteenth century, and the Bea tribe, speaking an archaic Romanian dialect, settled in the nineteenth century. Most of them became itinerant artisans (basket-makers, metal-workers, brick-makers) and lived apart from the rest of society. Under the Habsburgs a number of attempts were made to settle the semi-nomad Gypsies, more than once forcibly and by taking their children from them. In the nineteenth century Hungarian-speaking Gypsy musicians integrated most successfully, and the Hungarian-style art-music that they played was erroneously regarded by many as Magyar folk-music, and later (equally erroneously) as authentic Gypsy folklore. The spread of mass-produced articles rendered the traditional Gypsy handiwork redundant and from the early twentieth century itinerant work was restricted by law, making most of the Gypsies unemployed and leading to societal conflict. Institutionalised persecution of the Gypsies on a racial basis came later than that of the Jews, only after the Arrow-Cross took power, and some 5,000 fell victim to the period known as the porrojmos. Nowadays it is estimated that there are some 6–800,000 Gypsies in Hungary, constituting the largest ethnic minority in the country.*

He came from a successful family of Gypsy musicians. His father was a talented cimbalist, who had started in Budapest cafés and travelled with his band as far as Paris. There he had lived in a small flat with his wife and two small daughters until the outbreak of the First World War, when, as a citizen of a hostile country of military age he was interned in a prisoner of war camp; his wife and children were expelled from France, and were permitted to take a mere fifteen kilos of luggage on the train. Like others similarly expelled because of the war they found temporary accommodation in the slum quarter of Angyalföld, a working-class suburb of Pest, which became known as Tripolis. They were able to take shelter in wooden houses on stilts: each family had a room with no cooking facilities, with straw paliasses on the floor. After they had spent a long time there the father too was released and joined them. He tried to support his family, but could only obtain occasional work on the Danube wharves. What his wife earned as a charwoman was their only income, and so he slipped deeper and deeper into depression. A third girl was soon born, but died as an infant from malnutrition. Their son followed not longer after, in 1921. Little György hovered between life and death all the time as a child, as had his sister. He spent longer lying on the paliasses than he was able to be out of doors. No one knew what was wrong with him as there was no money for a doctor. Sometimes there was no food to put on the table. *At such times we went to bed at sunset,* he recalled later, *and said that anyone that was sleeping was also eating.* A charitable organisation sent one of his sisters to Holland to gain strength. She never came back: her hosts initiated the procedure for adoption and her parents gave their consent: let at least one of their children be rescued from poverty. The other sister, Jolán, managed eventually to find work washing up in a works kitchen, and brought home left-over food to the family. It was soon discovered that she also spoke French, and so was able to get office work with better money. One day she came home with a strange present: she had hired a piano to revive her piano-playing and cheer her father up.

The instrument so captivated little György as he lay sick that he imitated his sister's scale practice with his fingers. Eventually he stirred himself and, when she was out, sat down at the piano. A few days later he was playing tunes, and then his father began to teach him. He could not read music, but at the age of five he could do as much as a good adult amateur. He could play any tune that was sung to him, and improvise variations on it. Not only the neighbours heard him play, but so did circus people that came to the slum area, and they immediately said to his mother: *It would be a sin, madam, to deprive the audience of the chance to enjoy the little boy's exceptional musical ability.* Young György performed in the evenings between the flea circus and the strong man, and some days earned as much as a workman did in a month. A fortnight later, however, he was sick with overwork, and as he lay ill in bed the circus moved on. But after that the local people regarded him as a child prodigy, and he often entertained them through the open door. That was how he came to the attention of the travelling clothes salesman who sent him and his mother to see Ernő Dohnányi.

The eight-year-old found the daily six or seven hours of hard practice in the Music Academy a terrible strain, but he was persistent and diligent. At the age of thirteen he was giving successful concerts in Hungary and abroad. Because of his reputation as a child prodigy and because of his origins, however, the 'serious' artistic world of the concert halls did not accept him, and he was regarded as a sensation that would pass. From his early teens he also played in hotels and restaurants in order to support his family, as a result of which he had less and less time to study. *I got to know night musicians. It seems that they liked me, because it was with their assistance that I found my way into the world of dance music.* Gradually he dropped out of the Academy and sank into the world of nightclubs. Love saved him from wasting his ability: he was twenty when, in the famous Arizona music-hall in Budapest, he met Zulejka, a danseuse of the same age and of Egyptian background. After a couple of days acquaintance the dark-skinned foreign girl and the good-looking Gypsy pianist married – without their parents' consent. The witnesses to the marriage were people they asked in the street, and the wedding breakfast consisted of half a pound of salami eaten on a park bench. A year after they met their son, another György, was born. The boy did not see his father for three years: when he came into the world György was already fighting for his life on the Russian front.

It meant nothing to the officer in charge of his training that his new recruit was a pianist. *Your days are numbered, because you're going to die, you stupid animal!* he shouted, and ordered Cziffra to volunteer for the front. He was posted to the cavalry, and might soon have been sent, horse and all, against the Russian tanks if he had not been needed at a celebration in the German-Hungarian camp as a pianist. His playing so impressed one of the Wehrmacht generals that he offered to take him with him to Berlin, where he could make a career. Cziffra did not want to find himself on the battlefield, but in a few minutes he also considered what kind of life awaited him in Nazi Germany as a Gypsy with an Egyptian wife, and he decided, if the chance arose, to desert from the army. He stole a railway engine, and jumped from it in territory held by Ukrainian partisans. In no time he was awaiting his fate as their prisoner. He was kept for weeks in total darkness in a mine, where all that he was given to eat was watery soup every other day. He was dying from starvation when Russian soldiers found him. He was re-enlisted, and after brief training joined a force of Hungarian volunteers fighting with the Russians. He had not played for three years when the opportunity came to perform at a camp celebration, this time a Russian-Hungarian one. He looked at his frost-damaged hands and replied: *Not only would I be* incapable *of becoming a pianist to order, because that's what you're asking, but even the sight of a piano keyboard would disturb and trouble me.*

When he was discharged in 1946 he could not have thought that he would be engaged as a concert pianist anywhere. *I bent my back and sank back into the world of the night,* he wrote in his autobiography. On one occasion he had to play in total darkness in a secret brothel, and later he played in almost all the famous nightclubs in Budapest. The manager of an American jazz band on tour in Budapest

He never forgot his roots. Cziffra in France in 1961.

offered him a contract overseas, but he turned it down. *I had learnt the ins and outs of this profession, that is, I knew how to entertain the guests in nightclubs. Piano, cognac, humour.* At that time Cziffra was addicted to alcohol, and would play Chopin or dance music as required for a cognac, and on the way home on the early-morning suburban railway would gaze dismally at posters in the stations advertising concerts. A lot of people tried to rescue him. The actress Mária Mezey, for example, wanted him as her permanent accompanist, but after a while he was playing in bars again. His virtuoso extemporisations were legendary, and famous performers went to hear him to work out his secret. When a Russian pianist asked him why, with that talent, he did not play in concert halls abroad he made up his mind to shake off his way of life, which was leading to a certain breakdown, and to leave Hungary.

Early in 1950 he meant to cross the border together with his wife and seven-year-old son. They were caught, detained and beaten up. Not only were they prevented from crossing the frontier, they were also accused of spying. In the course of their interrogation one of the officers told Cziffra that he had been the travelling salesman who had sent him to Dohnányi on that occasion. Now, however, he had *brought disgrace on the country,* and was going to suffer for it. Cziffra was given three years, his wife two, and the little boy barely survived the beating. The authorities meant to teach the musician a sharp lesson. He had to break stones for eighteen months in a punishment labour camp so that his hands should be permanently useless for playing the piano. He was released in 1953 at the age of thirty-two with fingers that could hardly move and swollen wrists. Anyone else would not have tried to sit at a piano, but he decided not to give up. The joints in his hands were so damaged that for months he wore wristbands to practise. When he began playing in Budapest nightclubs again the rumour went round in musical circles that the secret of his virtuoso technique was simply the wristbands. Several other pianists acquired the same, but they brought them no luck! On one occasion György Ferenczi, a teacher of piano at the Music Academy, came into the bar, immediately recognised the wasted ability, and made Cziffra an offer. He would allow him three months in which to prepare, and after that he promised to organise a concert for him. Cziffra accepted: *I decided to give up the practice of 'fraudulent piano-playing'.* He returned to proper serious music after an interval of fifteen years. Crowds queued for tickets at his concerts, and the improvisations that ended his programmes received veritable ovations. When at one concert he played Liszt's *Rákóczi March* ten times in different variations the police eventually had to be called to clear the hall. On 22 October 1956 he performed Bartók's second piano concerto, which was considered unplayable. Many believe that the fiery performance was a significant preliminary to the revolutionary events of the following day.

HUNGARIAN COMPOSERS. Beyond question, Hungarian influence in the world at large has been greater in music than in the other arts. The first musical world star, Ferenc (Franz) Liszt, never lived in Hungary but was proud of his Hungarian roots, and frequently performed there. In the late nineteenth and early twentieth centuries Budapest was second only to Vienna as the capital of operetta, a genre sealed with the names of Imre (Emmerich) Kálmán and Ferenc (Franz) Lehár. It was at this time that the two defining composers of the twentieth century, Béla Bartók and Zoltán Kodály, were beginning their careers; both of them made the rediscovery of authentic Magyar folk-music fundamental to their work. Both of them studied at the Music Academy in Budapest, where Ernő (Ernst von) Dohnányi was their contemporary. The convoluted path of Hungarian history is shown by the fact that both Bartók and Dohnányi died in New York; the former emigrated because he wanted nothing to do with official Hungary as it became allied to the Nazis, while the latter was − baselessly − accused of war crimes after 1945. During the twentieth century numerous other great Hungarian musicians have left Hungary for fame abroad, such as György Solti (who was knighted in the United Kingdom) and György Ligeti.

When the frontier was briefly open during the revolution Cziffra would take no more chances and left Hungary with his family on a motorcycle combination. Ten days later he gave a hugely successful concert in Vienna. He was pleased to discover that in the West people knew precisely who he was, as his recordings had been published without his knowledge. He received invitations to the world's greatest concert halls and was spoken of as one of the most significant of pianists. He settled in Paris, where Charles de Gaulle himself conferred French citizenship on him. *Compared with what had gone before,* he wrote, *my life in my second homeland, France, has been virtually pure holy water,* but he never forgot how much he had had to struggle for it. He restored a ruinous chapel and made it into a concert hall in honour of Ferenc Liszt. It became the centre of the Cziffra Foundation that he established, which has helped hundreds of young musicians and other artists. He first re-visited Hungary in 1973, and the public received his concerts with thunderous applause. He was awarded many foreign distinctions and the greatest that Hungary can offer, but he was proudest of all of being elected President of the 100 Member Gypsy Orchestra of Hungary. The Gypsy cimbalist's son who was always capable of starting again died in Paris at the age of seventy-two.

Within the framework of the autumn musical festivities that annually commemorate Béla Bartók in Hungary the organisers had engaged a Chinese pianist to play Bartók's famous second piano concerto, which was at the time reckoned unplayable. My distinguished colleague had the reputation of having learnt all the thoughts of Mao in ten days and actually understanding them. He had six months to learn the work. He hesitated for six weeks before withdrawing. Thus I inherited that concerto, that astounding piece of work, which even today is one of the most complex items of our time for the piano. (…) So I set about it, gave it all I'd got, worked like a madman. But I also knew that if I managed to learn that harder than hard composition in the time available the ordeal would confer upon me an international career. The great day arrived, the concerto was a triumph pregnant with future. That music, with its almost crazy complexity, which is nevertheless crystal clarity itself, inspired me to excel myself, and the applause burst forth from the audience like red-hot lava. It was 22 October. Next day the frontier was opened, tens of thousands were roaring through cracks that were made in the frontiers. We didn't have much time to make our minds up. I voted to emigrate. Scarcely ten days after we left I gave my first concert in the capital of Austria.

György Cziffra,
Guns and flowers
1983

László Papp in 1946.
"I have never known a better boxer, nor yet a greater sportsman."
(Jean-Paul Belmondo)

László Papp

In October 1945 the nineteen-year-old railwayman had gone
with his friends to watch a boxing match. A few months previously he too had gone boxing at the Budapest Railwaymen's
Club, had actually fought a bout, but his main interest was in
football. He had not long returned from being a prisoner of war,
he was a poor man and could not find regular work – and like
many young toughs in Angyalföld he too saw in sport the chance
to advance themselves. Gyula Bicsák, the favourite of the Csepel fans, was waiting in vain for his opponent from the Railwaymen's Club, who had not turned up. The crowd, consisting mostly of working men, was becoming more and more restless, and
cat-calling started. In his despair the trainer began to plead with
the novice sitting in the audience – László Papp, nicknamed Gör-
be – to take on Bicsák. In that situation even an honourable defeat would be to his credit, he argued. After a little persuasion the
laconic young man shrugged, went and changed, and the match
began. After the second round the Csepel champion had to be assisted, reeling, from the ring. Next day *Népsport* (People's Sport)
reported the event under the headline *Who is this Papp?* The audience stamped their feet, hats flew in the air. Papp, 19, had won a
great victory. Happy and disappointed alike rushed to him, embraced and kissed him. Four days later Laci was fighting against
the Austrians in the senior team, and won by a first-round knock-

out. From being a complete unknown, he had become a star in minutes. Ordinary people saw in him a role-model, living proof that a working man could come to the top. The authorities too portrayed him as an ideal proletarian. And for that reason they, by a cynical political decision, took from one of the most successful boxers of all time the chance of a lifetime: that of becoming Hungary's first professional world champion boxer.

László Papp was born in 1926; his mother was a poor Székely girl who had escaped from Transylvania to Budapest after Trianon, and his father an industrious working man of Gypsy ancestry, who was keen to get on. They settled in Angyalföld. She undertook the duties of concierge in the run-down apartment block, and so augmented what he earned as a driver. *We were poor, but we never starved,* László remembered of his childhood. His father, however, had experienced want, and did his utmost for his son to do better than himself. He could see three ways ahead: his son might be a successful musician, a footballer, or perhaps a boxer. He had László taught the violin, for which he showed some ability, but the boy was more interested in football and kicked a battered ball around on waste ground with his friends whenever he could. Boxing was soon excluded from the list of possibilities: at the age of ten László unfortunately fell out of a tree, breaking a wrist. *Now you'll never make a boxer,* his father told him in the hospital. All the same, he did not give up fighting. When a boy, six years his senior, slapped his face at school he challenged him to a fight after lessons, and gave him such a thrashing that he never again bothered the younger ones. But he did not only take part in chivalrous encounters: along with street children in the neighbourhood he liked to cheek passers-by, and one in particular prophesied that he would end up in prison. Many of his friends did in fact end up there, but he was lucky.

He was eleven when his father died of pneumonia, and so his promising musical career too ended. *If father hadn't left us here so early perhaps my way would have led to the conservatoire. I could already play quite well when after his death mother made me promise not to take it out of the cupboard for three years.* His mother opened a tiny general store in the concierge's flat to keep her two children. László used to fetch vegetables from the market first thing in the morning, a little later brought in milk and fresh bread, then went to school and to football training in the afternoon. The family's material situation did not permit him to stay at school. At the age of fifteen he became an apprentice with Magyar Optikai Művek (Hungarian Optical Works) and played in the firm's football team. He dabbled at boxing again, but soon became uninterested. In those days people thought differently. The saying was: *On the first day he has to be beaten up. If he comes back, he'll be a good boxer. If not, he'll be none the worse for it. I got three huge slaps. My kisser was as ragged as a peasant's* gatya. (…) *I had no intention of going back. I'd still got football.*

Then it happened that he and a few friends were picked up on the riverside by the police on suspicion of stealing rabbits. They beat him up and demanded that he should confess what he had done. Afterwards the actual thief was caught and he was released without an apology. *I couldn't see why they slapped me about first and then told me what the problem was.* The war was at its height, so at the age of seventeen he and his fellow apprentices were called up. They did some shooting practice and then were put on the train and sent to Germany. He could not even let his mother know. The train was hit by a bomb and he escaped injury while many of his companions were killed. Eventually he deserted and was captured by the Americans. On returning home he found occasional work on the railway, and that was how he joined the boxing club of the Budapest Railwaymen's Sporting Association. When he went home the first evening with a bruise under his eye his mother forbade him to do any more fighting. *Son, if you need a slap in the face just let me know and I'll give you one every evening before bedtime.* He did not keep his word, and a few months later, after defeating Bicsák, found himself in the front rank. On the night that made his name he tried to tip-toe into the flat. *Mother was waiting for me and gave*

*me a good one with the rolling-pin for staying out late. At first I didn't dare
tell her I'd become a boxer.*

After the match with Bicsák Papp became a leading boxer at
once and never had to fight in youth competitions. He owed his
great popularity not only to the fact that of more than two hundred amateur bouts he lost only nine, but also to his immediate
style. He spoke the slang of the suburbs of Budapest, strongly fla-
voured with Gypsy, Swabian and Yiddish terms, and was never
conceited. At the start of his career he acquired the two most important allies in his life: his wife and his trainer. He married Zsó-
ka – who worked in a sweet-shop – only after a long courtship,
as his mother had initially opposed the marriage. She was soon
handling his extensive correspondence from fans, and on occasion
it was she that even replied to love-letters that he received. Papp
met his chosen trainer in 1946 – Zsigmond Adler, aged forty-five,
the former Hungarian heavyweight champion. As a trainer Adler
had had his first successes with Olympic competitors in the 1930s,
but after that had been cut out of sporting life because of his Jewish background. After the war he went back into the gymnasium,
where he noticed Papp; he had by then scored his first successes,
but was still technically untutored. In the years that followed they
won together results that brought the greatest fame to Hungarian
boxing. In all that time Papp addressed his master respectfully as
Uncle Zsiga, while Adler called his pupil Laci. It did not take long
for Papp to bring fame to another country or to achieve success
in another branch of sport. In 1946, together with a friend of his,
he left Hungary for Czechoslovakia in the hope of more rapid advancement. He found a team and in Hungary his licence was suspended, but eventually he came back home at his mother's request.
In 1947 he thought seriously about giving up boxing for football,
but in the end was persuaded to continue. From then on, his boxing career was more and more successful. The list of his victories
would fill many pages – to sum up, it will suffice to say that he
was one of the three boxers in the world that won three succes-

sive Olympic gold medals: in 1948 at middleweight, and in 1952 and 1956 at light middleweight. It is not surprising that politics too tried to make use of him for its own purposes, but these attempts made no impression on him. In one pre-Olympic training camp Mátyás Rákosi himself, the Secretary General of the party, called on him with an escort of journalists. Papp slapped the startled politician on the back and said, with his impish smile, *That's a nice hat you've got, you know, where'd you get it?* The propaganda report was never written. Every time that he won thousands celebrated, and after the London Olympics, for example, he was carried shoulder-high from the station.

HUNGARIAN SPORT IN THE YEARS OF COMMUNISM. It is a curious paradox that Hungarian sport went through a veritable golden age in the years of the darkest dictatorship, the 1950s. The communist state was well aware of the propaganda value of sport, and supported to the full young people for whom sport represented the only opportunity of advancement. The 1952 Helsinki Olympics were the most successful ever for Hungary; with sixteen gold medals, ten silver and sixteen bronze the Hungarian team was behind only the USA and USSR in the medals table. At the same time, in fact, Hungarian football too achieved its best ever results. In addition to the gold medal at Helsinki and the European Cup in 1953, the so-called Golden Team achieved its greatest success in a friendly match, beating England 6:3 at Wembley. The captain of the team, Ferenc Puskás, who attained international fame as 'goal king' of Real Madrid after he emigrated, has even since then been reckoned one of the Hungarians best known abroad. His story too typifies the way in which the communist leadership in sport did not encourage professionalism, with the result that many successful Olympians were forced to leave the country if they wished to continue their sporting careers.

He seemed untouchable, but the authorities tried very hard to influence his life. Adler was not allowed to travel to Warsaw for the 1953 European championships. The official explanation was that his training methods were outmoded, but in reality the authorities feared that the pair would remain abroad and begin Papp's professional career. He went alone, and in the final suffered the only serious defeat of his life. Two years later, however, before the European Championships in West Berlin, a strictly confidential note was written in the party central committee: *It is very likely that Papp and Adler meant to use the European Championships to abscond. Papp's wife and his circle of friends are markedly reactionary, and have a bad influence on him. (…) Papp knows very well that without a manager he would be cheated in the West, and so has not dared to go by himself.*

(…) Recommendation: On the basis of the above we have to consider whether to permit László Papp to go to the West in future. Zsigmond Adler must in no circumstances be authorised to leave Hungary. Papp only found out that his trainer could not travel with him when the team was actually on the coach. He immediately took his suitcase and went home. As a punishment his sports funding was withdrawn, and his trainer was dismissed from the team for a period. Papp and Adler had indeed been thinking that after winning two Olympic medals it would be worth his while testing himself as a professional. They could not, however, imagine doing it otherwise than as Hungarian citizens, under Hungarian colours. Papp had already had a couple of opportunities to leave the country but never did, even in 1956 when several Olympians did not return from Melbourne. He won his third Olympic gold and at once received dozens of offers of professional contracts from the biggest clubs in the world. He turned them all down. When he phoned home after winning, his wife asked whether she should come after him and bring their eighteen-month-old son. *No, I'm coming home,* he replied. *If every Hungarian came out, if ever we were needed there'd be no Hungarians left in the country.* When, however, György Marosán, the party leader responsible for sport, asked him at the airport whether there was anything that he would like, he did not hesitate: *I'd like to see how I get on among the professionals.*

Even after those successes the sporting authorities did not easily agree to Papp's trying his luck as a professional. According to the official explanation, only amateur sport had a place in 'socialist morals'. In reality the opposition was caused by a combination of hypocrisy, minute personal revenges and political games. In the end, however, because of Marosán's promise Papp was given the necessary permission and at the age of thirty-one could set his sights on the world championship belt. Beginning in 1957 he had twenty-nine professional fights, of which he won twenty-seven and two ended in draws – in other words, he was undefeated. His fan Jean-Paul Belmondo remembers his first more significant fight, against the French champion Anewy, in Paris: *I was sorry that he only joined the professional ranks late because the communist régime obstructed him. (…) I was able to see with my own eyes that László Papp had been a quite exceptional boxer.*

He trained for every match modestly and thoroughly. *I used to arrive for training when there was no one else there yet, and when I left everyone else had already gone home. In my professional competitive days I followed the simplest of routines.* Such strength-building routines as wood-cutting, which he included in his training on Adler's advice. He moved quickly up the rankings in the professional world too. In 1962 he defeated the legendary American Ralf 'Tiger' Jones, and in the same year took the European Championship from the Danish Chris Christiansen. This last was his only match to be shown on Hungarian television – the rest were mentioned only briefly on the back pages of newspapers. His victories rather attracted regretful comments on the fact that he had gone astray. In *Népszabadság* a derogatory article entitled *Moral Tale* told of an unnamed boxer who owed his successes to good luck and had then sold himself for cash. Meanwhile his popularity in Austria reached its peak, as he fought his 'home' fights in the Stadthalle in Vienna instead of in Budapest. Altogether he successfully defended his European title six times, and opinion was unanimous that he could crown his career by winning the World Championship.

To this day there is no knowing why the Hungarian political leadership withdrew his licence when he was at the peak of his success. The fact is that the contracts had been signed for the world championship match against Joey Giardello when Papp was informed in a curt letter from the Hungarian Physical Education and Sport Association (OTSH) that it would not agree to any further matches. The decision had been taken at the highest level. The president of the sport office merely told Papp's wife: *In the USSR there is no professionalism. What will the workers say? What you are after is sheer greed.* To that Mrs. Papp replied that her husband would donate half of his winnings to an orphanage. The sporting official informed her that *The Hungarian state can maintain the orphanages, and they should come home before there is trouble.* After that she was not even allowed to go out to Vienna to help her husband move back to Hungary for fear that they would stay there. After coming back Papp went in to the sport official's office; he defended himself, saying that it was wrong for a boxer to earn tens of thousands of forints in half an hour when a labourer earned a couple of hundred. *When you're paid the same as a labourer, I'll box for that much as well,* replied Papp, and slammed the door as he left. When he was banned from boxing he was told that his expertise was needed in Hungary, and so he was given nothing at all to do for two years and had to do pointless office work. During those years boxing could not even be mentioned in his hearing, and his wife was afraid that he was going to have a nervous breakdown. Eventually he resumed his career as a trainer, but first even had to go through a humiliating course for trainers. Even so he remained successful: in the last great period of Hungarian boxing he helped several Hungarian sportsmen to Olympic victory.

He could never get over his career being terminated in its prime. In later years too he showed his feelings in a number of interviews when he had to speak about his ban, but he never accused anyone and endured his injury with head unbowed. When on his sixty-fifth birthday the World Boxing Association – as a consolation prize – offered him a world championship belt he told them: *Even as a professional I represented Hungary. (…) I have never brought shame on the Hungarian people.* He was also present at the sessions of the Gypsy organisations when they were formed, showing that he had never forgotten where he came from. Then, in the mists of Alzheimer's and Parkinson's disease, he tolerated the celebrations only passively as he did the fact that no official forgiveness was ever asked of him by the Hungarian state for the opportunities that had been taken away. Max Schmelling, the German heavyweight world champion, said of him: *Not only have I never known a better boxer than him, I've never known a more sportsmanlike man. (…) László Papp was the greatest gentleman in boxing.* That he certainly was, an impeccable gentleman with an impish smile from the depths of Angyalföld.

László Papp declined all the opportunities offered to him. In the course of conversation he stated that he harmed no one by what he did and that he wished to continue and to fight for the title of world champion. The opportunities offered, however – having regard to his qualities – will always be open to him. (…) Standing orders require that we settle this question in accordance with the decision of the Political Committee. Specifically the situation, working conditions and future of László Papp. And in principle the question of professional sport in general.
1. If all attempts remain fruitless we must then prohibit administratively his further functioning as a professional boxer.
2. More space must be provided than hitherto in the work of agitation and propaganda in the whole Hungarian sports movement for enlightening work against professional sport.

Memorandum of the deputy president of OTSH
on László Papp

"Live on, laugh aloud, for that is how we meant to live."

István Angyal

When the Soviet army poured into Hungary on 4 November 1956 the leaders of the revolution soon realised that the fate of the country was sealed. In a few places in Budapest, however, such as the working-class district of Ferencváros, armed struggles continued for some days more. Led by the twenty-eight-year-old István Angyal the insurgents of Tűzoltó utca fought an urban guerrilla war against the tanks. They differed from the majority of the revolutionaries not only in that they did not lay down their arms even in the most hopeless situations, but also in that they were all communists. On 7 November, at Angyal's suggestion, they put Hungarian flags and red banners out in the streets for the Soviet soldiers to see that they represented real communism, not the Kádár authorities. When the armed struggle was over Angyal still did not retreat: in a hospital cellar he wrote and reproduced handbills. By that time he had not slept for days and was keeping himself awake by injections of caffeine. His fellow sufferers tried to persuade him to escape abroad with them, but he would not.

He was the last revolutionary, the one who held out longest. When armed police stormed the hospital on 16 November and began to arrest suspicious persons, he rushed at them from his hiding-place, begging for his companions to be released. Even from the interrogation room he threw out notes to the police guarding him. He was informed that he was to be executed next day and would be given one night to write down what he had done in the revolution. He wrote down absolutely everything. In the end he was not killed immediately but three show trials were conducted against him. His fellow prisoners considered the former star-worker revolutionary, who had been in Auschwitz under the previous régime, the most pure-souled man that had ever been. He sent poems and love-letters from prison to his ex-wife. The authorities hated him because he really was a communist, and so executed him with special cruelty at the age of thirty. As far as age is concerned he might still be among us.

He was born in 1928 in a penurious provincial Jewish family. His father made shoelaces and had three children to keep. The family was marked by a strong Magyar identity: religion and Jewish traditions were not important to them. The parents would have liked their son to continue to study after his four years at grammar school, but the anti-Jewish laws prevented that. Aged sixteen, he was looking for manual work when the deportations began. His father and one of his sisters were in Budapest at the time, and so only his mother, the other sister and István were bundled off to Auschwitz. The fact that his sister did not die in the same way as did most of the victims in all probability contributed to the formation of István's character. Vera Angyal tried to escape from the camp, and for that the authorities hanged her publicly in front of the inmates. István soon became known to his fellow prisoners for his courage. The Polish prisoners intended to beat a boy, two years his junior, to death when it turned out that he was uncircumcised. István shouted a word of command in German from the back of the crowd, at which the Poles sprang to attention. The boy was able to escape, his face bleeding, and his rescuer argued with the attackers in his stead. István only discovered after the camp was liberated that his mother had died as well as his sister. He had typhus and recovered, and returned home with chronic eating and sleeping problems. He passed his matriculation and the university entrance examination, to study in the Hungarian and History Faculties.

At the age of eighteen he considered himself a convinced communist, and believed that a more just world could be created. Unlike many of his fellow students, however, he never joined the party, and his communism sprang from a profound inward faith. For that very reason he had to be quite early disappointed in the system that called itself communist. When his professor at university, György Lukács, was attacked for not being sufficiently respectful of Soviet literature, István rose openly in his defence at a university assembly. In his speech he said that the wish to exclude Lukács because of his views was unacceptable. He was immediately expelled from the university. In his disillusionment he hung a photograph of Stalin upside-down in the lavatory, an act not without risk at the time. He was sent as a building worker to the showplace town of Sztálinváros, then under construction. He did not take this as a punishment, but learnt how to handle reinforced concrete, and because of his hard work was promoted first to technician in charge, then to clerk of works. He was a real Stakhanovite[14] model worker and was awarded the decorations to prove it one after another. His workers were enthusiastic about him because he worked hard along with them. He treated those under him as his equals, and if he felt that anyone was treating them unfairly he was capable of ringing up the management at night to stand up for them. As a committed communist he read them excerpts from Marx and Lenin during breaks – most often such as could be taken as criticism of the Rákosi regime.

Outside work, Angyal also belonged to an amateur dramatic group. He was twenty-two when he met there a grammar school girl of seventeen, Ágnes Sánta, and they fell in love during rehearsals. Her parents did not care for the communist Jewish boyfriend, but that did not prevent the young people marrying a year later. *Two obstinate people who loved each other very much but could never get along together,* was how Ágnes described their marriage, and in fact painful quarrelling and even violence often alternated with romantic times. In 1953 they moved to Budapest, and in their flat in Üllői út lived a very sociable life with workers, artists and university people among their daily visitors. Their friends included the writers Endre Fejes, Erzsébet Galgóczi and Béla Abody together with István Eörsi, with whom Angyal became life-long friends. The stormy marriage, however, could not be saved. *We were married for five years: five splendid years, throughout which we quarrelled. He loved me and yet was constantly hurting me. I loved him, and still I left him*, recalled Ágnes, who, a few months after the divorce, married her family friend Béla Abody. Even afterwards Angyal remained in contact with Ágnes and on good terms with Abody.

THE PRELIMINARIES TO THE 1956 REVOLUTION. After the death of Stalin in 1953 the communist dictatorship began to ease in Hungary too. On orders from Moscow Mátyás Rákosi resigned, and his place was taken by Imre Nagy, the former Minister for Agriculture, whom Rákosi had earlier forced out of the party leadership. Nagy declared an amnesty for political detainees, closed the internment camps, and carried through increases in wages and reductions in prices. The Petőfi Circle, which was full of reforming left-wing intelligentsia, was allowed to reopen. In 1955 Rákosi and the élite of the Communist Party, who had been excluded from power, arrived with their hard-line Moscow allies to order Nagy to the Kremlin and call for the withdrawal of part of his reforms. As he was not prepared to do that his party membership was suspended at a session of the party leadership. It proved impossible, however, to reinstate the Stalinist dictatorship, and under Soviet pressure Rákosi resigned from the post of Party Secretary. The reburial of László Rajk, the Minister for the Interior whom he had had executed in 1949, grew into a mass demonstration, and the left-wing intelligentsia, who demanded reform, criticised the regime more and more openly.

Although he attended Petőfi Circle debates and had a sympathetic regard for Imre Nagy, Angyal did not personally believe that the regime could be reformed. According to István Eörsi, he was the only one of their friends that saw the possibility of a revolution before 23 October: *As certain animals can sense a coming earthquake and sniff all round with nerves stretched to breaking-point, so his over-refined sensitivity indicated that the times would soon be out of joint. The three of us were walking in the Károlyi garden in September when he told us in deadly earnest: 'There's going to be a revolution'. We looked at him as if he'd gone mad.* Angyal was working on a building-site in Esztergom on 23 October when news reached him of the imminent student demonstration. He went to Budapest and joined the crowd heading for the Parliament. That evening he went to the radio building because he would not believe the news that unarmed demonstrators were being fired on. Nevertheless, next day, when someone told him that communism had failed in Hungary, he replied: *What's happened here is that communists, young people fuelled by the principles of socialism and brought up on it, have moved in opposition to the distortion of socialism and those that have distorted it, so now there'll really be socialism in Hungary.* He took an ever more active part in the events of the revolution. First he distributed revolutionary news-sheets and fliers in the city, then delivered food and bandages to the insurgents and to families with children. Then he became involved with the resistance group in Tűzoltó utca, most of whom were, like him, young working men that considered themselves genuine communists. Although he was never elected to the position, after a while everyone in the group looked on him as the commander. Not only the young insurgents, but also people thirty and forty years his senior looked up to him and did as he said. The Tűzoltó utca people were successful in the armed defence of the city, and destroyed several tanks. One day Angyal and his companions captured a squad of ÁVO soldiers. He would not permit anyone to take revenge on them, but fed them and protected them until the fighting ended. One of them later said of him: *He's a real angel.* With the same purpose in mind he placed a guard at the door of a terrified communist official so that no harm should come to him. It shows that he was becoming more and more acceptable that he discussed the maintenance of order with Imre Nagy and his Minister of Defence as a member of a delegation of insurgents. Of the communist leaders that took the revolutionaries' side he trusted most of all János Kádár, whom Rákosi had imprisoned. After the lynching that followed the occupation of the Communist Party Headquarters he actually went to see him in the Parliament building and promised him that he would place an armed guard on the party offices. He even invited Kádár to Tűzoltó utca to meet the armed left-wing young people, and indeed offered him the honorary leadership of his group. Kádár promised to come, but in the end did not visit the insurgents but went off to the USSR. He never forgave Angyal for witnessing his betrayal.

THE 1956 REVOLUTION AND FREEDOM STRUGGLE. On 23 October 1956 the university youth announced a demonstration of solidarity with the Polish workers. Out of the action there developed an openly anti-party demonstration calling for the election of Imre Nagy as Prime Minister. By the evening they had knocked down the notorious statue of Stalin, cut the communist cypher out of flags, and besieged and occupied the radio building so as to be able to read out their demands. The party leadership could not gain control of the situation and declared the events a counter-revolution, but yielded to the pressure of the crowd and elected Nagy Prime Minister. Two days later armed police fired on demonstrators who were assembling peacefully outside the Parliament, and some hundreds were killed and injured. The bloodshed swept events towards armed revolution, and poorly armed groups of insurgents organised themselves against the Soviet military and ÁVH units. On 30 October Imre Nagy announced that the party-state and the one-party system were no more, and that free elections were to be held. That never happened: Khrushchev, who had previously supported Nagy, had the government's Minister of State, the communist János Kádár, taken to Moscow and entrusted him with the leadership of the anti-government. The Kádár government, which called itself 'revolutionary', called in Soviet forces and the crushing by force of the revolution began. In the course of a few weeks more than two hundred thousand escaped to the West through the briefly opened frontiers.

During the days of the revolution Angyal was ill with pneumonia and bronchitis. Even so he set aside time to visit his small son regularly. During these visits his ex-wife fell in love again with her ex-husband and an emotional relationship began. We cannot say how their fate would have run had history allowed their relationship to develop, but time did not permit that. Kádár called in the Soviet troops and the revolution was put down. Angyal fought to the last minute against superior odds. When he was arrested in the hospital where he was hiding he knew precisely the fate that awaited him. As commander of a group of armed insurgents he was considered *leader of an organisation intent on bringing down the people's democratic regime*, and could not avoid a death sentence. He made no attempt to exonerate himself in his written confessions, and so they constituted the firm basis of the charge. He put on paper such things as: *The Soviet tanks are an insult to our national pride, our socialist self-awareness and our human equality.* He also gave a detailed account of his meeting with Kádár, and that finally sealed his fate. In court too he gave a full account of his revolutionary role, proudly and sincerely. *Pista was calm and disciplined. One might even say, contemptuous,* wrote Béla Abody later; he sat with Ágnes throughout the hearings. In all probability Kádár himself had the final say in the handing down of the death sentence. Angyal did not ask for mercy, but his defence lawyer lodged an appeal. He wanted to have Kádár called as a witness in the higher court, and addressed him in the later proceedings: *You approved everything for which you are now sending a man to death while you lie low.* During the speech that Angyal made, exercising his right to have the final word, the court stenographer – a woman who had seen a lot – burst into tears: *I did not wish to be a leader of men, just to be a citizen. I have always regarded myself first and foremost as a citizen, but for me the law meant death until 1945, and in many cases after then too. I have searched for justice somewhere between the two legal systems. I have not found it. I wished to live as a free man, I shall not be able to endure prison. I beg the court to pass sentence.*

319

"I would rather die than live in shame like you."
István Angyal before his judges in 1957

He took care to say good-bye to everyone. He had already been sentenced to death when he managed to get a farewell note – written with a stub of pencil on a piece of toilet-paper – to Eörsi, who was also in prison, and who memorised the words and destroyed the paper. He wrote frequently from prison to Ágnes, who was sometimes able to see him at visiting times. He also sent her his poem *Még élek* (I'm still alive): *(…) I seek you as the memory does the past / As the wandering mind does faith / Which might alarm the cruel powers / While I knew that we would be parted.* Béla Abody wrote sincerely that his love for his wife had come back to life. On his son's fourth birthday he sent a handkerchief embroidered with a quotation from Radnóti, which he sent out with a fellow prisoner who was released. As his final day came closer he wrote a brief farewell letter to Ágnes: *This I sing: The cedar-tree is with its leaves and branches, still, my angel, we are to be separated …* I love you very very much. I love everyone very very much. You too. Everyone who loves me. But those too who don't know that I'm worthy of love. I embrace, embrace, embrace you, Angyal."

He was executed on 1 December 1958 in the presence of the public prosecutor and of the notorious Tutsek the 'hanging judge', who pronounced dozens of death sentences. *I'd rather die than live a life full of shame like you,* were his last words to them. Perhaps it was because of that sentence, perhaps because of his unshakeable communism, that he had to suffer for twenty-eight minutes on the gallows. The popular actor Iván Darvas, who was also a fellow prisoner, remembers him: *He could preserve a kind of sovereignty, an aloofness, untouchability − indeed − a kind of personal freedom, in that hell of communal misery. I like to think that he died that way too.*

Pista, I'm still alive, though the spiritual slothfulness that goes with the fourth month of transubstantiation is troubling me. Like it or not I have to be too preoccupied with myself, and that is loathsome for a practical man. I would like to be active, of use − that is very much lacking. Győző asks, what message shall I send? I might send no message at all, and that would be best. But I'm still frail, and love binds me excessively to the world and strongly to you too, Pista, and makes me send word. Nowadays these final words are expected as in olden days pieces of the rope were from the hangman. People would like us to make statements to the world, but the only thing that still bothers us, if anything still can bother us, is that perhaps 'grateful posterity' will make martyrs or heroes of us to torment itself. If such a thing happens, protest, protest! We don't want that, let them not rummage in their dustbins, their past made up by us. Let the memory of the nameless mob from which we came, with which we were one and with whom we shall return, be a great rough rock. But that too is foolishness, like all brooding over the past. Forget us, forget us, that is what will help. Recollection either ties down the arm that would act or spurs it on to foolish, futile deeds. All of you, live on, laugh out loud, because that is how we meant to live. Don't allow recollection to dominate you. Every day is long until we die and every day that we live is short. It's very hard, but I haven't changed, and like this it's bearable. I've become more of a man, perhaps so much so that now I can go away. If it hurts, it hurts because it causes pain to those who loved us. I embrace you, Pista, heaven be with you.

István Angyal's letter of farewell to István Eörsi,
1958

"I'm not a Gypsy writer but a Gypsy that writes."
Menyhért Lakatos in the 1970s.

Menyhért Lakatos

The engineer Menyhért Lakatos, aged thirty-eight, wanted to build a little house for his family, but at the time it happened to be hard to come by bricks. He remembered that his Gypsy grand-parents had lived by making mud-bricks in their time. Togeth-er with a few local Gypsies he began to manufacture bricks in a disused building that belonged to the collective farm – first only for his own use, later for sale. A year later there were 150 work-ing there and making good money. *I consciously tried for the Gyp-sies to do every job themselves, not so that they should increase their knowl-edge but because I believed that one only respects the piece of work that one has produced oneself,* he stated. *And they, who had a different view of ownership from other people, gradually reached the stage at which morality played a decisive role in the definition of property.* Two years later houses with bathrooms were being built beside the brick-works, and after three years a nursery and a school too. Including the family mem-bers he brought 500 people out of penury. In the fourth year the collective farm became alarmed at a Gypsy building capitalism on the rented plot, cancelled the lease, dispersed the machinery and drove the people away. From then on Lakatos helped the Gypsies in another way – he became a writer, the best known among the Gypsies and the first whose works appeared in hundreds of thou-sands of copies in Hungary and abroad. And he was almost killed twice because of the colour of his skin.

He was born in poverty beyond imagination, though on his father's side the family had been landowners in Transylvania. His grandfather, Miklós Boncza, had been a member of the National Assembly, and father-in-law of the famous poet Endre Ady. "My father was a child of rape," he said later. His Honour had needed a Gypsy girl from the mansion staff only for a single night, if that. He did not even look at his son, that is how things were in those days. In the Gypsy settlement, however, everyone called the light-skinned boy Boncza, as they later did his grandson, born in 1926. Menyhért Lakatos was born in a field next to a rural Gypsy settlement, as was stated in his personal record: his mother was just on her way home when she gave birth. His parents dealt in horses, feathers and pottery, and, if necessary, worked as day-labourers. His illiterate mother felt that her son deserved better than to remain in the settlement, and sent him to the village school from their hovel in a white shirt that she washed every day. He was the only child among the Gypsies that went to school. *I was constantly abused, and the adults could not understand my mother either: what did she mean with all that schooling when the other children actually earned a pengő and a half at the autumn hunts. (…) She would not hear of my missing a single day.* He did not much enjoy going to school, but became very fond of reading. The other children called him 'Pagey' because he was always leafing through books. The teacher often boasted of him to the school inspector. *Just listen to the little negus!* There was, of course, no chance of his continuing after the six elementary classes, that was too expensive.

Thanks to a cruel piece of luck, however, he did have that chance. At a village hunting fellowship celebration, to which the Gypsy children had been invited as clowns, the gentlemen drank more than they should have and began shooting. The headmaster of the grammar school, blind drunk, fired at little Menyhért: the ranger later picked seventy-three pieces of shot out of him with a knife. The village doctor would not so much as look at the injured boy. He would have died but for another hunting fellowship, who wanted to cause trouble for their opponents. They persuaded his mother to take legal action. The headmaster took fright and offered her money. She refused it, but asked for something all the same: *If we might be able to send him to the senior school, we wouldn't mind being in rags if we could only have him educated. But I don't really think that a Gypsy boy would be accepted there.* The next offer was that he should be admitted to the grammar school free of charge, and that was accepted. And so Menyhért was the first Gypsy boy in the county, and perhaps in the whole of Hungary, to go to grammar school.

His father was not very pleased: *He could have been a double bass player, a mud-brick maker, even a horse-dealer, but none of these, he prefers all those rotten books. God forgive me, but I went to school until I was kicked out.* There was something in what he said, and the boy did not feel comfortable in the strange place and was homesick. His mother, nevertheless, persuaded him: *All we Gypsies place our hope in you. If you become an educated man, everybody'll be able to see that a Gypsy can rise in the world, be successful.* The free education, however, cost a lot: the expense of clothes and study materials left the family literally starving. He was an outstanding pupil, but in other respects might not put a foot wrong. *If the school porter came in and said that someone had made a mess in the WC the eyes of the class turned on me (…), and if I couldn't prove my innocence I wasn't spared the teachers' remarks.* He was lonely, and no one would befriend the pupil on account of whom the other boys nicknamed Class C 'the Gypsy class'. *Not a pencil disappeared without the contents of my pockets and my bag being turned out.* Although there was never an instance of anything being found on him they still wanted to get rid of him. His classmates sneaked a *pengő* into his pocket so that he should be expelled as a thief, but he found the coin in time and handed it in to a teacher. He watched as first the poor peasant children dropped out of school because they could not last the pace, and later as his hard-working Jewish classmate was expelled because of his origin. Finally he too had to go. In

1943 a schoolmate tried to make him tidy up, and he refused. *We wanted to save you for the fatherland, we thought that you'd show greater respect for it than the stinking Jews that have been expelled,* shouted the young gentleman. Lakatos boxed the loudmouth's ears, with the result that next day the police called on him in the Gypsy settlement.

His studies had broken off just before the matriculation examination. He suffered a twinge of conscience as he hid from the police because, following his example, another woman from the settlement had sent her son to school; his classmates had only intended to humiliate him, but in the end had drowned him in the school lavatory. A grim time followed. Several inhabitants of the Gypsy settlement died because of overdoses injected against a typhus epidemic. Instead of medicine or food, the authorities issued quicklime so that the corpses could be crammed into a pit without coffins. The hungry people of the settlement were actually delighted when, in 1944, the town clerk called on them to assemble because they would be taken to where they would be fed. They climbed happily into the cattle-trucks. Menyhért and his two siblings were deported to Birkenau. *We were herded, barefoot and in rags, towards the trucks, which had been sprinkled with powdered quicklime, while in the main street 'gawping public opinion' accompanied our column with a malicious smile.* In the camp they were treated like laboratory animals. *People were cheaper than white mice,* he said later. They were used for sterilisation, bacterial infections and chemical experiments. Menyhért was strapped down in a tub and his body temperature lowered to 22/23°; he was then placed naked between two others: the object was to see whether they would be able to transmit the warmth of their bodies to him. Anyone that could stand it, survived. Any that could not, was frozen to death. Menyhért survived, one of his siblings died. Years later in Germany a German reader of his asked him whether he hated the Germans. *Not now,* came the answer. *In those days we didn't hate just the Germans but the Hungarians as well.*

On coming home he finished the grammar school and continued studying, qualifying as a planning engineer. He was already writing at that time, mostly for the table drawer. At first he wrote down old Gypsy tales that he herd from his illiterate uncle, then poems and stories. *I really never meant to write. I'd been jotting things down for a long time — the paper didn't answer back — but for a long time I didn't consider writing. Rather I had it in mind somehow to help my people, to bring them into more humane circumstances, to change things. So that skilled work, rather than social assistance, should be the basis of life. That was why I started the brickworks.* In 1964 he rented land from the collective farm with money which he had saved, and started the Gypsy Brickworks, of which he became manager. *Who would have dared to tell your fathers that they were lazy Gypsies?* he used to persuade the locals. *They built up a whole empire with the bricks that they made. From spring until late autumn they weren't short of work.* There were some that were not pleased to see the experiment. Their first efforts were ruined because people from the village drove cattle onto the drying bricks. The Gypsies too had to be convinced: there were Gypsy men who were ashamed at their wives' going to work in the brickworks. Then, when he succeeded in selling the first consignment, they began to believe him. More and more came and joined him; one elderly man even brought his favourite horse so that he should have the means of delivery. Demand for good quality bricks grew and grew all over the country, and half of the money that came in was spent on developing the works while the rest went on wages, so that everyone had an interest in the joint success. Second-hand machinery too was bought, but no one knew how to use it. Lakatos bought technical books and learnt how to operate the machines, and then began to pass on his knowledge to the Gypsies, who were mostly illiterate. And if the adults were now having to sit on the school benches the schooling that their children had to be organized as well. Lakatos was with the Gypsies day and night; his wife divorced him because he was spending all his money on the brickworks.

The late Kádár régime and the most cheerful barracks. From the mid-60s onward the communist régime in Hungary became a sort of soft dictatorship, which many Western analysts,
comparing it with the harsher régimes in other socialist countries,
called 'the most cheerful barracks in the Soviet camp', or 'goulash
communism'. Although it was not permissible to find fault with the
basis of the system, and so the leading role of the Communist Party, the person of János Kádár or the fact of the Soviet occupation,
otherwise most subjects could be debated by the intelligentsia. Instead of censorship the party expected a kind of self-censorship, and
official cultural policies categorised artists into the 'three t's' – *tűrt,
támogatott* or *tiltott*, tolerated, supported or banned – depending on
the degree to which they could restrain their tendency to criticise
the régime. Western politicians too looked kindly on Kádár, who
rejected the cult of personality and was considered to have a human
face, and they assisted the stagnant Hungarian economy with financial credits. Thanks to these it was possible artificially to maintain
a standard of living higher than that of the neighbouring countries,
so that most families could afford a Trabant, a weekend house, or
even a trip to the West every three years. At the same time, behind
the apparently more liberal facade the populace was watched by the
secret police, and dissident thinkers were suppressed or forced into
exile. Kádár was ousted in 1989, but unlike other twentieth-centu-
ry leaders of the Hungarian state died peacefully at home. Surveys
indicate that even today he is the most popular historical figure in
Hungarian circles.

Then one day the head of the collective farm visited Lakatos and
informed him that he was pleased with the results but did not agree
with the management style, which was "excessively Gypsy-cen-
tred". As Lakatos did not change his ways he was summoned to
the headquarters and there told that his business licence was withdrawn because he did not have enough trained workers. He had to
yield to *force majeure*. The workers had to register with the collective farm, and those that refused were dismissed. The elderly Gyp-

"People were cheaper than white mice."
Gypsies being checked for identity before deportation in 1944.

sy who was having to leave his horse in collective ownership was
so embittered that he killed the animal with a sickle. Eventually a
new manager was appointed who put an end to the workers' sharing in the proceeds. A year later the works was financially ruined
and had to be closed. *It was taken from us, and all the money that we
had invested was squandered. A business was wrecked that even had national importance. I'll never forget it as long as I live,* Lakatos recalled later.

He started over. He began to publish on social questions concerning the Gypsies, and then became a member of the sociology
research group of the Hungarian Academy, as a specialist on Gypsies. He soon gained a reputation in the academic world, and this
brought him international recognition too: he was elected deputy President of the International Romani Union. In addition to
his academic work he wrote his short stories on blank pages in
his daughters' exercise-books. He was forty-four when his children entered for a literary competition things that he had written

which they had found in a drawer. He won! From then on commissions came in one after another for poems, stories, fairy-tales, and finally even a novel. He was frightened of the task and refused it, at which the editor sent him an advance. He felt that there was nothing more to be said: his *Füstös képek* (translated as The Colour of Smoke), describing his youth in the Gypsy settlement, was an outstanding success. Four editions ran to a hundred thousand copies in Hungary and more abroad.

HUNGARIAN LITERATURE. The Hungarians are traditionally a literature-loving people, but there are few branches of art in which the list of practitioners also known abroad differs as radically from that of those considered important in their own country as does that in literature. One notable exception is the poet of the 1848 revolution, Sándor Petőfi, the Hungarian writer who has been translated into more languages than any other, and who has been a cult figure in Hungary for more than 150 years. Hungarian poetry is in any case difficult to translate, so that only Hungarian speakers are aware that such poets as Endre Ady, Mihály Babits and Dezső Kosztolányi, who published in the periodical *Nyugat* (West) in the first third of the twentieth century, have a place at the summit in the world of lyric poetry, as has their younger contemporary Attila József, who is regarded by the greatest number of Hungarians as the finest poet. The plays of Ferenc Molnár are still performed today on the stages of the world, but in Hungary he is rarely ranked among the ten most important authors. Best known abroad of the masters of prose is Sándor Márai, who died as an emigré in America, while the works of Antal Szerb, his contemporary who fell victim to the Holocaust, have only recently become available to the English reader. Of the writers of the second half of the twentieth century, the works of the recently deceased Magda Szabó may be found in many foreign bookshops, while Tibor Déry, Miklós Mészöly and István Örkény are little known. Of contemporary writers, the books of the late Imre Kertész, the only Hungarian Nobel Laureate for Literature, are well known outside Hungary.

From then on he lived by his pen. He wrote in fairy-tales the missing myths of the Gypsies, and in his later years showed himself to be a poet too. He was one of the few Gypsy intelligentsia to be honoured by every tendency and clique alike. He attempted more than once to intervene in the internecine strife of the Gypsy intelligentsia of Hungary – mostly without success. He founded the Gypsy Cultural Association of Hungary, of which he was the first President. He was extremely proud of the fact that he played a part in the Gandhi Foundation, which runs the world's first Gypsy grammar school – and which was actually founded on his birthday! He said of himself in an interview: (…) *I'm not a Gypsy writer, but a Gypsy that writes, because I cannot deny my origins. Not from the point of view of literature: that means my make-up as a person, myself. I know this community better that I do the starlight. I want to reveal the life of the Gypsies, their destiny, their position in society.* He died in 2007 at the age of eighty-two, a veritable Methuselah by Gypsy standards.

As the days went by, as the rows of green-grey bricks grew, so dreams too began to assume a semblance of reality. Passers-by no longer tried to make out what the Gypsies were up to, they ventured down among the pits to find out, down to where bricks ready for firing dispelled their previous doubts. We too believed that we were soon going to surprise the village with ringing red bricks. There were quite a few unbelievers too, but that merely strengthened our resolve. By now we meant to provide proof, as people who knew very well that nobody gave tuppence for what they said. And then, because the weather was good, why should we not have believed that we had become the specially favoured of the Creator, Who had stretched out the summer and dried our bricks bone-hard with its blazing, scorching heat. True, the Gypsies had dried out with them, the skin hung in furrows on their slender bodies, they had become as hard and tough as dry meat.

Menyhért Lakatos,
Akik élni akartak (Those that meant to live)
1982

"He even calmed me." Ferenczy and his wife in the 1960.

Béni Ferenczy

In November 1956, a few days after the Soviet tanks had snuffed out the revolution, the sixty-six-year-old sculptor went out for a walk in devastated Budapest. On returning home Béni Ferenczy said nothing to his wife, just looked into space for a long time. Soon afterwards the phone rang and he picked up the receiver. His wife saw that he had stopped speaking and that only gurgling sounds were coming from his throat. He was immediately taken to hospital where his condition was stabilised, but there was no knowing how much damage the stroke had caused. When he recovered consciousness it turned out that his one side was completely without feeling and that he had lost the power of speech. He was given a book, and by eye movements he indicated that he could read. A few weeks later, by which time he could say a word or two, his family began to hope that he was going to pull through. They kept him from bad news, but in 1957 there was plenty. For example, he happened to come upon the news of the death of his twin, the tapestry artist Noémi Ferenczy, in a newspaper that had been left lying about. From that point his condition deteriorated rapidly, he lost his speech again, and in the doctors' opinion another blood clot had moved in his head. It was believed that he did not want to read because of grief, but it became apparent that this time he had also lost the ability to read.

For a long time it seemed that his mind too was affected, and one could not be certain whether he understood what was said to him. They put pictures in front of him and tried to communicate in that way. A visitor handed him a copy of *Paris Match* with an illustrated report of the revolution in Hungary. Ferenczy looked over the pictures and began to move his mouth. He put the paper down and said loudly and clearly *Oui*. It became clear that the stroke had wiped from his brain his native Hungarian together with his perfect command of German and Russian – but not the French that he had learnt at grammar school. From then on he read French papers and novels. He could not regain the power of speech but used just a few short words, but if he sang he could construct whole sentences. In a few months' time he took a turn for the worse and also lost his knowledge of French, but by then no one thought that the stricken artist did not understand what was happening around him. His wife discharged him from hospital on her own responsibility and by a superhuman effort very gradually taught him to walk again, and put paper and pencil in front of him. At first he did not know what they were for. Then he began to draw, using only his left hand. It was reckoned a medical miracle, and was explained by saying that *he was able to use the free capacity of his brain to force the right-handed habits of a lifetime over to the left hand.* After the initial childish drawings there gradually emerged elaborate graphics, and later watercolours too. Three years after the stroke he reached out for the first time for clay that had been placed in front of him. With a tremendous effort, with his paralysed leg propped up, he shaped a statue: an angel gracefully poised on one leg. It was an unmistakeable work of Ferenczy's genius, and he gave it the title *Golden Age*. Reflected in it was admiration for the human form and beauty, just as it was in his other work which followed. An artistic career similar to that of the deaf Beethoven lasted for a decade, the worthy climax of the life of a peerlessly humane, courageous and persistent man.

Ferenczy was born in 1890 into an artistic family of exceptional talent. His father, Károly Ferenczy, came from the Bánát and had the greatest influence on the revival of Hungarian painting. His mother, Olga Fialka, came of a Czech-Austrian family, and had had a successful early career as a painter but after marrying had only smoothed the way for her husband's career, while bringing up their three children. The eldest son, Valér, became a painter like his father, and the twins that followed became world-famous – Noémi as a textile artist and Béni as a sculptor. Béni spent a blissfully happy childhood in Nagybánya (today Baia Mare, Romania), the Transylvanian mining town, where his parents brought him up in accordance with the most modern principles. *I inherited from my mother the destiny of a wanderer, never at home anywhere, polyglot ways, an interest in world literature and music and a democratic sympathy with the simple children of the people. From my father I inherited physique, humour and a critical faculty. And, obviously, the fact that art is what matters most to me,* he wrote later in his autobiography, which has remained in a fragmentary state.

THE FINE ARTS IN HUNGARY. *Hungarian painters and sculptors have not become founders of international schools as Liszt and Bartók have in music. In the nineteenth century Mihály Munkácsy, the realist painter who worked in Paris, and the Tsar's court painter Mihály Zichy were known abroad. A number of the Nagybánya painters who gathered around Károly Ferenczy (such as Béla Iványi-Grünwald and Simon Hollósy) lived for shorter or longer periods in Munich or Paris; their styles bore marks of impressionism and naturalism. The post-impressionist József Rippl-Rónai too brought the most modern style of portraiture from Paris. The French tendency continued into the twentieth century: the work of A Nyolcak (The Eight), the first Hungarian avant-garde group who adopted the principles of fauvism and cubism, is compared by many to Bartók's search for a way ahead. The paintings of Róbert Berény, Béla Czóbel and Károly Kernstok change hands nowadays for substantial amounts at international auctions. Experimental Hungarian avant-garde artists such as László Moholy-Nagy, a representative of the Bauhaus school who worked in photography and design, are listed in the international forefront. Among the most significant Parisian photographers of the first half of the twentieth century are the Hungarians André*

Kertész, Lucien Hervé, Brassaï, Martin Munkácsi and Robert Capa, who later went to America. The leading figure in op-art, Victor Vasarely, also went to Paris from Hungary.

There was not a moment's doubt that he would opt for a career in art. Likewise, that he was not going to follow either his parents or his brother. As a child he spent hours at quarries, watching the workers drill into the granite. As a teenager he wanted to study sculpture, and so his father sent him to Florence when he was eighteen; two years later he went to the Munich Academy. The artistic experiences that affected him most, however, came in Paris, where he met the works of Cézanne, Matisse and Rodin. He heard Apollinaire lecture – he held a derogatory opinion of classical sculpture, and so Ferenczy's first independent works were in the cubist style. *Béni Ferenczy will be a force to be reckoned with in the future of Hungarian sculpture,* prophesied the periodical *Művészet* (Art) in 1916, when the young artist exhibited his work to the Hungarian public. By his own admission he was twenty-seven before he read any contemporary literature or took an interest in politics: such had been his father's advice. After Károly Ferenczy died in 1917 his son threw himself into reading and public life. He attended the *soirées* of the new literary periodical *Nyugat* (West) in the salon of that patron of the arts, baron Lajos Hatvany, and became acquainted with the progressive intelligentsia of the time. He was at the bedside of the mortally sick Endre Ady, considered the father of lyric modernism, and drew one of the last portraits of him. In 1919 he accepted the invitation of the Artistic Directorate of the Republic of Councils and became head of the Department of Sculpture. In that capacity he designed the new 10 and 200 *korona* coins, by which he scandalised the leaders of the Republic of Councils: he had portrayed nude figures on the obverse. The dispute was never resolved as the Republic of Councils collapsed. Ferenczy and his twin sister, however, moved to join their mother, who was cut off beyond the Trianon frontier in Nagybánya, where they took part in the organisation of the general pit strike against the Romanian state, and so in 1920 had to leave. As there was a warrant out for his arrest in Hungary, because of his part in the Republic of Councils, he emigrated to Vienna as did many other left-wing intelligentsia too.

In Vienna he rented a studio and also took on pupils. Among others, he taught Yvonne von Ungermann, the daughter of an Austrian army officer, who became not a sculptor but his wife. They had two children, Rosie and Mátyás. All of Vienna knew the studio, not only because of the statues that came from there, but because the Austrian police kept it under surveillance as the place of assembly of emigré Hungarian communists and other left-wing persons. The communist leaders regarded the tenant – whom they put at risk – as a naive dreamer. Meanwhile Ferenczy worked constantly, exhibiting his work at the gallery of the progressive *Képzőművészek Új Társasága* (New Association of Artists). He frequently went to Berlin too, where *Der Sturm*, the most important forum of expressionism, held an exhibition for him. Despite his artistic successes, these were years of hardship. *Unfortunately my material situation is so bad that I would be able to deliver only if I received my expenses in advance*, he wrote to one gallery. His private life too was in ruins: his wife left him for an Austrian ski instructor, with whom she emigrated to Moscow on a sudden whim, taking with her the children.

In 1930 Ferenczy travelled to Nagybánya, as his mother had died. As he was walking in the town he met an old friend of his, Miklós Kovács, and his wife, Erzsébet Plop. As a girl she had spent a lot of time in the Ferenczy family's constantly teeming house and had fallen in love with the older boy, Valér: he, however, had paid her no attention. Some years later she had married: her husband was the son of a well-to-do local family, and at the same time a member of the illegal Communist Party. During the brief conversation Ferenczy could not take his eyes off his friend's wife. *We just looked at each other and couldn't speak*, she reminisced later. Next day a fellow party member who had been caught betrayed

337

Kovács, and he and his wife had to run away. They made an adventurous escape to the USSR.

Ferenczy had therefore three reasons for going to Moscow: the attraction of his friend's wife, he wanted to be near his children, and, of course, he believed fervently in the unfamiliar world which was proclaimed as more just. Erzsébet disillusioned him of that at their first meeting in Moscow: *Have you gone mad? You want to stay here? Go straight home!* The Kovácses had had their Romanian passports taken from them, and as Soviet citizens were not allowed to leave the country. As an Austrian citizen Ferenczy could still have left, but he was in love and so wanted to stay. He soon found out that the Soviet authorities were unreceptive to modern styles in art. Disappointed in the regime, he obtained no commissions, and because of an insufficiently idealised portrait of Marx that he had painted his work was removed from an exhibition. From then on Erzsébet was his most important model, and he immortalised her in several dozen statues and hundreds of drawings: every one was a confession of love. By that time the Kovácses had separated, and the husband had started a relationship with a Russian woman. Ferenczy and his lover moved in together and brought up her small son Miki. Like most of the intelligentsia that had come from the West they too wanted to go home, but it was not so simple. Ferenczy's ex-wife Yvonne, for example, only managed by leaving her partner and returning to Vienna with the children. Not long afterwards she died of septicaemia at the age of thirty-two, and the children went to relatives in Vienna. Ferenczy immediately wanted to go after them, but first he married Erzsébet so that he could obtain a passport for her son too, unite the families, and they could all move in together in Vienna. The boy's passport was a long time coming, and after a year's waiting Erzsébet's had almost expired. He left for Vienna by himself in the belief that she would soon come after him bringing the boy. That was in 1936, the year of the great purges. If they stayed perhaps they would not have escaped. Miklós Kovács stayed and was executed for espionage. Friends looked in vain for the little boy but could find no trace of him.

On returning the Ferenczys lived a life divided between Budapest and Vienna. They were Austrian citizens, and had to go home to Vienna every three months to renew their visas, but most of the time they lived in Hungary. They had no children of their own, but Ferenczy adopted Karl, his first wife's son by her second marriage. They did not regain Hungarian citizenship. One actress friend who intervened on their behalf was told by the Minister for the Interior: *Madam, your friends are Bolsheviks!* At the time, however, Ferenczy was equally critical of bolshevism and fascism alike. When they woke up one day to find that Hitler's forces had entered Vienna and that they had become German citizens they moved finally to Budapest. Ferenczy worked in silence, abstractedly, mostly making little bronze figurines and medals of artists that he admired, Bartók and El Greco among others. *Monumental quality doesn't depend on the size of a piece of work,* he said. *One too big might be an astonishing 'wonder', but man can only give birth to man, not to giants.* Little wonder that dictatorships of the left and right alike did not look with favour on Ferenczy and his art.

His German citizenship brought Ferenczy one terrible loss. His son Matyi, then a boy at school, was conscripted into the Wehrmacht, and was killed fighting with the Germans in the battle for Paris. At the same time, his German passport saved the lives of many persecuted persons. In 1944 friends from Vienna and Budapest, forced to hide because of their origins and their political views, had the good fortune to escape in the Ferenczys' flat in József Attila utca – it was a long time before the Hungarian authorities called on them. After a while that protection too vanished, as the long awaited Hungarian passports arrived. Even then the Ferenczys did not stop hiding the persecuted. When the father of a friendly Jewish family was sent to Mauthausen and the mother to Auschwitz, the Ferenczys extracted their three children from the 'starred house' and took them home. When they suspected that their flat was being watched they asked their friends to accommodate the Jewish children for them. After the Arrow-Cross came to power the friends found the situation too risky and so asked Ferenczy to take the children back. The Ferenczys preferred to abandon their own flat and go into hiding with their protégés. That may have in fact saved their lives: during the siege Ferenczy's studio and flat sustained a direct hit, and many statues and drawings were destroyed, and his books and notes burned.

After the war they had to start a new life from scratch. Ferenczy was full of hope for a more liberal world, and in 1946 was appointed a lecturer at the Fine Arts Academy. *He didn't give us great, long lectures, he preferred to draw what he was thinking*, one of his pupils recalls. It was in the Academy workshop that Ferenczy made the statue of Petőfi which he intended to be his masterpiece. He meant to distance himself from the empty pathos of the out-door statuary of the preceding period, and so he portrayed the poet-revolutionary of 1849 as a short, sunken-chested but definitely youthful man, his belt weighted down by his sword. He was still working on the statue when in 1948 he and his twin received the award, recently established by the new regime, of the Kossuth Prize. A few months after the prize-giving the communist culture-potentates saw the plaster model of the statue: the air froze around Ferenczy. His sometime guest in Vienna, József Révai, the communist Minister for Culture had not long previously declared the slogan of the movement to be "Our Banner: Petőfi", and with that in mind found the statue insufficiently heroic. *It turned out that the Secretary of State that had ordered Petőfi (…) had cancelled the order,* Ferenczy wrote in his diary. *Therefore I shall go on more willingly, as if only on my own account, and with growing courage!* He had just finished it when one morning the porter would not let him into the workshop of the Academy. Thus it was that he learnt that he had been dismissed. The Petőfi statue gathered dust in the Academy basement.

Ferenczy's philanthropism and intellectual independence were not acceptable to the authorities; in 1949 he was compulsorily retired, and in 1950 his workshop was taken from him. In the following years he lived by illustrating books – work found for him by writer friends – and in addition had some income from the sale – also mostly to friends – of sweaters knitted by his wife. At the same time he also worked for churches, carving the marble statue of St Teresa for the Basilica in Budapest and a funerary monument for his father. In 1956 came a change of fortune for the Ferenczys, not only because of the revolution. In October a Soviet Air Force officer called on them – it was Kolya, the son that Erzsébet had thought was lost, who had been brought up in an orphanage in Siberia, and had found his mother after twenty years of searching. Their delight in finding each other was short-lived, as Ferenczy's stroke changed everything in the life of the family.

THE SUPPRESSION OF THE REVOLUTION AND THE EARLY KÁDÁR REGIME. In a matter of days the Soviet forces called in by János Kádár had swept through the country. By mid-November fighting had ceased everywhere. Although Kádár had promised an amnesty, over the next three years some 400 were executed for their part in the revolution, among them Imre Nagy and several members of his government, and almost 20,000 were imprisoned. At the same time, as the regime became established it did not introduce a Stalin-type dictatorship: while Rákosi's watchword had been *He that is not with us is against us*, Kádár was satisfied with *He that is not against us is with us*. Because of the way in which the revolution had been crushed Hungary was at first internationally isolated, but in the early 1960s the authorities declared a general amnesty and the "Hungarian question" was dropped from the agenda at the United Nations. During this period Kádár still carried through the forcible collectivisation of peasant land-holdings, in the course of which owners were forced, in many cases by blackmail or violence, to hand over their land to the collective farms. After that, however, the Kádár regime was characterised by economic and political consolidation and became more and more popular among the population.

After eighteen months Ferenczy's wife took him home from hospital. At that time he had a vocabulary of only eight or nine words – yes, no, of course, good, this, that, here, there, etc. – but verbs, nouns and pronouns had been lost. Even so, by various stresses he could express a lot of things. *Béni has permanently lost a whole dimension of his being, his individuality,* wrote a friend. He would often pick up his lifeless right hand in his left and wave it with a laugh: *no good.* Then, with astounding persistence and will-power he nevertheless learnt again what had been the most important thing to him: artistic self-expression. His main subjects were animals, flowers, mythological figures, fairytale beings, all creativity radiant with optimism. He would hold a conversation with his friends by listening to them and replying with sketch-like pictures. It was, however, with the Cupid-like figure of *Golden Age*, gracefully balanced on one leg, that he expressed his inexorable will to live. The Petőfi statue was eventually exhibited on the main square in Gyula,[15] from where, years later, it went to Milan, into the Ambrosiana Library collection, where the works of the world's greatest sculptors are displayed.

In the last years of his life too his home was open to artist friends, Sándor Weöres, Gyula Illyés, János Pilinszky and László Nagy among others. He would receive them seated in his armchair, freshly shaved, with a loosely tied silk cravat in the open collar of his freshly ironed shirt. He mostly listened to the music of Mozart and Bartók, while listening with interest to what people had to tell him. Only his short interjections of a brief word or two gave any indication of his illness. In the late spring of 1967 his wife was about to take him away on holiday, and they were in the middle of packing. Ferenczy suddenly pointed to his abdomen with his left hand, indicating that something was the matter. An ambulance was called and a perforated appendix diagnosed, requiring immediate surgery. During the operation he suffered a brain embolism, and died in hospital eleven days later. He was seventy-seven, and his wife lived on for thirty-three years more. *He was a past master at calming the whole world,* said she of her husband before her death. *He even calmed me.* In the half-century that has passed since his demise no detailed biography or monograph has been written about one of the most significant figures in Hungarian sculpture, who as a man too lived an exemplary life.

János Pilinszky

Pietà
for Béni Ferenczy

The corpse laid out across your own frail body,
it fell like thunder from the heavy air
and landed in your lap and broke your strength
and slipped from you, a weight you could not bear.

And as a startled herd fleeing the axe
turns round in panic to defy the threat ,
your feelings sprang instinctively to face
the death your senses struggled to reject.

Now only down the blind crazed passageways
of kisses could your own sick heart approach
the heart it madly beat for, the dead heart
it sought to join in body and to touch.

It can't have merited sufficient grace.
because in your rebellion and dole
you gnawed the very flesh from your own bones
a foreign flesh of which you'd lost control

so that you might be worthy of the death
that in your lap had come to make its bed.
You stripped yourself down to eternal grief.
And he, on the third day, rose from the dead.

(Translated by George Szirtes)

Notes

1 Modern Budapest is historically a city of two halves – Pest on the left bank of the Danube, Buda on the right. The two were only formally united (together with Óbuda, a little farther north) in 1873. Before that Pest and Buda were independent municipalities. In these essays this distinction will be preserved as dates require. The term Budapest may therefore not be used before 1873.

2 From the Turkish invasion of 1526 until 1873 Pozsony was the capital of Hungary. Nowadays known as Bratislava, it is the capital of Slovakia.

3 'Banner mother' – an archaism denoting a lady of importance who was called upon to assist in the dedication of a banner.

4 A distinctive item of headgear once worn by unmarried girls.

5 The modern Oslo – the medieval name which was restored in 1925.

6 As in English one finds titles such as Lord (someone) of (somewhere), so the Hungarian common nobility used to use styles of territorial designation, indicating association with or ownership of some village. This was done by suffixing -i to the name of the place in question, and prefixing the result to the nobleman's name – Saági Gudbrand Gregersen. There are in Hungary about a dozen places named Ság(h), and which one is referred to here remains unclear.

7 The proverbial *Aki nem tud arabusul, ne beszéljen arabusul*. Don't talk about what you don't understand.

8 The Feyerick Prize of the International Fencing Federation for honesty and integrity in athletic competition.

9 Hungary shorn of the territories ceded under the Treaty of Trianon; in effect, modern Hungary.

10 The territory west of the Danube.

11 The ÁVH labour camp with the harshest régime and highest death-rate of all. It operated only from 1950–1953, when all 100 or so such camps were closed by the Imre Nagy government.

12 In Zala county, near the Slovene border.

13 The *főispán* was the representative of the Crown in a Hungarian county, somewhat similar to the English Lord Lieutenant. Hungary was still a monarchy at the time, and Kolozs county had recently been returned from Romanian possession. Márton was a Hungarian by birth but a Romanian citizen by virtue of alteration of frontier.

14 Alexey Grigoryevich Stakhanov (1906–1977) was a miner in the Soviet Union, Hero of Socialist Labour (1970), and a member of the CPSU (1936). He became a celebrity in 1935 as part of what became known as the Stakhanovite movement – a campaign intended to increase worker productivity and to demonstrate the superiority of the socialist economic system.

15 A town in south-eastern Hungary, on the Romanian frontier.

Picture Credits

Blanka Teleki: brunszvikterez.hu; Manó Gozsdu: Nemzeti Portrétár; Domaniczky Tivadar, Ábrahám Ganz: Öntödei Múzeum; Lipót Löw: Magyar Zsidó Múzeum és Levéltár; Ignác Semmelweis: Orvostörténeti Múzeum; Gregersen Gudbrand: Ferencvárosi Helytörténeti Gyűjtemény, Halmos Lászlóné Berkó Carmen hagyatéka; Vasárnapi Újság, 1894/41; Mihály Fadlallah el Hedad: Bábolna Nemzeti Ménesbirtok Kft.; Ármin Vámbéry: Magyar Nemzeti Múzeum Történeti Fényképtár; Vilma Hugonnai: Semmelweis Ignác Orvostörténeti Múzeum; László Rátz: Budapest-Fasori Evangélikus Gimnázium; Rózsa Bédy-Schwimmer: ro zelia.schwimmer.collection; Róbert Feinsilber: Kieselbach Galéria; MTI; Gedeon Richter: Richter Gedeon Nyrt.; Attila Petschauer: Magyar Olimpiai és Sportmúzeum; Olivér Halassy: Magyar Olimpiai és Sportmúzeum; Gábor Sztehlo: Evangélikus Országos Múzeum; Margit Schlachta: Magyar Nemzeti Múzeum Történeti Fényképtár; László Ocskay: http://vox-nova.hu/pic_viewer.php?view=hirek/ocskay%20fotoo.jpg&m=2; http://www.centropa. org/sites/default/files/styles/max_quality/public/photo/orig/huid0032.jpg?itok=jmvxspN1; Imre Reviczky: Magyar Nemzeti Múzeum Történeti Fényképtár; Géza Soos: reformatus.hu; Ilona Elek: Magyar Olimpiai es Sportmúzeum; László Kozma: MTI, Patkó Klári; Sára Karig: Magyar Nemzeti Múzeum Történeti Fényképtár; Simon Papp: Magyar Olaj- és Gázipari Múzeum; Áron Márton: Márton Áron Múzeum – Csíkszentdomokos; György Cziffra: Cultiris; László Papp: Magyar Olimpiai és Sportmúzeum; István Angyal: Eörsi László gyűjteménye; Menyhért Lakatos: Petőfi Irodalmi Múzeum; Béni Ferenczy: Ferenczy Család Művészeti Alapítvány.

Appendix

Recommended books in English:

Bellák, Gábor et al.: *A Thousand Years of Art in Hungary*. Budapest, Corvina, 2012

Birnbaum, Marianna D.: *1944: A Year Without Goodbyes*. Budapest, Corvina, 2016

Braham, Randolph: *The Nazis' Last Victims: The Holocaust in Hungary*. Wayne State University Press, 2002

Hanák, Péter et al.: *A History of Hungary*. Bloomington, Indiana University Press, 1994

Hargittai, István: *The Martians of Science: Five Physicists Who Changed the Twentieth Century*. Oxford, Oxford University Press, 2006

Herman, Arthur. *What Life Was Like: At Empire's End: Austro-Hungarian Empire 1848–1918*. New York, Time Life, 2000

Hoensch, Joerg K.: *A History of Modern Hungary: 1867-1994*. New York and London, Longman, 1995

Kontler, László: *A History of Hungary*. Budapest, Atlantisz Könyvkiadó, 2006

Kósa, László: *A Cultural History of Hungary*. Budapest, Corvina, 2000

Lázár, István: *A Brief History of Hungary (with 62 Pictures in Colour)*. Budapest, Corvina, 2010

Lendvai, Paul: Hungary: *Between Democracy and Authoritarianism*. London and New York, C. Hurts & Co., New York, Columbia University Press, 2012

Marton, Kati: *The great escape: nine Jews who fled Hitler and changed the world*. New York, Simon & Schuster, 2006

Molnár, Miklós: *A Concise History of Hungary*. Cambrigde, Cambridge University Press, 2001

Romsics, Ignác: *Hungary in the Twentieth Century*. Budapest, Corvina, 2013

Sebestyen, Victor: *Twelve Days: The Story of the 1956 Hungarian Revolution*. New York, Pantheon, 2006

Szita, Szabolcs: *The Power of Humanity – Raoul Wallenberg and his Aides in Budapest*. Budapest, Corvina, 2012

Ungváry, Krisztián: *Battle for Budapest: 100 Days in World War II*. I. B. Tauris & Co. London and New York, 2005

List of references:

Blanka Teleki

De Gerando, Antonina: *Gróf Teleki Blanka élete*. Budapest, Légrádi testvérek, 1892
Hornyák, Mária: *Brunszvik Teréz "szellemi gyermeke": Teleki Blanka (1806–1862)*.
Martonvásár: Brunszvik Teréz Szellemi Hagyatéka Alapítvány, 2001
Nemeskürty, István: A hírszerző regénye: Teleki Blanka titkos élete. In: (Halmos
Ferenc ed.) *Száz rejtély a magyar irodalomból*. Budapest, Gesta, 1996
Solymos, Beatrix: *Kufsteini rózsák: gróf Teleki Blanka élete*. Budapest, Athenaeum, 1943
Teleki Blanka és köre: Karacs Teréz, Teleki Blanka, Lővei Klára. (Sáfrán Györgyi ed.).
Budapest, Szépirodalmi, 1963

Manó Gozsdu

Berényi, Mária: "A magyarországi románság mecénása: Egy román magyar: Gozs-
du Manó". In: *Rubicon*, Vol. XXI. No. 209. 2010, pp. 64-65.
Berényi, Mária: *Istoria Fundației Gojdu (1870–1952) / A Gozsdu Alapítvány története
(1870–1952)*. Comp-Press Kft., Budapesta-Budapest, 1995
Berényi, Mária: "Macedorománok, románok Pesten és Budán a XVIII-XIX. Szá-
zadban". In: *Napút*, 2013, No. 9. pp. 61-74.
Gozsdu, Manó: "Rejtett szavak", "Ny. Zs. kisasszony halálára". (Szépliteratúrai
Ajándék, 1826) In: *Napút*, 2013. No. 9. p. 60.

Ábrahám Ganz

Gajdos, Gusztáv: *Kempelen Farkas, Ganz Ábrahám. Magyar feltalálók, találmányok*.
Budapest, Műszaki Könyvkiadó, 1997. pp. 22-39.
Gajdos, Gusztáv: "Ganz Ábrahám, a kéregöntés meghonosítója". In: *Honismeret*,
1990, No. 4. pp. 48- 50.
Klement, Judit: "Ganz Ábrahám". In: (Sebők, Marcell ed.): *Sokszínű kapitalizmus:
pályaképek a magyar tőkés fejlődés aranykorából*. Budapest, HVG Könyvek, 2004,
pp. 44- 57.
Kovács, László: "Ganz Ábrahám". In: *Rubicon*, Vol. XXI. No. 2009. pp. 38-43.

Lipót Löw

Hídvégi, Máté: "Löv Lipót 1849-es börtönnaplója" In: *Múlt és Jövő*, Vol. 10.
No. 1. 1998
Löw, Immánuel – Kulinyi, Zsigmond: *A szegedi zsidók 1785-től 1885-ig*. Szeged, 1885
Löw, Lipót: *Történelmi és vallástudományi értekezések*. Szeged, 1861
Komoróczy, Géza: *Zsidók a magyar társadalomban: írások az együttélésről, a feszültségek-
ről és az értékekről, 1790–2012*. Pozsony, Kalligram, 2015
Varga Papi, László: *Babilon folyói mellől a Tisza partjáig: zsidók és zsidó magyarok*. Sze-
ged, Bába, 2002
Zakar, Péter: "Tábori rabbik 1848–49-ben".In: Múlt és Jövő, Vol. 10. No. 1., 1998

Ignác Semmelweis

Antall, József: "Semmelweis Ignác életútja". In: *Orvostörténeti közlemények,* Suppl. 13-14. 1984, pp. 15-26.

Czeizel, Endre: *Tudósok – Gének – Tanulságok.* Budapest, Galenus, 2006, pp. 16-69.

(Gazda, István ed.): *Semmelweis Ignác emlékezete.* Budapest, Semmelweis Orvostörténeti Múzeum, 2003

(Gazda, István ed.): *Semmelweis Ignác munkásságáról.* Budapest, Neumann Kht., 2007

Nuland, Sherwin B.: *The doctors' plague: germs, childbed fever, and the strange story of Ignác Semmelweis.* New York – London, W. W. Norton, 2003

Semmelweis, Ignác: *A gyermekágyi láz kóroktana, fogalma és megelőzése.* (trans. Rákóczi Katalin). Budapest, Akadémiai, 2012

Gregersen Gudbrand

Gönczi, Ambrus: *The Gregersen Family Integration into the Hungarian social group of upper-class entrepreneurs during the 19th century.* PhD Dissertation, Budapest, 2013

Gönczi, Ambrus: *Gregersen építőmester.* A Ferencvárosi Helytörténeti Gyűjtemény kiállításának katalógusa, Oslo, 2003

Halmos, Károly: "Gregersen Gudbrand: ácslegényből építési nagyvállalkozó". In: (Sebők, Marcell ed.) *Sokszínű kapitalizmus: pályaképek a magyar tőkés fejlődés aranykorából.* Budapest, HVG könyvek, 2004

Sveaas, Per Aunen: *Familien Gregersen og Gudbrand Gregersen, ungarsk adelsmann fra Modum.* Drammen, 1993

Mihály Fadallah el Hedad

Fadlallah el Hedad, Mihály: *Utazásom Mesopotámiában és Irak-Arábiában.* Budapest, Pallas, 1904

Hecker, Walter: *A Bábolnai Arab Ménes.* Bábolna, Magyarországi Arablótenyésztők Egyesülete, 2014

Szakács, Ferenc: "Fadlallah el Hedad Mihály". In: *Bábolna újjászületése,* Bábolna, 2010

Ármin Vámbéry

Dobrovits, Mihály: *Vámbéryval a harmadik évezredben.* Dunaszerdahely, Lilium Aurum, 2010

Hazai, György: *Vámbéry Ármin: 1832–1913.* Budapest, Akadémiai Kiadó – Zrínyi Kiadó, 1976

Kovács, Sándor Iván: *Batu kán pesti rokonai: Vámbéry Ármin és tatárja, Csagatai Izsák.* Pozsony, Kalligram, 2001

Mandler, Dávid: *Kelet és nyugat mezsgyéjén: Vámbéry Ármin és a Brit Birodalom.* Budapest, Múlt és Jövő Könyvek, 2014

Vámbéry, Ármin: *Dervisruhában Közép-Ázsián át.* Dunaszerdahely, Lilium Aurum, 2013

Vámbéry, Ármin: *Küzdelmeim.* Dunaszerdahely, Lilium Aurum, 2001

Vámbéry, Ármin: *Oroszország és a kelet.* Dunaszerdahely, Lilium Aurum, 2012

Vilma Hugonnay

Estók, János – Szerencsés, Károly: "Hugonnai Vilma". In: *Híres nők a magyar történelemben.* Budapest, Kossuth, 2007. pp. 92-93.

Hugonnai, Vilma: *A nő mint háziorvos: az egészség ápolásának kézikönyve, különös tekintettel a női- és gyermekbetegségekre, valamint a szülészetre és gyermekápolásra.* Budapest, Minerva, 1907

Hugonnai, Vilma: *A "Művelt Nők Otthona" jótékony egyesület története.* Budapest, Thália, 1912

Kertész, Erzsébet: *Vilma doktorasszony: Az első magyar orvosnő életregénye.* Budapest, Móra, 1965

Pivárcsi, István: "Hugonnay Vilma". In: *Híres magyar asszonyok kalandjai.* Palatinus, 2003. pp. 68-71.

Szállási, Árpád: "100 éve szerzett oklevelet az első magyar orvosnő: Hugonnai Vilma". In: *Orvosi hetilap* Vol. 120. No. 32. 1979, pp. 1950-1952.

László Rátz

Czeizel, Endre: *Tudósok, gének, dilemmák.* Budapest, Géniusz, 2002

Czeizel, Endre: *Tudósok, gének, tanulságok.* Budapest, Géniusz, 2006

D. Kenedli, Eszter: "A »fasori csoda«: Az iskolai élet alapegyenlete: jó tanár, jó iskola (3.): Rátz, László". In: *Tanító. Módszertani folyóirat,* Vol. 51. No. 1. 2013, pp. 7-10.

Dobos, Krisztina – Gazda, István – Kovács, László: *A fasori csoda.* Budapest, Országos Pedagógiai Könyvtár és Múzeum, 2002

Némethné Pap, Kornélia: "Rátz László tanár úr". In: *A fizika tanítása. Módszertani folyóirat.* Vol. 15. No. 3. 2007, pp. 33-34.

Rózsa Bédy-Schwimmer

(Bédy-Schwimmer, Rózsa ed.) *A nő és a társadalom:* a Feministák Egyesülete és a Nőtisztviselők Országos Egyesülete hivatalos közlönye. 1907–1913

(Bédy-Schwimmer, Rózsa ed.) *A nő:* feminista folyóirat. Budapesti Feministák Egyesülete, 1914–1928

Csizmadia, Edit: "»Ki a lövészárkokból karácsonyra!«. A Ford békehajó legendája". In: *Vasváry-gyűjtemény hírlevele,* No. 53. 2015

Flowers, Ronald B. – Lahutsky, Nadia M.: "The Naturalisation of Rosika Schwimmer". In: *Journal of Church and State,* Vol. 32, No. 2, 1990

Kereszty, Orsolya: Bédy-Schwimmer Rózsa, a Nő és a társadalom szerkesztője". In: (Palasik, Mária, Sipos, Balázs eds.) *Házastárs? vetélytárs? munkatárs?: a női szerepek változása a 20. századi Magyarországon.* Budapest, Napvilág, 2005

Robert Feinsilber

Búza, Péter: "A leves". In: *Budapest.* Vol. 20. No. 2.(1982), pp. 18-19.

Szilágyi, György: "A tolsztojánus Feinsilber: Róbert bácsi regénye". In: *Remény.* Vol. 9. No. 3. 2006, pp. 77-80.

Szilágyi, György: "»A városnak ez a ritka jó bolondja«: Róbert bácsi regénye". In: *Új élet.* Vol. 59. No. 12. 2004, p. 6.

Gedeon Richter

Csontos, Jolán et al.: *A Richter Gedeon Rt. 100 éves története.* Richter Gedeon Vegyészet Gyár Rt., Budapest, 2001

Hajduska, István: "Richter Gedeon". In: *Magyar gyógyszerek – magyar kutatók.* Gondolat, Budapest, 1976

Nemere, István: *A megszállott: Richter Gedeon élete.* Magánkiadás, Budapest, 2012

Rasztik, Tibor: *Történelmi üzletembereink: Richter Gedeon.* Richter Gedeon Nyrt., Budapest, 2010

Spáh, Dávid (director): *Nem tűntem el – Richter Gedeon története.* Színes magyar portréfilm, 2014

Attila Petschauer

Dávid, Sándor: Arany évtizedek: a magyar vívás története: a Magyar Vívó Szövetség 75 éves jubileumára. Budapest, Magyar Vívó Szövetség, 1988

Hámori, Ottó: Egy kardforgató élete: filmnovella Petschauer Attiláról. Budapest, Sportpropaganda, 1983

Kő, András: *Pengevilág.* Budapest, Magyar Vívószövetség, 2004

Réti, Anna: *Mi lett velük?* Budapest, Sport, 1967

Syposs, Zoltán: *Villanó pengék.* Budapest, Sport, 1975

Olivér Halassy

Németh, János: *Komjádi aranycsapata: a magyar vízilabda útja a kezdetektől a világelsőségig.* Cleveland, Ohio, Classic Printing, 1981

Nyáry, Krisztián: "Munkaszolgálatos tanúk – Hol halt meg Petschauer Attila?" In: *BBC History,* Vol. VI. No. 11, pp. 7-9.

Szakály, Sándor: "Vissza a dokumentomokhoz – Hol halt meg Petschauer Attila?" In: *BBC History,* Vol. VI. No. 11, pp. 6-7.

Szöllősy, Marianne: "Egy újpesti úszó- és bajnok emlékezete" In: *Újpesti helytörténeti értesítő, Vol.* 14. No. 4. 2007, pp. 29-31.

Verrasztó, Gábor: "Halassy Olivér, a »féllábú gazember«: A világ első mozgássérült olimpiai bajnoka, vízilabdázó, gyorsúszó parasportoló". In: *Humanitás.* Vol. 33. No. 8. 2013, p. 13.

Verrasztó, Gábor: "Az olimpikon halála". In: *Napút.* Vol. 15. No. 3. (2013), pp. 110-112.

Gábor Sztehlo

Bartosné Stiasny, Éva: *Háborúban békességben: A Bogár utcai gyermekotthon lakóinak csodás megmenekülése.* Budapest, Luther Kiadó, 2005

Koren, Emil: *Sztehlo Gábor élete és szolgálata.* Budapest, Országos Evangélikus Múzeum, 1994

Miklya Luzsányi, Mónika: *Frontvonal: Sztehlo Gábor élete.* Budapest, Harmat Kiadó, 2003

Miklya Luzsányi, Mónika: *Hogy véget érjen a sötétség: Dokumentumok Sztehlo Gábor gyermekmentő munkájáról a II. világháború idején.* Budapcst, Harmat Kiadó, Budapest, 2003

Sztehlo, Gábor: *Isten kezében* (Bozóky Éva ed.). Budapest, Sztehlo Gábor Gyermek és Ifjúságsegítő Alapítvány, 1994

Margit Slachta

Balogh, Margit: "Ínségakcióktól a politikai közéletig: Slachta Margit (1884-1974) szociális testvér pályaképe." In: (Szilágyi Csaba ed.): *Szociális kérdések és mozgalmak Magyarországon (1919-1945),* Budapest, Gondolat, 2008, pp. 213-230.

Balogh, Margit: "Slachta Margit és a keresztény nőkép". In: *Rubicon*, Vol. 20. No. 4. 2009, p. 10.

Estók, János – Szerencsés, Károly: "Slachta Margit". In: *Híres nők a magyar történelemben.* Budapest, Kossuth, 2007, pp. 206-209.

Majsai, Tamás: "Iratok a kőrösmezei zsidódeportálás történetéhez 1944." In: *Ráday Gyűjtemény évkönyve,* IV-V., Budapest, 1986, pp. 195-237.

Szécsi, József: "Megtagadok minden közösséget a földi bálvány-istenekkel és a sátán hitvallásával: a gyűlölettel!". Slachta Margit a szlovák zsidókért. In: *Egyházfórum,* Vol. 25. No. 4-5. pp. 47-53.

Vadász, Ferenc: "Slachta Margit nagyívű, hősies életútjáról: Beszélgetés Mona Ilonával". In: *Szombat,* Vol. 2. No. 9. 1990, pp. 10-12.

László Ocskay

Ablonczy, Bálint: "Ocskay listája". In: *Heti Válasz,* 2007. 5. April

Danieli, Dan: *Ocskay százados, egy igaz ember...,* Riverdale (USA), self-published, 1996

Fonyó, Gergely: Ocskay László, az elfelejtett hős. (Hungarian documentary film), 70 min., 2008

Szita, Szabolcs: *"Ocskay László története a háborús embermentések tükrében."* Budapest, *Vox-Nova,* 2008

Imre Reviczky

Deák, István: "Tisztesség és becsület a II. világháborúban: Zsidókat mentő magyar katonatisztek" In: *História,* 2010/8.

Randolph L. Braham, Tibori Szabó, Zoltán: *A magyarországi holokauszt földrajzi enciklopédiája,* I. Budapest, Park Könyvkiadó, 2010

Reviczky, Ádám: *Vesztes háborúk, megnyert csaták: emlékezés Reviczky Imre ezredesre.* Magvető, Budapest, 1985

Tóth, Sándor: *A lelkiismeret parancsára: Reviczky Imre posztumusz vezérőrnagy, a "Világ Jámbora".* Nyíregyháza, Nyíri Honvéd Egyesület, 2006.

Géza Soos

(Horváth, Erzsébet ed.) "A hitet megtartottam...": Soos Géza, 1912–2012. Budapest, Magyarországi Református Egyház Zsinati Levéltára, 2012

Kiss, Réka: "Soos Géza, a kiemelkedő ifjúsági vezető és politikus". In: (Kósa, László ed.) Reformátusok Budapesten: tanulmányok a magyar főváros református-ságáról. Budapest, Argumentum – ELTE BTK Művelődéstört. Tanszék, 2006.

Koncz, Lajos: "Zsidómentés és nemzeti ellenállás". In: *Beszélő*. Vol. 6. No. 9. 2001

(Soos, Gézáné Tüdős, Ilona ed.) "Evangéliumot Magyarországnak!": Soos Géza emlékkönyv. Ráday Gyűjtemény, Budapest, 1999

Soos, Gézáné Tüdős, Ilona: *Mint a Jézus Krisztus jó vitéze: Emlékezés Soos Gézára*. Budapest, author's edition, 1989

Ilona Elek

Dávid, Sándor: *Arany évtizedek: a magyar vívás története. A Magyar Vívó Szövetség 75 éves jubileumára*. Budapest, Magyar Vívó Szövetség, 1988

Kő, András: *Pengevilág*. Budapest, Magyar Vívószövetség, 2004

Elek, Ilona – Elek, Margit: *Így vívtunk mi*. Budapest, Sport, 1968

László Kozma

Keviczky, László: "Kozma László". In: *Magyar Tudomány,* Vol. XLVIII. No. 3. 2003, p. 378.

Kovács, Győző: "Dr. Kozma László elektromérnök, a távbeszélő-technika és a számítástechnika magyar úttörője". In: *Magyar Tudomány,* Vol. XLVIII. No. 3. 2003, pp. 379-388.

Kozma, László: *Egy Kossuth-díjas börtönévei*. Budapest, *Új Mandátum,* 2001

Sára Karig

Karig, Sára: *Sarkövezet:* Versek. Budapest, Philobiblon, 1995

Karig, Sára – Gergely, Ágnes: "Szibéria nincs olyan messze" (interview). In: Gergely, Ágnes: *Közép-Európa ígéret volt*. Budapest, Balassi, 1994

Oral history interview with Sara Karig, purchased and received by the United States Holocaust Memorial Museum Archives in November 1994

Palasik, Mária: "Alkotó élet, hányatott sors. Karig Sára életútja". In: (Balogh Margit, S. Nagy Katalin eds.) *Asszonysorsok a 20. században*. Budapest, BME Szociológia és Kommunikáció Tanszék – SZCSM Nőképviseleti Titkársága, 2000

Palasik, Mária: "A Life Lived for Progress and Democracy: Sára Karig (1914–1999)". In: *Hungarian Studies Review,* Vol. XXXIX, Nos. 1-2, 2012

Simon Papp

Dobai, Gábor: "A magyar olaj és földgáz története". (III-IX..) In: *Víz, gáz, fűtéstechnika: épületgépészeti szaklap,* Vol. 14. Nos. 1-11. 2013

F. Tóth, Géza: "125 éve született Papp Simon, »a kőolajkutatás atyja«". In: *Honismeret,* Vol. 39. No. 3. 2011, pp. 9-11.

Meskó, Attila: "Papp Simon munkássága". In: *Magyar geofizika,* Vol. 40. No. 4. 1999, pp. 86-90.

Papp, Simon: *Életem*. Budapest, Magyar Olajipari Múzeum, 1996

Áron Márton

(Marton, József ed.) *Márton Áron emlékkönyv születésének 100. évfordulóján*. Kolozsvár, Gloria, 1996

Márton, Áron: *Válogatott írások és beszédek*. Hargita, Csíkszereda, 2013

Poszler, György: "Hagyomány és korszerűség – Márton Áron törvényei: vázlat egy elmaradt monográfiához". In: *Az eltévedt lovas nyomában*. Balassi, Budapest, 2008

Venczel, József: "Márton Áron püspök népnevelő rendszere". In: *Erdélyi föld, erdélyi társadalom*. Budapest, Közgazd. és Jogi Könyvkiadó, 1988

(Virt, László ed.): *Márton Áron, a lelkiismeret apostola*. Budapest, Ecclesia, 1988

(Virt, László ed.) *Márton Áron breviárium*. Budapest, Kairosz, 2009

György Cziffra

Böhm, Kurt Adolphe: *Hommage à György Cziffra – le journal d'une amitié*. Paris, Verlag La Pensée universelle, 1995

Cziffra, György: *Ágyúk és virágok* (transl. Fedor, Ágnes és Herczeg, György). Budapest, Zeneműkiadó Vállalat, 1983

Horváth, Jenő: "A művész, a diplomata meg a Kádár-huszár – Dokumentumok Cziffra Györgyről és Magyarországról, 1958-ból". In: *Muzsika*, Vol. 37. No.4. 1994, pp. 13-17.

Némethné Őri, Irma: "Cziffra György és Madame Soleilka. (Emlékeim a művészről és feleségéről)". In: *Vasi Szemle*, Vol. 66. No. 3. 2012, pp. 286-296.

Wilheim, András: "Cziffra György". In: *Mozgó Világ*, Vol. 8. No. 5. 1982, pp. 38-39.

László Papp

Czeizel, Endre: "Az ökölvívás: Papp László". In: *Családfa*. Budapest, Kossuth, 1992, pp. 180-181.

ifj. Papp, László: *Édesapám, Papp Laci: Harc ringen belül és kívül*. Budapest, Tinta könyvkiadó, 2004

Kő, András: *Papp Laci*. Budapest, Budapest-Print, 2004

Vad, Dezső et al: *Papp László hatvan éves*. Sportpropaganda, Budapest, 1986

István Angyal

Abody, Rita: "Halottas szoba – (Magzati emlékek 56-ból)". In: *Lettre* Vol. 54, 2004

Angyal István sajátkezű vallomásai (1956. december). In: *Múltunk*, Vol. 40. No. 4. 1995, p. 133.

Eörsi, István: *Emlékezés a régi szép időkre*. Budapest, Napra-forgó Kft, 1988

Eörsi, László: *Angyal István (1928–1958)*. Noran, Budapest, 2008

Eörsi, László: "Egy hithű forradalmár: Angyal István". In: *Rubicon*, Vol. 6. No. 8. 1995, pp. 32-34.

Tóbiás, Áron: "Angyal István balladája". In: *Kapu*, Vol. 10. No. 10. 2013, pp. 68-71.

Menyhért Lakatos

Lakatos, Menyhért: *Füstös képek*. Budapest, Magvető, 1975

Lakatos, Menyhért: *Akik élni akartak*. Budapest, Magvető, 1982

Lakatos, Menyhért: "A cigányok sorsa 1944-ben". In: (Orbán, Sándor ed.) *Magyarország 1944-ben: Tudományos tanácskozás*. Kossuth, 1984, pp. 54-58

Szénási, Zsófia: "Interjú Lakatos Menyhérttel." In: *KönyvHét*, Vol. IV. No. 11. 2000, pp. 9-10.

Varga, Ilona: "»Egy ideig bírtam, tűrtem...«: találkozás a nyolcvanéves Lakatos Menyhérttel" In: *Barátság.* – Vol. 13. No. 3. 2006, pp. 4994-4996.

Béni Ferenczy

Földes, Mária: "*... a szelídség szobra*": *Válogatás Ferenczy Béni szobrászművész hagyatékából.* Budapest, Magyar Nemzeti Galéria, 2005

Hubay, Miklós: "Aranykor". In: *Aranykor*, Budapest, Szépirodalmi Kiadó, 1972

Kontha, Sándor: *Ferenczy Béni.* Budapest, Corvina, 1981

Szabó, Katalin: *Ferenczy Béni.* Budapest, Corvina, 1967

Vajda, Miklós: *Ferenczy Béni estéje.* Budapest, Tótfalusi Kis Miklós Nyomdaipari Szki, 1999